Shortlisted for the *Sunday Times*/Peters Fraser & Dunlop
Young Writer of the Year Award

A *Daily Telegraph*, *Times* and *Spectator*
Book of the Year, 2018

'[A] beautifully written hyb'... criticism ... This book i... itten by a bookworm unfu... derable power' ... *The Times*

'A miraculous memoir ... one who has encountered anorexia, either first hand or in someone they love, will recognise this harrowing yet heartening portrait. *The Reading Cure* is a book for the bookish, for those hungry for self-knowledge, or for those who are just hungry'
Daniel Johnson, *Standpoint*

'*The Reading Cure* is a tale of joy winning against piety, and the triumph of life over death ... both a stimulating argument for the power of fiction as a force for personal change and a wise memoir of anorexia. Moreover, it is never pat, always intelligent, full of enthusiasm, and almost entirely free of self-pity'
Craig Brown, *Mail on Sunday*

'Enchanting and original ... an illuminating and highly engaging way to think about all kinds of literature'
Amanda Craig

'*The Reading Cure* is devastatingly close to the bone for anyone who has had an eating disorder and knows its power to warp the mind. Gripping, moving, healing, mouthwatering'
Ysenda Maxtone Graham

'Warm and insightful, Freeman takes us on an exhilarating journey'   Bel Mooney, *Daily Mail*

'Laura Freeman is unflinchingly honest about the loneliness and misery of suffering from an eating disorder ... But her pleasure in the food of literature is infectious. *The Reading Cure* will speak to anyone who has ever felt pain and found solace in a book'   Bee Wilson

'Wonderfully uplifting'   *Sunday Times Style*

'*The Reading Cure* is a painful exploration of anorexia but also a love letter to the healing power of books written with expert care, talent ... and hope'
                                    Francesca Brown, *Emerald Street*

'Freeman's writing throughout is beautiful and bountiful; her descriptions of food are full of flavour and temptation; her journey to wellness an inspiring one'
                                    Lucy Pearson, *The Literary Edit*

'A story of salvation and picnics, ravioli and freedom, Dickens and survival. Laura's recovery is testament to the power of literature, the love of a concerned family and the tenacity of a woman on a mission'   Kate Leaver, *The Pool*

'Lyrically written, raw and honest'   Eithne Farry, *S Magazine*

'Clear-eyed, ambrosial, impassioned, bountiful ... it's impossible not to be seduced by Freeman's love of prose. It's essential reading not just for those who love food, but words. Come dine with her'   Tanya Sweeney, *Irish Independent*

The
Reading Cure

How Books
Restored My Appetite

LAURA FREEMAN

WEIDENFELD & NICOLSON

First published in Great Britain in 2018

This paperback edition first published in 2019
by Weidenfeld & Nicolson
an imprint of The Orion Publishing Group Ltd
Carmelite House, 50 Victoria Embankment
London EC4Y 0DZ

An Hachette UK Company

1 3 5 7 9 10 8 6 4 2

A CIP catalogue record for this book is
available from the British Library.

ISBN (paperback) 978 1 4746 0465 9
ISBN (ebook) 978 1 4746 0466 6

Typeset by Input Data Services Ltd, Somerset

Printed and bound in Great Britain by Clays Ltd, Elcograf S.p.A.

www.orionbooks.co.uk

To my parents Michael and Clara,
and my brother Edward

Contents

Introduction

'A good supper and strong tea restored their strength'

There is nothing like hunting a tiger to work up an appetite. So Bevis and Mark find after a day punting a raft around their island, tracking prints at the water's edge. Some tiger or Red Injun or Man Friday has been stealing their rashers of bacon and they are out to find him.

The boys, heroes of Richard Jefferies' *Bevis*, return to their camp an hour after sunset, defeated by a rising gale. No sign of the bacon thief. Morale is low. There is only one thing to be done. The boys lose not a moment. 'The gate was padlocked, the kettle put on, and they sat down to rest. A good supper and strong tea restored their strength.' When I read *Bevis* for the first time, aged twenty-seven, on a July day as hot and clear as boys with a raft could wish for, I paused at this island picnic.

'A good supper and strong tea restored their strength.' Such a throwaway sentence. All the more so in a book in which Bevis's eager imagination conjures sea voyages to the Tropics, battles between Roman legionaries, spitting cobras, witches and genies, without ever leaving his father's grounds.

Other readers would have pressed on to find out if Bevis and Mark, taking turns on the night watch, manage to shoot the tiger through their stockade. (They don't. Bevis

falls asleep with his back to the wall. That's what comes
of a good supper.) I kept turning the line over and over.
'A good supper and strong tea restored their strength.' It
seemed to strike at something that had eluded me for a
long time. Fifteen years.

A day later, I was still worrying away at the sentence,
as if it were a linseed stubbornly stuck between two teeth.
What comfort, what warmth there was in that supper and
strong tea. What a lifting effect it has on the boys. And
what a strange and unfamiliar idea it presented to me: that
a good meal might restore a tired body and defeated spirits.

For fifteen years before taking *Bevis* off the shelf, I had
been hungry. Sometimes acutely so, sometimes less, but
always going to bed each night empty and cold. For two of
those fifteen years, I had been starving. How we misuse the
word. 'I'm starving!' we announce over elevenses biscuits
because breakfast was at seven and lunch won't be till one.
'Starving' – it sounds so overdone. But I was. I cannot pretend to know what it is like to starve because your country
is in famine or because you are held political prisoner. But
I do know what it is like, slowly and with quiet and determined purpose, to starve your body near to death.

Let us call it by its proper name from the beginning.
Anorexia. It is a difficult word. It does not come easily.
Anorexia nervosa. You cannot mumble it under your breath
and hope no one has heard. I do not like the length or
unfamiliarity of the word, nor its harsh X, like a pair of
crossed femur bones. You think of X-rays and skeletons.

Obese, plump. These are rounded, greedy words: well-
fed vowels and full, buxom Ps and Bs. Peter Paul Rubens
lends his name so seductively to fleshly bodies – *Ruben-
esque* – not just because his painted ladies, his Graces and

Delilahs, are so comely, so peaches-and-creamy, but because that rolling R, that bouncing B insist on ampleness and appetite. Skeleton, starving, anorexia. These are thin words. Their Ks, Ls and Ts are like spines. That V is a pelvic bone. The X of anorexia is angular and alien.

Through my many years of anorexia I have shied away from the word. When I have told people of my thin, starved teens I have often couched it in some feeble half-truth: 'I had some difficulty eating.' At other times I have been vague. I talk of a mystery 'illness' or 'an eating disorder'. This is too general. It might describe an illimitable appetite for junk and sugar, or bulimia with its bingeing and purging. No, anorexia is the only faithful description of my particular illness.

Besides, 'eating disorder' is wrong. This baggy catch-all is to blame for many of the failings in the way such illnesses are treated. It is the mistake of some doctors to treat only the disordered habits of eating. A patient is admitted to a clinic and prescribed a meal plan. If she eats what is advised, she will gain weight, and, all boxes ticked, can be sent home. But left to her own devices, left to feed herself, the anorexic reverts to the old, destructive ways. It is not disordered eating which defines this illness. It is the disordered mind.

How can I fully describe the chaos, misery and misrule of an anorexic's thinking? The mess and devastation of an illness that, while starving a body of its flesh, strips the mind of all rational thought?

Imagine a healthy mind as a library. As pleasant a room as a reader could wish. The books are shelved in glass-fronted cases, alphabetically and by subject. High, shuttered windows give a view of the sea, a garden square, or chalk downland. There is an armchair, with a table and lamp, and a polished top stacked with favourite titles. In an ordered mind, this light, tidy library is a refuge, a retreat from a tiring world, a room where you can sit and read and gather your thoughts.

Now let me describe a different sort of library, this one belonging to the disordered, anorexic mind. The bookcases have fallen, their glass fronts smashed, their contents in disarray across the floor. The windows, too, have shattered. Rain and damp have got at the books, spoiling their bindings and soaking the pages. The chair, in which you have been accustomed to sit your whole life, has been knocked on its side and cannot be righted under the weight of the toppled cases. The table is splintered and the lamp cracked. What is to be done with a room as desolate as this? What is there to salvage? It is not a retreat, it is wreckage. At fifteen, this was the state of my mind.

Anorexia is an illness of wretched isolation. It traps you inside your thoughts and those thoughts become more and more frightening, less and less in your control. You want desperately for someone to help, to heave cases upright, set your chair by the window, return books to their shelves, while at the same time fearing more than anything that intervention might mean being forced to eat. I would sooner have taken my chances with the chaos than be made to eat a baked potato.

One of the great unfathomables of any mental illness is why this person and not that? Why are some people equable, cheerful, take misfortune in their stride and others subject to irrational glooms and torments? Another is: why that manifestation? Why anorexia, and not depression?

Self-harm, and not drugs? Drink, and not gambling?

In my own case, I can only answer that it was temperament. I take things to heart; berate myself for past mistakes; feel my own failures keenly. I am anxious, perfectionist by nature and dismayed by any falling short. These are traits common to many anorexics. The wish to impose checks on one's body – to make it lean, unobtrusive, spare – is the result of this sort of character losing its grip on reason. So, when I experienced a prolonged period of unhappiness in my early teens, more lowering and debilitating than the usual adolescent growing pains, it was anorexia which seized me, not drink or drugs or an obsessive compulsive disorder.

It is difficult, when it comes to any illness of the mind, to mark the moment between well and unwell, before and after – the tipping point between low spirits and consuming depression. But in my case, there is a date in the diary. Every day before was without anorexia, every day after marked by it.

I was thirteen and it was towards the end of the 2001 summer holiday. An eight-week release from a school which was to me more hateful than Nicholas Nickleby's Dotheboys or Jane Eyre's Lowood. At eleven, I had moved from a cheerful, mixed primary school to an academic, unsisterly, all-girls' school. I did not take to it. I was small, slight, shy, sick with nerves on the school bus each morning, and sicker as we approached the gates.

I had some friends and an adored Latin teacher. But it wasn't – I wasn't – a good fit. I felt diminished and oppressed by the dark-red brick of the main school building and the chequered marble of the central hallway.

The first year was unsettled, the second miserable. It

was a brutal, competitive place. Two-thirds of the girls in each year group went on to Oxbridge and there was what the school called 'plenty of healthy rivalry' and I would call bullying. It was generally dismissed as 'high spirits' or 'hormones'. Whatever it was, it was soul-destroying. I was more shrunken – only mentally, not yet physically – and more cowed each term.

Late in that summer holiday between the second and third years, anxious about the September start of term, something in my mind gave way. It was a fine, amber August day of high blue skies. Gloucestershire, where we were spending the holidays, might have been Granada. We had been swimming outdoors and I was wearing a black swimsuit. Standing on the edge of the pool, wet from the water but drying off quickly in the sun, I felt, for the first time, that there was something wrong, irreparably wrong, with my body.

My skin didn't seem to fit. I was ugly, formless, lumpen. I was revolted by the heaviness of my limbs and my swollen, inflated stomach. To any outward observer, I was the same slim girl I had been ten minutes before. But there had been some internal tremor, some shaking of that carefully ordered library, and a bookcase, perhaps more than one, had come crashing down.

I had been happy and relieved to be away that summer, out of school, in the garden with my brother Ed. It was the contrast of that relief, I believe, with the prospect of the return to school the following week that impressed so heavily. I had been unhappy before, but something new had asserted itself. I went back to school troubled by new compulsions. I must be smaller. I must be quieter. I must be less conspicuous.

I resolved not to visit the tuck shop at morning break. I was not to eat sweets or chocolate, biscuits or crisps. There was to be no wavering, no giving in to temptation. It was easy, remarkably so. Once gone, I didn't miss them. How firm I was in my determination. But how plump and ungainly I was, how lacking in self-control when it came to other foods. I made a new resolution. I would give up all red meat: steak and hamburgers, salt beef and bacon. That, too, was easy.

I gave up chicken and fish, then pasta, potatoes, bread and rice. But even on this restricted diet I was fatter, slower, more lumbering. I gave up eggs, cheese, butter, yogurt and dairy milk. I gave up any snack between meals and all desserts. I would not eat in the school dining room or in the street or on the bus.

Through that third year at school, I pared my diet thinner and thinner. The summer between my third and fourth year, when I was fourteen, we went to France, where I was aware for the first time of an anxiousness before meals. I trailed Dad around the French supermarket filling the trolley with tofu, mushrooms, soya milk. What a relief that they had such things even in *foie-gras* and *cassoulet-de-canard* France. I was skittish when lunch out at a restaurant was proposed and frantic when the meal arrived with chips.

Those two weeks in France also mark the first time I felt hungry. Not hungry immediately before meals, but hungry all the time. I went to bed hungry and woke up hungry. I was hungry every hour in between, a distracting, preoccupying hunger that ate into every thought. When I could no longer concentrate on the book I was reading – it was the summer of *I, Claudius*, *Great Expectations* and *Blandings* – I would go down to the kitchen, take one *reine claude* plum from the bowl on the counter and tell myself it must last until dinner.

I was stricken by any family member taking a photo. I did not want my thunderous thighs on camera. Though I flinched from the lens at the time, some photographs were taken. I can look at them now and see pale, spindly legs beneath a denim skirt and a narrow body in a white jersey.

By the time I went back to school in September 2002, I was in a bad way. I would not eat dried fruit, fresh fruit, tomatoes or rice cakes. I would not eat any food cooked in olive oil. I would not use seasoning – not salt, not pepper, not vinegar, not soy sauce, not herbs, nor any garnish – on my food. I would not have any meal cooked with garlic or onions when I could have it plain. I would not have soup, unless clear broth. I would not drink anything but water or mint tea.

I had been taking vitamin C and cod liver oil tablets, but I would not take them any more. Each contained two calories, according to the packaging, and I was an exacting reader of packaging. No monk every laboured over his manuscript as devotedly as I did over tables of calorie, fat and sugar content. I would no longer take the Nurofen tablets – in a sugar casing – I had been relying on to ease appalling headaches. I had them every day, screaming, crippling hunger headaches. And still I seemed to swell, growing fatter even on this lean diet.

You might reasonably ask why no one had noticed. No parent, teacher or friend. I can't blame those around me for not seeing what I was doing to myself. Anorexia makes schemers and deceivers of its sufferers. I had always had a 'huge lunch' at school, an 'enormous sandwich' on the way home. And you do not see incremental change. If I lost a steady pound a month and wore great baggy jeans that trailed on the pavement, any difference in my weight was not obvious.

There came a point, though, early in the New Year, when no pair of jeans, however baggy, and no amount of bluster about 'vast helpings of lasagne' would help me. Brushing my hair pulled whole skeins loose. There was soft, grey down all over my stomach, back and arms. My clothes hung on shrunken arms and legs. My chest hurt when I walked up the three flights of the school fire escape between lessons in the January cold.

So disturbed was my thinking that I convinced myself that if my lungs ached, it was because I was unfit. If I was tired, it was because I was lazy. If I was cold, it was because I was not running far enough on the treadmills in the school gym. I took up jogging in my lunch hour to improve, as I reasoned it, my circulation. I certainly didn't need that hour for lunch.

The physical distress, though, was nothing compared to the mental. Every shelf in my mind's library smashed; every book splayed, spine bent back; the glass in all the lamps cracked; wreckage and ruin from skirting board to skirting board. Every day the clamour in my head was louder. I was fat. I was disgusting, sluggish, worthless. A pig. Blubbery, blubbering, not fit to be seen.

In February 2003 I was taken to see a doctor. No girl of fifteen should be so tired, nor so cold. My parents were worried, though uncertain of the diagnosis. I was certain: I was too fat, ate too much and exercised too little. I was prepared for the doctor to weigh me, measure me, calculate my BMI and tell me that I was overweight, grotesquely obese.

I had given in to an apple the previous week, I recorded in my diary, hating myself for having been so weak-willed.

I was weighed, I was measured and I was found wanting. My body was skeletal, nearly two stone underweight. I told the doctor my hair had been falling out and perhaps this was because I had stopped taking the cod liver oil. He shook his head, called Mum in from the waiting room and made his diagnosis. Anorexia.

Writing this does not come easily. When I think of the worst of my illness, it still stirs something close to grief, mourning those years lost to hunger. I want to write of my recovery, of learning not only to eat again, but to take pleasure in food and in cooking. To relish, as Bevis and Mark do, on the first day of their expedition, a picnic of 'huge double slices of bread-and-butter done up in paper, apples, and the leg of a roast duck', which the boys have pinched from the pantry.

I settled on the image of a library to describe my mind. I wonder how others would understand theirs: as a garden, a greenhouse, a painter's studio, a cricket pitch and its pavilion, in greater or lesser states of repair. It would depend on the person.

I am a bookish person. I always have been. At primary school, I borrowed the permitted eight books a week from the Swiss Cottage children's library every Wednesday and read them after lights-out in the shaft of light from the hallway which fell across the foot of my bed, feet tucked under the pillow.

At university, studying history of art, I lugged crates of books back and forth each term, more than there was ever room for in the car or in my cramped first- and second-year rooms. Today, my attic flat is always out of book space. Once a year I ring Max the carpenter and ask him to put up shelves in some new cranny under the eaves. If the floors collapse, the books will be to blame. Even at my weakest and most frail, confined to bed, invalided out of school, I read with a ravening appetite that I was missing in all other respects, devouring books at a rate of one a day.

Mum took me once a week to the doctor, twice a week to a therapist, a specialist in anorexia, and once a week to the Daunt bookshop on Marylebone High Street. In between, I was put back to bed. No running on the treadmill, no walks in the cold. What else was there to do but read? And so I did, piling books on the floor by my bedside table. If words had been calories, I would have been gorged. Reading was an escape when I was most desperate. Later, it was medicine of a different sort.

When I was first diagnosed with anorexia, at fifteen, the doctor warned that I faced a five- to ten-year recovery. It seemed impossible at the time. So long a treatment and convalescence was to my mind unending and unconquerable. But he was right.

The first three years were often so frightening, so exhausting that I swore again and again to abandon recovery and let the disease do what it might. Every mealtime was a battle, every new food a cause for terror and panic. That I survived those three years is thanks to Mum's nursing, her inexhaustible patience. She sat with me at every meal, coaxing and reassuring, as I picked my way through small portions of despised foods. How did she endure with such outward calm those awful mealtimes? I would weep until I choked with tears over a bowl of yogurt or a slice of toast, raging that I would not, could not eat it.

I remember with shame the day she baked a fruitcake and offered me a slice at teatime. Hysterical, screaming that I did not eat cake, I threw the piece she had cut me on the floor. At meals, when I was told I must try some new food I behaved like a captured animal chained to the table leg, wild with distress.

Little by little, though, I did eat. A slice of wholemeal bread and ham, a grilled chicken breast, milk, vegetables, smoked salmon, even, eventually, a slice of fruitcake. By the time I went to university at nineteen, I could feed myself without Mum cheering me on. Not a lot, but enough. I ate with mechanical routine, small helpings of a very narrow range of foods, and never with any savour. I would try new foods with friends, but when eating alone over my books I would return to matchbox portions of a predictable, plodding diet. The same lunch every day for a term, known and reassuring. The same breakfast for three years. A tendency to prod and poke any meal dished up in college hall, more prodded and poked than eaten.

I might have gone on this way my whole life, eating just enough, not really at ease having dinner in company, not varying from safe staples: a little muesli, pasta with tomato sauce, chicken, sweet potatoes, roast vegetables, yogurt. A diet to keep one alive, but not one to relish.

I might never have struck the top of an egg with my teaspoon and hurried to catch the lava of yolk from the crater. I might never have smoothed melting butter onto toast with the side of a knife or fried sardines with salted capers for a midnight snack or nursed a cup of Earl Grey – 'strong tea' – in a favourite china mug with its superglued handle. I might have been deprived of all this if I hadn't, a year or so after university, read Siegfried Sassoon's description of a breakfast of boiled eggs, eaten in winter. In *Memoirs of a Fox-Hunting Man*, the first volume of his First World War trilogy, the poet recalls cold mornings before a hunt: 'We got up at four o'clock, fortified ourselves with boiled eggs and cocoa, and set off on bicycles to a cubbing meet about eight miles away.' Stopping in a copse, he has sandwiches, and on the way home keeps himself warm with thoughts of poached eggs on toast, tea and more cocoa.

All those eggs! All that bread! Hot chocolate! (I hadn't had a cup of hot chocolate in a decade.) Sassoon's exhilaration in the hunt, the fortifying effect of the eggs and cocoa at dawn, planted a thought: that hearty, warming food might lead to a richer life than the mean, restricted one I had been living. With Sassoon's help, I was on to something. But I didn't yet know what it was.

When I read Sassoon's cubbing-meet breakfast, I was twenty-four. I had nearly reached the ten-year recovery mark that had seemed so daunting in the doctor's office. I was better than I had been, but not wholly well. What was the state of my mind's library at this point? The chair had been righted, the lamp repaired, the glass in the windows and bookcases replaced. Some semblance of order had been restored, but the books, my thoughts, were still maddeningly disordered.

When anxious or upset, I saw myself as fat, and, under pressure from a job interview or a break-up with a boyfriend, as monstrously obese. My dresses and jeans may all have been the smallest size in the shops, but the reflection in the mirror belonged to another person. I thought of most foods with fear and disgust and lashed myself with a cat-o'-nine-tails when I thought I had eaten to excess. 'Excess' was not a packet of crisps or a takeaway burger,

but a handful of dried apricots or a single roast potato at
Sunday lunch.

It has been the work of the last five years to pick up
each of those mind's library books in turn and shelve them
in their rightful place. To learn – and it has been a long,
hesitating lesson – to eat not with grudging duty, but with
delight. It began with Sassoon's eggs. His ham sandwiches
eaten perched on a country gate. His slice of cherry tart
at a very good cricket tea. My curiosity was piqued. Dare
I say my stomach rumbled? I wondered: were there other
writers with as hearty an appetite? There were.

This is not a book about the anguish – and it is anguish – of anorexia. Others have reported the worst of the
illness with searing clarity and honesty. But their memoirs
often stop at the first signs of recovery. This book is about
what comes next. About the pouring in of sunlight after
more than a decade of darkness and hunger. About Charles
Dickens giving me the courage to try a spoonful of Christmas pudding. About crumbling saffron buns on a walk
with Laurie Lee, and spooning yogurt, honey and walnuts
at a breakfast with Patrick Leigh Fermor. About keeping
the cold out with Robert Graves's bully beef, and picking
teeth-staining mulberries with Elizabeth David. About
(rapture, this!) stirring whole milk into my porridge with
the Swallows and Amazons. About ginger biscuits broken
in half with Virginia Woolf.

I want to write about the solace of reading, and through
reading, putting my mind's shelves in order. About restoring my library, one book at a time.

I

'A shocking thing hunger, isn't it, Mr Nickleby?'

Through the winter months of the worst of my illness, eating peas and scraps of tofu, I never once skipped breakfast. I had a conviction – and I must have read the phrase in a magazine because the wording is so precise – that 'a good breakfast is the key to successful weight loss'. I could starve as I pleased as the day went on, but mornings began with the good breakfast of the rubric.

While my definition of breakfast remained the same – I did eat something every morning – I chipped away at the 'good'. Porridge and milk and a banana and honey: that is a good breakfast. Take away the honey, and the porridge and banana will set you up for the day. Take away the banana, and the porridge will keep you warm. Swap dairy milk for soya, and you lose the benefit of the calcium. I did myself lasting harm this way. A scan, insisted on by my doctor after his diagnosis, showed osteopenia – the beginnings of brittle bone disease – at the base of my spine.

Halve the portion of porridge, and you will be hungry by eleven. Halve the portion again, and you'll be hungry by nine. Halve it again – we are down to three level table-spoons now – and the cold when you leave the house for school is cruel. Replace the soya milk with water, and you are mottled and shivering even in six layers of clothes.

God, how cold I was. Fingers and toes blue, wearing gloves in lessons, and sinking into a bath sobbing at the end of the day. I was driven wild with cold at the bus stop. Let the driver come round the corner with the next change of lights, let me not stand here on a January morning for a minute longer.

But still I had eaten a *good breakfast*. The anorexic mind is perversely logical. I had a talent for convincing myself that my regime was admirable. I scoffed at the girls at school who missed breakfast. What dolts! They would be much better off having hot porridge, as I did. How often they stumbled at morning break, buying chocolate from the tuck shop. But, I, with my *good* breakfast, hardly needed my lunchtime Ryvita, taken in broken pieces from inside a locker so no one would see me eat. Nor was I hungry for my pea soup at dinner – peas in the water in which they had been boiled.

A good breakfast – it sounds absurd now. By the time I'd finished my refinements, you couldn't truly call it porridge. It had become the thin, workhouse gruel ladled from the copper in *Oliver Twist* for the benefit of poor parish boys. Unlike Oliver, it never crossed my mind to want more.

The workhouse children of Charles Dickens's Mudfog have a porringer of oatmeal and water three times a day. Oliver and his fellow starvelings polish the bowls clean with their spoons and lick their fingers for stray splashes of gruel. In some ways they are fortunate. There are worse breakfasts in Dickens. In *Nicholas Nickleby*, the pupils of Dotheboys Hall have their porridge – 'which looked like diluted pincushions without the covers' – from Mrs Wackford Squeers, who first doses each boy with brimstone and treacle because it spoils his appetite.

Wackford Squeers, headmaster of Dotheboys Hall, is all for good breakfasts – but only if he's the one who is eating them. In the dining room of a coaching inn, Squeers lines up before him the five little boys, unlucky all, who will shortly go up to his Yorkshire school. He orders two penn'orth of milk in a blue mug, thinned with lukewarm water. 'Why the milk will be drowned,' protests the waiter, mindful of five boys with empty stomachs. Mr Squeers is unmoved. 'Conquer your passions, boys, and don't be eager after vittles.'

The lukewarm milk and water arrives and Squeers tells his charges how they will proceed. '"When I say number one", pursued Mr Squeers, putting the mug before the children, "the boy on the left hand nearest the window may take a drink; and when I say number two the boy next him will go in, and so till we come to number five, which is the last boy. Are you ready?"' 'Yes, sir,' cry the little boys, eager and hungry. '"That's right," said Squeers, calmly getting on with his breakfast; "keep ready till I tell you to begin. Subdue your appetites, my dears, and you've conquered human nature. This is the way we inculcate strength of mind, Mr Nickleby."'

Mr Squeers, mouth full of beef and toast, keeps his boys in 'torments of expectations' until he has finished his own breakfast. Then: '"Number one may take a drink." Number one seized the mug ravenously, and had just drunk enough to make him wish for more, when Mr Squeers gave the signal for number two, who gave up at the same interesting moment to number three, and the process was repeated till the milk and water terminated with number five.'

Was there ever such a torture scene? After a decade of diluting my milk with the meanness of Mr Squeers, I read this passage with horror. Dickens makes clear that Squeers, by his miserly husbanding of the milk, is as rotten as they come. Worse still, we have Ralph Nickleby, the novel's villain – and we know he is a villain by *his* breakfast habits – boasting to the widowed Mrs Nickleby: 'When I first went to business, ma'am, I took a penny loaf and ha'porth of milk for my breakfast as I walked to the city every morning; what do you say to that, ma'am? Breakfast! Pshaw!' And I bet he had his ha'porth of milk watered, too.

I joke now, but I found the scene of the coaching inn breakfast genuinely unsettling. Did my eating habits align me with characters like this? Bullies and misanthropes? Had I not inflicted on my own body what Wackford Squeers inflicts on his boys? For the two penn'orth of milk is only the beginning of his cruelties.

The kitchen Mr Squeers keeps at Dotheboys Hall is by no means a lean one, at least when it comes to feeding his own family. There is Yorkshire pie and cold beef when he arrives with his cargo of small boys from London, and, later, an 'uncommon juicy steak'. Downstairs, meanwhile, it is porridge and brimstone for the boys. In morning lessons, the children sit 'crouching and shivering together, and seemed to lack the spirit to move about'. 'Crouching and shivering'. That is another phrase which, once read, has lodged in my memory. A breakfast of anorexic's porridge – scant tablespoons of oats, thinned and thinned again with water – leaves you fit for nothing but crouching and shivering.

At the worst of my anorexia, I did lack the spirit, certainly the strength, to move about. A few weeks after the doctor had made his diagnosis, during which time I staggered into school with a deranged determination, shaking

and light-headed from hunger, I was taken out of my own
Dotheboys Hall, and put to bed. There I more or less remained, broken only by outings to doctor, therapist and
Daunt, from March until September, when I started at a
new school taking just five GCSEs and going home to bed
between lessons. If the first school had been a Dotheboys,
then this light, high-ceilinged college was more like the
village classroom kept in *Great Expectations* by the good
and kindly Biddy.

You might think I take Mr Squeers and his hungry
boys too much to heart. After all, he is only fictional. But
when he says to Nicholas, smacking his lips over the two
penn'orth of milk, 'A shocking thing hunger, isn't it, Mr
Nickleby?' I find myself nodding in appalled agreement.

That I was so gripped by *Nicholas Nickleby* and that
its wickeder scenes seemed so vivid was because Dickens
had taken me over almost completely. In 2012, the bicentenary of his birth, I made it my January resolution to
read all sixteen novels – I had managed only *A Christmas
Carol* and *Great Expectations* at school – before the year was
out. This tendency to turn any gentle pursuit – reading a
bedside novel, say – into a gauntlet and endurance test is
not uncommon in anorexics. I could always have worked
harder. Three hours' homework, four hours, five. Always
have taken on another project, done it better, more neatly,
read another dozen books from the reading list. Always
have been up earlier. Still, since I was no longer allowed to
make New Year's pledges to lose weight, exercise furiously
or banish this food or that from my diet, reading all of
Dickens's novels in a year was a kinder undertaking.

I almost managed it. If I hadn't been waylaid by *Sherlock
Holmes* in May (having picked up *A Study in Scarlet*, I then,

seized by a completist's mania, had to read every one of Arthur Conan Doyle's *Holmes* mysteries) I might have done it. As it was, I ran over into 2013 by six weeks.

When I started the Dickens marathon, I was twenty-four. I had got myself through university, managed the first year of a job as a commissioning editor on a newspaper, found a balance, just about, between well and unwell. I was, I suppose, what doctors call a 'functioning' anorexic. I had an unhappy truce with the illness. I'd eat enough to get by. I'd eat old stalwarts – cereal, tomatoes, rye bread – but nothing new. A chatty, happy dinner with friends had to be checked and paid for by a fast the day after.

I was funny about cookbooks, cooing over pictures and recipes, treating myself to imagined ingredients, dishes and places – saffron, soba, fenugreek, kohlrabi, Otto-lenghi, Moro, the Orient, the Levant, Aleppo peppers and Chinese pears. When I'd had my fill I'd close the pages, return the books to the shelf, and cook something plain and under-seasoned: pasta and cherry tomatoes, white fish and greens. At weekends I'd make a great parade of baking – flour, icing sugar, syrups, glazes, pomegranate this and orange blossom that – and admire my trays of rising muffins, before pressing them on friends, colleagues, my brother, party hosts and finding – the lies we tell – that there wasn't one left over for me.

While I was reading Dickens something changed. I didn't want to be on the outside, looking at pictures, tasting recipes at one remove, seeing the last muffin go to someone else. I began to want to *want* food. To share it, savour it, to have it without guilt.

That year, I read with an unbounded appetite, bean-feasting on hundreds of pages in a sitting, entire books in a week, heavy and surfeited with words. Mr Pickwick never tucked into a meal with as much eagerness as I did sixteen courses of Dickens. *Edwin Drood*, which I read last, and which was unfinished when Dickens died, was the small glass of port wine after the figgy pudding. If I hadn't been so possessed by Dickens in that year, not been so immersed in his London, his Yarmouth, his Yorkshire, if I had read the books piecemeal over a lifetime and not in a single great banquet, one course after the other, he might not have left such a mark. But in waking up with Dickens, breakfasting, lunching, walking, suppering, going to bed with him, reading a few pages while the kettle boiled because I was falling behind in my year's timings, in being completely rapt by Dickens, I began to see all manner of things through his lens.

It struck me, as I ticked off *Nicklebys*, *Copperfields* and *Chuzzlewits*, that not one of his novels is carried off without a meal or two, or indeed a dozen along the way. No great enterprise is undertaken without the promise of pie and porter at the end of it and no celebration complete without a tureen of mock-turtle soup marbled with fat. Marbled with fat – what an idea. After so long thinking of any hearty meal, any food which would find a place on the table of the 'gorging and gormandising' Mr Pumblechook (another man for watering the milk of hungry boys – poor Pip) with something between terror and revulsion, I read Dickens's passages of supper-conjuring with a famished curiosity.

I did not – yet – have any great desire to eat a whole 'haystack of buttered toast', such as the one prepared by the Aged Parent in *Great Expectations*, nor Mr Crummles's hot beef-steak pudding and potatoes. But I liked the thought of them, and took vicarious pleasure in others' enjoyment of fried sole, shrimp sauce, watercress and young radishes.

I was following the example of Mr John Browdie in *Nicholas Nickleby* who, vexed at being made to wait to start on the tea table, ventures 'to dip a tea-spoon in the milk-pot and carry it to his mouth, or to cut off a little knob of crust, and a little corner of meat, and swallow them at two gulps like a couple of pills'. That was all I wanted for the time being, to taste, to sample, to dip just a tea-spoon in the milkpot of Dickens's meals.

Recovering from anorexia is about more than just eating enough and continuing to eat enough to keep yourself alive. You have to pick up, order and shelve all the thoughts that have been scattered, upturned, torn and damaged. Though I had started to eat again, I still thought of food as something fundamentally bad and unnecessary. There was a part of me that still believed I could get by – if I was steel-willed enough – on air and water alone. The smell from any takeaway shop I passed in the street turned my stomach and I inwardly recoiled when I watched friends eat a curry or hamburger.

In uptight moods, I privately tutted at others asking for second helpings, or ordering pudding, or spooning rich gravy over their meat, and I was neurotic about being of-fered such things myself. I half coveted and half resented the chocolate bars eaten by girlfriends and the caramel popcorn taken into the cinema. How did they eat with such ease?

Hunger, restraint, iron self-command conferred a mis-placed moral superiority. *I* was virtuous because I did not eat. Others were wanton, reckless, wild, polluted because they did. That had been my way of thinking from the age

of thirteen to twenty-four. It took a year of Dickens to
shake me out of this wrong-headedness. There is no virtue
in hunger in Dickens. It is a symptom of want, deprivation
and poverty. I flinched when I read the passage in *Oliver
Twist* when Oliver, apprenticed to an undertaker, arrives at
a house where a young woman has died. Her father, mad
with grief, tells them: 'I say she starved to death. I never
knew how bad she was, till the fever came upon her, and
then her bones were starting through the skin.'

Having so long fetishised 'bones . . . starting through
the skin', so long wished for a thinner and thinner body
– though the curse of the illness is that you are never thin
enough, that the closer you are to bone, the greater the
flesh you imagine – reading these words shook me. A new
thought rose: that there is no beauty, nothing brave in
starvation. It brings no happiness, confers no blessings,
has no goodness in it. I had aspired for so long to skeletal
thinness, but here was a young woman, starved so thin
that, as her father, puts it: 'The worms would worry – not
eat her, – she is so worn away.'

The strange thing is that if you had asked me at fifteen
what I made of this woman, I might have told you I *envied*
her. Wracked with hunger, my mind harum-scarum with
headaches and desperate impulses, I thought there was
something good in death. I would have welcomed it as
respite from the clamouring in my head and the pains of
my starved body. But reading *Oliver Twist* at twenty-four,
better nourished and a great deal calmer, I cringed from
this scene. Hunger, as it was here, was horrible and pitiful.
I wanted no part of it.

We tend to remember Oliver's hunger, his polite request
– 'Please, sir, I want some more' – for workhouse gruel and

his being hit on the head with the ladle and carted off by the Beadle for his pains, but we forget the unnamed young woman, starved and taken away by the undertakers only a chapter later.

I found myself dwelling on this poor tenement house. It exposed just how fractured my anorexic thinking had been. How privation and deathly hunger had acquired a glamour – and I mean glamour in the sense of a dazzling illusion, a mirage – they did not deserve. It went some way towards explaining what a task I was up against, to drive out such thinking and restore sanity and reason.

There is a misunderstanding that anorexia is a disease of vanity. That the anorexic aspires to the maypole body of the catwalk model or the red-carpet Amazon. Not at all. It is not prettification of self that drives the illness, but annihilation of self. It is the scraping-back of flesh from bone, it is punishment, will to destruction. It is the belief that you are not worthy of food, nourishment, life. Vanity, beauty? They have nothing to do with it.

After visiting the Mudfog slum house without coal or bread, we are in need now of something reviving, something of the sort Pip and Mr Wemmick have before setting out from Wandsworth for Mr Wemmick's clandestine marriage to Miss Skiffins in *Great Expectations*. 'We had fortified ourselves with the rum-and-milk and biscuits,' says Pip, and we must have the same: rum-and-milk and biscuits to recover from the early, hungry chapters of *Oliver Twist*.

Mr Wemmick is a great one for biscuits, which he pops into his mouth as if they were letters into a postbox; and not just biscuits, but buttered rolls, sausages speared on

a toasting fork, loin of pork, home-grown greens and cucumbers raised on a garden frame. Wemmick, a lawyer's
clerk, has the pick of the choicest fowls from the cook's
shop, having relieved the cook of jury duty. He makes an
excellent steak stew.

We know Mr Wemmick is good, just as we know Mr
Squeers is bad, by the table he keeps. When Pip goes to
Wemmick's for tea, there is not just the 'haystack of buttered toast' prepared by the Aged Parent, but a 'such a
jorum of tea, that the pig in the back premises became
strongly excited and repeatedly expressed his desire to par-
ticipate in the entertainment'. I was taken with that jorum
of tea, circling it with a pencil in my book and copying
from the dictionary: 'a large drinking bowl or vessel, esp. a
bowl of punch' in the space at the top of the page. Had it
been only a 'pot' of tea I might not have taken such notice,
but I like new words, collect and keep lists of them in the
back of my diary, and use them, however obscure, if I think
I can get away with it.

I was sold, too, on Herbert Pocket's 'pottle' of strawberries ('a small basket, esp. one of a conical shape used
for holding strawberries or other soft fruit, now rare') in
Great Expectations, bought at Covent Garden market, carried back to Chancery and fast turning to jam in his hands.
A pot of tea or a punnet of strawberries I would not have
wanted to share, but a *jorum* of tea and a *pottle* of strawberries . . . 'We ate the whole of the toast,' recalls Pip of Mr
Wemmick's spread, 'and drank tea in proportion, and it
was delightful to see how warm and greasy we all got after
it.' The idea that food could be companionable, delightful,
warming ('greasy', I admit, had less appeal) was new and
tantalising.

In *David Copperfield* I met Mr Micawber, an admirable guest at a party: affable, eager and deft with a gridiron. When a planned supper at Davey Copperfield's lodging goes awry (his cook, Mrs Crupp, is taken ill while frying the soles), it is Micawber to the rescue. Mr Micawber's Mustard Mutton would not disgrace the menu in any cookhouse. Davey tells us: 'Traddles cut the mutton into slices; Mr Micawber (who could do anything of this sort to perfection) covered them in pepper, mustard, salt and cayenne; I put them on the gridiron, turned them with a fork and took them off, under Mr Micawber's directions; and Mrs Micawber heated, and continually stirred some mushroom ketchup in a little saucepan.'

They roll their sleeves up at the wrists and fall to, as more mutton slices sputter on the fire. It wasn't so much the mutton or the ketchup or even the cayenne that stayed with me after I'd closed the book, but, as with the buttered toast, the conviviality, the game of it all. Here is how Davey sums up the party:

> What with the novelty of this cookery, the excellence of it, the bustle of it, the frequent starting up to look after it, the frequent sitting down to dispose of it as the crisp slices came off the gridiron hot and hot, the being so busy, so flushed with the fire, so amused, and in the midst of such a tempting noise and savour, we reduced the leg of mutton to the bone. My own appetite came back miraculously.

Bustle, a flushing fire, tempting noise, laughter, and an appetite miraculously restored. I read this passage with stirrings of appetite no less miraculous.

There were times, though, when I rebelled against Dickens's mutton and beef, perspiring hams and 'blisterous' Yorkshire puddings. When Mr Hubble (that is not a thin-sounding name and Mr Hubble is not a thin-looking man) in *Great Expectations* announces 'a bit of savoury pork pie would lay atop of anything you could mention, and do no harm,' I all but closed the book and put it back on the shelf in protest. No, there were no circumstances in which I could imagine a pork pie being eaten as a dainty morsel, a palette-cleanser, an after-dinner mint to finish a meal of pickled pork, roast stuffed fowls, mince pies and boiled Christmas pudding. I could just about face a (small) one if it constituted the whole meal and a long walk to follow, but, no, I could not join Mr Hubble in a post-prandial pork pie.

By instinct and appetite I am more on the side of the Little Dorrits than the Mr Hubbles. Amy Dorrit has 'a great anxiety' about eating, 'an extraordinary repugnance to dining in company'. She is a furtive eater, taking her plate off to odd corners, or eating standing on tiptoe at the mantelpiece instead of a table. With her back to the room, she can squirrel away her food to take home to her father, locked in the Marshalsea prison for the worst of bad debts.

In *Little Dorrit*, characters lose or recover their appetites in line with their fortunes. A lack of appetite for food is the first sign of a weakening of will, a growing, cooped-up fear of the outside world. When we meet Amy Dorrit, she is employed as a paid companion to Mrs Clennam, a woman listless and incurious in her eating. She never leaves the house, never sees a new face, never tries any new titbit brought to her in her isolation. Her evening meal is a dish of little rusks carried up on a tray. Half of these she dips in a hot mixture of port wine, lemon, sugar and spices; half she has softened with butter. Her retainers, the tyrannous Mr Flintwich and trembling Mrs Affery, try to tempt her with a dish of oysters, 'eight in number, circularly set out on a white plate on a tray covered with a white napkin, flanked by a slice of buttered French roll,' but she refuses, and sends the briny supper back to the kitchen.

After her son, Arthur Clennam, is ruined in business and condemned like Mr Dorrit before him to the Marshalsea, he rapidly falls ill. All food turns to dust. John Chivery, son of the gatekeeper and Arthur's rival for Amy, brings a picnic to lift Arthur's spirits: fresh butter kept clean in a cabbage leaf, slices of boiled ham, bread, a basket of watercresses and salad herbs. Arthur does his best, but 'the ham sickened him, the bread seemed to turn to sand in his mouth. He could force nothing upon himself but a cup of tea.' At John's urging – 'Try a little something green' – Arthur manages a sprig or two of watercress, but nothing more. 'The bread turned to a heavier sand than before, and the ham (though it was good enough of itself) seemed to blow a faint simoom of ham through the whole Marshalsea.'

Arthur knows that it must have cost the slighted John much to bring him that cabbage-leaf supper: 'It was very kind of you to think of putting this between the wires; but, I cannot even get this down today.' In his misery and abasement Arthur no longer thinks it worth taking care of himself. He falls idle, mopes, pines, can no longer even lose himself in books. He cannot sleep, nor breathe except at the window. He eats nothing and sinks into a low fever.

There is a difference in *Little Dorrit* between mind-sickness and body-sickness. The Clennams, mother and son, are mind-sick: hounded by the past and held hostage by guilt. They see no reason to eat. Their opposite is the simple, trusting Maggy, on whom Amy keeps a tender eye. Maggy was once body-sick. She had a bad fever when she was ten, and has never grown any older in her thoughts. She is so simple, so trusting and childish, that she feels no dejection, no regret, no disgrace. She looks back at her fevered stay in hospital – 'Ev'nly place!' – with bliss: '"Such beds is there!" cried Maggy. "Such lemonades! Such oranges! Such d'licious broth and wine! Such Chicking! Oh, AIN'T it a delightful place to go and stop at!"' The greatest compliment the chuckling Maggy can pay the supper offered her by Arthur Clennam – cakes, fruit and wine – is: 'Oh ain't it d'licious! Ain't it hospitally!'

When I was most ill, at fifteen, when all meals might have been sand and when I would not have eaten even a grain if Mum had not sat with me taking up John's cry of 'Try a little more something,' I did not want to see anyone. I was convinced that visitors were keeping score of my weight. Had I lost or gained that week? It was easier to hide in my room, making a Marshalsea of the house. Easier to read alone. No book has ever given me a look up and down and said, 'You look better.' I always took this badly. 'You're looking better' to me meant: 'You're definitely fatter.'

In those Marshalsea months, a family friend came to visit. She said something that upset me very much at the time, though I knew she had meant well. Gallows humour. She said that her husband – a gourmet, a Pickwick, a Hubble – had always wanted to be anorexic. Because what fun he would have had eating himself fat and well again. I managed a smile while she was there, but I was angry after. You wouldn't wish anorexia upon yourself, not on your worst enemy. It isn't fun. Recovery wasn't a game, an all-you-can-eat spree at the cheeseboard and wine cellar. Every mouthful was a struggle, from buttered toast down to the last sand-dry sprig of watercress.

My sickness was mind-sickness, Clennam-sickness. Body-sickness, Maggy's sort of sickness, can be, if not cured, then at least bettered and soothed with lemonade and cakes. Anorexia is a very devious sort of illness, and it needs wilier medicines. You would not find a copy of *Little Dorrit* in any dispensary. Doctors write no notes for Chuzzlewit pills and Dombey tinctures. But Dickens *was* making me better.

If I had been a functioning anorexic, still enslaved by old rules and measures, Dickens made me an agitating, questioning one. Why did I have to be hungry? Why eat dry rusks? Why waste away on meals pushed between the wires? If I went out for supper it was always soup, salad, fruit. Why not a roast leg of something feathered with sage and onions and mashed potatoes?

Dickens made me brave. Could I have eaten the Cratchits' Christmas goose? One of Mrs Clennam's oysters? No, not yet. But just reading about them, just broaching the thought of them, and of Mr Pancks's bread and butter pudding and Amy's basket of grapes and jelly, was beginning to slacken the knots of my illness.

The very worst of Dickens's creations eat lustily and well while keeping food from others. Wackford Squeers does it to his captive pupils, Mr Pumblechook does it to Pip, and Miss Charlotte does it to Oliver as she feeds him the 'dainty viands' that the dog has rejected.

One of the nastiest examples of this is Miss Sally Brass in *The Old Curiosity Shop*, a bully of the first order, who starves the servant girl in the kitchen while pretending to charity. When it comes to the sainted Little Nell, I am afraid I am with Oscar Wilde that one would have to have a heart of stone not to laugh at her syrupy, sentimental last illness, but my heart did break for the 'Marchioness' (she has no other name) in her basement kitchen. This is how she takes her dinner – 'a dreary waste of cold potatoes, looking as eatable as Stonehenge':

> 'Do you see this?' said Miss Brass, slicing off about two square inches of cold mutton, after all this preparation, and holding it out on the point of the fork.
>
> The small servant looked hard enough at it with her hungry eyes to see every shred of it, small as it was, and answered, 'yes.'
>
> 'Then don't you ever go and say,' retorted Miss Sally, 'that you hadn't meat here. There eat it up.'
>
> This was soon done. 'Now, do you want any more?' said Miss Sally.
>
> The hungry creature answered with a faint 'no.' They were evidently going through an established form.
>
> 'You've been helped once to meat,' said Miss Brass, summing up the facts; 'you have had as much as you can eat, you're asked if you want any more, and you answer, "no!" Then don't you ever go and say you were allow-anced, mind that.'

Was there ever such a Gorgon? Later, when the Marchioness is rescued by Dick Swiveller, she tells him: 'They kept me very short ... Oh! you can't think how short

they kept me.' So short that she used to walk around the
house in the dark looking for bits of biscuit, 'sangwitches'
left in the office and curls of orange peel. These she would
put in cold water and make believe it was wine. 'If you
make believe very much,' she tells Dick, 'it's quite nice.
But if you don't, you know, it seems as if it would bear
a little more seasoning, certainly.' I knew a little of that.
One could make believe that peas in their boiling water
made pea soup. But really it wasn't the same as thick pea
soup with bacon cooked into it and a haystack of buttered
toast to mop the bowl. Eaten as the whole of dinner, it did
leave a hungry body very short indeed.

As I read my way through Dickens I made a tally of
the Squeers and Pumblechooks, Miss Charlottes and Miss
Sallys, each keeping those in their care short: not one
with an ounce of goodness in them. Why, then, when I
shuddered at their viciousness, did I think it right and
reasonable to keep my own body so short and so cold, fed
on thin gruel and make-believe? Could I go on my whole
life aligning myself with Squeerses and Miss Sallies and
meting out their punishments?

If there was a moment of clarity, it came at Christmas. I
had read the books in any old order as they appealed, but
A Christmas Carol I had saved for the holiday.

Christmas, since I had first been ill, had been a strain.
More than a strain: a cause for panic and distress. I hated
any disruption to my careful, measured eating. The ex-
pectation that for a week between Christmas Eve and the
New Year I might have to join in with turkey and buttered
carrots, roast parsnips and potatoes, pigs-in-blankets and
devils-on-horseback, Christmas pudding and mince pies,
iced fruitcakes and stollen, Quality Street and gingerbread,

filled me with terror. If terror sounds hysterical, well, I *was* hysterical. I was ill with worry each year, miserably filling my plate on the day with Brussels sprouts and cabbage. Mum did me great kindness year after year, laying out plates of smoked salmon and dishes of clementines, which I could eat and so give the impression of joining in. But the dread of being around so much food – as if I might grow fat on the very fumes of hot mulled wine – remained.

Where Mrs Freeman faltered, Mrs Bob Cratchit prevailed. Out Mrs Cratchit goes after the goose and apple sauce to fetch the pudding from the kitchen. ('Suppose it should not be done enough! Suppose it should break in turning out!') Off comes the pudding cloth. ('Hallo! A great deal of steam!') And back again to the table with her prize. 'In a half a minute Mrs Cratchit entered: flushed, but smiling proudly with the pudding, like a speckled cannon-ball, so hard and firm, blazing in half of half-a-quartern of ignited brandy, and bedight with Christmas holly stuck into the top.'

I read the chapter of the speckled cannon-ball on the train home on Christmas Eve 2012. Two days later, when the Boxing Day pudding came through the doors of the kitchen, lit up with brandy, I clapped with the others. I left my usual clementine in the bowl and I shared with the others a spoonful of that Christmas's plum pudding. It was only half of half a spoonful, if I am scrupulously honest, but it was a start.

2

*'Home-made bread and honey had indeed caused
us to forget that there was a war on'*

I'd like to write that once I had eaten my spoonful of Mrs Cratchit's plum pudding, it was on to Fagin's sausages, Kit Nubbles's oysters and Miss Pinch's peppered beefsteak pie with hand-raised pastry. But the great frustration of recovery from my illness, I suspect from any illness, was that it was rarely as simple as that. For every two strides forward there was a lurch back. I would conquer one old, bad tendency, only to find myself with some new phobia or folly. These would become habit and I wouldn't notice the damage until they were entrenched.

So it was that I could only justify my hard-won spoonful of Christmas pudding if it was followed a two-hour walk in the cold. My 'calorie-offsetting' defied any mathematical logic. One digestive biscuit was an hour's walking, a bowl of fruit crumble two. Walking in itself was no evil – it was often a joy – but too often I was walking miles and miles with little or nothing to sustain me.

If the year of Dickens had made me a more curious eater, it had also turned me into a prodigious walker. Reading his essays about night walking in London, I followed his routes: along the river; down with the tide; to Wapping; through Clerkenwell; Mr Clennam's walk from Covent

Garden to Twickenham in *Little Dorrit*; Thomas Pinch's walk from Camberwell to Islington in *Martin Chuzzlewit*. Dickens had taken up the sport after a spell of sleeplessness. This disorder, he wrote, was 'defeated by the brisk treatment of getting up directly after lying down, and going out, and coming home tired at sunrise'.

Washed as I was in his London fogs, I wanted to see the city as he had seen it. The first line of *The Old Curiosity Shop* ran in my head as I walked. 'Night is generally my time for walking.' I liked the solitude and relative empty quiet of the city, liberated from its daytime crowds: 'that constant pacing to and fro, that never-ending restlessness, that incessant tread of feet wearing the rough stones smooth and glossy'.

I started walking home to Paddington from the newspaper offices and from meetings in town, and then from further afield. From Holborn (an hour), from Highbury (an hour and a half), from Turnham Green (two hours.) I remembered what it had been like, at fifteen, to be too thin to walk. To be taken by Mum once around the communal garden, a loop of the gravel path, a rest on a bench, then back to bed. To feel that my legs were fat and must be exercised, though the truth was they were too wasted to support me.

When, ten years on from those circuits of the garden, and guided by Dickens, I started walking miles of London and finding my legs *would* carry me, I became addicted. On a soft, enveloping night in June it was exhilarating to have the city to myself and discover new energy after so many years of being first house-bound and later unable to keep up with friends. But in November, in sheets of rain and wearing thin-soled boots that let the water in, it became a new sort of punishment. I was no longer allowed to starve myself – that I clung to – so I made up new penances.

One night, coming back from Queen Square, I walked home in a bitter wind without a scarf or coat. I had had no dinner, had not eaten since lunch, and I was pinched with the cold before I'd even turned out of the square onto Southampton Row. Every bus that went past, every taxi, winked and beckoned. But I kept home to Paddington on foot, numb with cold and hunger. Too worn out to cook supper, I went to bed empty and shivering. There were other nights like it. I had only half learnt my lesson from Dickens. I had adopted his striding city walks – and revelled in newfound stamina – but had failed to reward myself with the mashed potatoes and anchovy toasts that greet his characters when they reach their lodgings. I needed a new model to follow.

Finishing *Edwin Drood* over a weekend in February 2013 left me floundering. What was I to read if not Dickens? For a year I had not had to think about which book to take to bed, there had always been a *Nickleby* or *Dombey*. I found myself bereft, listlessly starting on books before giving up after a few pages. Unread, half-read, abandoned books stacked up by my bed. I wanted a project.

The newspapers and radio schedules were full of the coming centenary of the start of the First World War, so at Daunt I bought the war poets: Siegfried Sassoon's *Memoirs of a Fox-Hunting Man, Memoirs of an Infantry Officer* and *Sherston's Progress*; Robert Graves's *Goodbye to All That*; and Edmund Blunden's *Undertones of War*. I already had a copy of the Welsh poet and painter David Jones's epic poem *In Parenthesis* – a 1978 Faber edition with dry glue and falling-out pages, bought while writing about

Jones's watercolours at university. It joined the pile. Suitably kitted, haversack filled with paperbacks, boots and puttees laced, I marched out.

I did not set off expecting to find anything tempting. If you had asked me what the Tommies had eaten in their billets and trenches, I would have said bully beef, biscuits and tea. I had a half-memory of a history lesson at school on trench rations. Yet here was Siegfried Sassoon and his unit in Amiens lunching *'like Dukes'* in a green-shuttered private room on langoustes, duck and two bottles of the house's best bubbly.

But, in starting at Amiens, I am racing ahead. Sassoon's memoirs do not open in a dug-out in battle-lined France. Our hero does not even cross the Channel until the last few pages of *Memoirs of a Fox-Hunting Man*. Sassoon's war trilogy – part-fictionalised, with Siegfried replaced by Sherston, and his mother by an unmarried Aunt Evelyn – opens on the Kent Downs, in the halcyon summers of an Edwardian childhood. Sherston remembers the smell of strawberry jam being made and the quince tree that grew beside the pond. There is the village vegetable show to be judged – 'You never saw such tomatoes and cucumbers!' – and delicious roast chickens ordered by Aunt Evelyn when he is home for the school holidays.

Waking early in summer, he steals down to the pantry, cuts himself a piece of cake and, 'yawning and munching', creeps back to bed for a few more hours' sleep before breakfast. He is hopelessly spoilt – 'What, no more asparagus, sir? Why it's the first we've had this year!' – and while sometimes lonely (Sassoon had two brothers, Sherston is an only child) with just his aunt and the servants, not unhappy.

Much of his childhood and adolescence is passed in what
was formerly the day nursery. Sherston devotes a good deal
of thought to what it should be called now that he is a
young man of letters:

> 'Study' was inappropriate and sounded elderly. 'Smok-
> ing room' wouldn't do either, because I hadn't begun
> smoking yet, although puffing my pipe by the fireside
> on winter evenings was a comfortable idea. 'Library', I
> thought (pausing in the dark passage with a hand on the
> brass door-knob) was too big a jump from 'schoolroom'.
> Besides, there wasn't any library. 'Library' meant glass-
> fronted bookcases with yellow busts of Julius Caesar and
> Cicero on the top. Entering the fire-lit room, I pounced
> on the bulky package which Miriam had deposited on
> the table. 'Book-room', I thought, as I tugged impet-
> uously at the thick string. And 'book-room' it rather
> tentatively became.

Here was a writer and reader after my own heart. I could
put my faith in Sherston and follow him into battle.

When he isn't reading, Sherston's two great pursuits are
cricket and fox-hunting. In his memoirs no cricket match
is ever won, no fence jumped, no fox run to ground without
a stomach full of a good breakfast, a better lunch and a top-
notch tea. The luncheon tent at the village cricket match
is a spectacle. Its trestle tables buckle under slices of cold
lamb and beef, veal and ham pie and a joint of gammon.
There is ginger beer and cold cherry tart for pudding. One
would willingly sit through a day's cricket and marrow-
judging for such a meal.

Cold cherry tarts and gooseberries as large as hen's eggs

came as a surprise. I had thought it would be all marches and mortars and trench foot and shell shock. It had never occurred to me that in between barrages the men would have had to have their tea or that the great consolation of dug-out life would be toasted cheese and a square of chocolate. Reading Dickens had made me receptive to breakfasts, lunches and teas, and as I picked my way along the duck-boards with Sassoon, Blunden, Graves and Jones, I found myself noticing what they ate and what meals meant to them.

For the young Sherston food was fuel for an afternoon's batting (forty-three not out – his highest score yet for the village), or for a morning's fox-hunting on ground flaked with frost, sandwiches stuffed into pockets. Sherston's hunting breakfasts are something special. The groomsman Dixon, worrying that a first breakfast at home has not done its job, takes his pupil to an inn and orders a large glass of hot milk, which Sherston '*should be jolly glad of, he said, before the day was out*'. Later, there are two boiled eggs eaten in the snug parlour of another inn in celebration after the hunt. What a difference between Mr Dixon and Mr Squeers.

Sherston eats an uncommon number of eggs – boiled and poached – and drinks cup after cup of cocoa. When the weather comes on wet, all he can think of is how far he is from the train station and poached eggs for tea. There are banana fritters after one hunt meet, and a brace of pheasants, spoils of a day's covert shooting, after another. His friend and fellow huntsman Denis Milden talks with his mouth full of bread and butter and '*munches*' – a favourite Sassoon word – brown biscuits brought from his pocket in a twist of paper when they stop to catch their breath. Sherston is more of a sandwiches man.

There is something admirably unselfconscious about the way Sherston and Milden eat. No thought of fat or sugar or whether they should or shouldn't be eating bread and fritters. No backs of packets to consult. No kilojoules or kilocals. No 'recommended daily intake'. If they are caught talking with their mouths full, who's to chastise them? If they bolt their sandwiches, it is only in their eagerness to be on to the next fence.

Sherston wouldn't waste a moment's thought on how he looked in his hunting jacket or army uniform. A body is not there to be despised and criticised. It is there to field cricket balls, swing its legs over a cob, march into battle. After my own teenage years in a girls' school where hunger and self-loathing were as expected as a dozen A-stars, I warmed to this energetically omnivorous adolescent boy. Sherston's energy is irrepressible. When he is invalided out of France to recuperate at Somerville College in Oxford, he escapes his nurses and their ministrations of beef tea to hire a canoe, which he paddles happily up and down the Cherwell. Food is never fretted over, it is wolfed down as ballast for the next adventure.

There's a word Sassoon uses which I have circled in my paperback. 'The mornings I remember most zestfully', he writes, 'were those which took us up on to the chalk downs.' Zestfully! What a thing to wake up full of zest. Such mornings are made possible by an early breakfast of boiled eggs and cocoa mixed from two spoonfuls ('not a grain more') of powder. Thus breakfasted, Sherston is off and over the Downs, revelling in skies and landscape 'stolen from the lie-a-bed world and the luckless city workers'.

My pencil circles multiplied. Eggs – circled. Ham sandwiches – circled. Bacon – circled. If I was going to walk for two hours on a frost-hardened morning in January or an unwelcoming, damp night in November, I was going to have to do better than watery porridge. And so, I learnt, at the age of twenty-five, how to boil an egg. Eggs had been one of the first foods to go when the anorexia took hold – some misguided idea about fat and cholesterol – and I had never reinstated them. With Sassoon as my guide, I introduced one boiled egg in the morning, in a white eggcup with a chipped lip, and two eggs if I had been out late walking. Three and a half minutes for soft-boilers. Crowns knocked off. Two turns of the pepper grinder.

There was a difference between the way I had read Dickens and the way I was now reading the war poets. The meals in Dickens, while invitingly described, were not easily recreated. Where was I to order Mrs Jorley's cold knuckle of ham? Or Peggotty's cowslip wine? Or the ingredients for tripe, cowheel and sparrowgrass stew, the house special at the Jolly Sandboys Inn? Even mutton is seldom sold in the supermarkets. His meals, then, were fantasies. I could dream them, taste them vicariously, but needn't muster the means to cook them at home.

Sassoon's eggs were different. They could be had from the corner shop, and with an inch or two of water, made a breakfast fit for a cricketer, huntsman and warrior-poet. When I took my egg out of the pan in the morning I thought of Sherston, already up and stealing a march on the world. If I wavered, thought I hadn't earned my egg, I told myself I had his blessing. Eggs for zest.

Sassoon is not a refined eater. Joints of beef and eggs and ham sandwiches are the stuff of his larder. He writes about the meals he ate as a schoolboy cricketer with a schoolboy's appetite – the more the better, never mind the recipe. It is his fellow soldier-poet Robert Graves who is the epicure: when they meet after the Battle of Loos, Sassoon and Graves go straight to a Béthune cake shop for cream buns.

In *Goodbye to All That*, Graves remembers 'the lemonade glasses, the cucumber sandwiches, the petits fours, the drawing-room knick-knacks, the chrysanthemums in bowls' of afternoon tea at home in Wimbledon in the 1900s. I can see Sherston incredulous in front of a tray of *petits fours*. What good are French fancies after a point-to-point over the Downs?

Graves's teatimes were of a different order. If Sherston is rather a provincial, village-bound soul, the Graves children are cosmopolitan, expected to present themselves at drawing-room salons, and well travelled. They are taken to Germany for their holidays, where they find the Bavarian food richer and spicier than the under-seasoned cooking at home:

> We liked the rye bread, the dark pine-honey, the huge ice-cream puddings made with fresh raspberry juice and the help of snow stored during the winter in an ice house, my grandfather's venison, the honey cakes, the pastries, and particularly the sauces made with different kinds of mushrooms. Also the pretzels, the carrots cooked in sugar, and summer puddings of cranberries and blueberries.

The children have the pick of the apples, pears and greengages in the orchard and of the blackcurrant and gooseberry bushes. There are 'enormous' trout from the stream and a local jam made from wild rosehips.

Even after the family's return to England, where the milk pudding comes to the table burnt, there are compensations. P. G. Wodehouse, visiting the Graves family, gives young Robert a penny and tells him to buy himself marshmallows. In Wales, at his mother's house, they find plover's eggs. And when George Mallory, then an assistant master at Charterhouse school, not yet a climber of Everest, takes Graves walking on Snowdon, they sit in the lee of a cairn and eat candied Carlsbad plums and liver-sausage sandwiches. I've been looking for Carlsbad plums in teashops and food halls ever since. (Less so the liver sausage.)

If Sassoon and Graves dwell on childhood meals, remember them with a clarity that you might have thought dimmed by the years, it is because those gooseberry-and-rhubarb-jam teatimes of the decade before the war were so often replayed and imaginatively recreated later when every dry biscuit, every tin of sardines came up in a ration wagon, approved by headquarters and signed for by the quartermaster. How much more sparkling the lemonade glasses of old Wimbledon must have seemed when each cup of lukewarm trench tea might have been the last. Graves laments the same cup of char spilt three times and filled with dirt by a bombardment.

Edmund Blunden, a peaceable, bird-watching soul, nineteen when he was sent to Flanders, almost loses his life to a cup of cocoa. 'I was genially desired by Corporal Worley to take cocoa with him,' he recalls in *Undertones of War*, published in 1928. 'He was just bringing it to the boil over some shreds of sandbags and tallow candles. Scarcely had I grasped the friendly mug when a rifle-grenade burst with red-hot fizzing on the parapet behind me and another on the parados behind him; and we were unhit.'

The 'friendliness' of food assumed a new importance for the men at the front. It was comfort, warmth, a taste of home, a reminder that you were still alive when the batman returned from Givenchy with beer and chocolate. Sitting down to Christmas dinner in 1917, Blunden remembers that the quartermaster's roast pork made them forget, if only briefly, the wind darting through the torn canvas of their tent. This was food as friend not foe. An ally in the worst of times.

The men are consoled by bread, fatty bacon, rum and 'bitter stewed tea sickly with sugar'. There are helpings of Maconochie stew – tinned meat and vegetables – which Sherston and his men eat 'in morose discomfort', and tinned tomatoes, tinned sardines and tinned peaches. Blunden, out of boredom, makes himself a connoisseur of the different brands of bully beef and 'Sunshine' sausages. These were eaten from the tin, standing upright in a shell hole fast filling with rain.

David Jones, a sensitive, sparrow-bodied boy who felt the cold and damp severely – 'Give the poor little sod some char,' says one kindly corporal – writes a sorrowful ode to inadequate rations in *In Parenthesis*. The tea leaves come tied in the heel of a sandbag, congealed and clinging to the mesh. The cheese is clammy, pitted with earth and hairy with hessian. The bread is waterlogged, and he carries a tin of sardines around in his pocket for insurance against hunger, along with two grenades. What little the men have is shared. Jones recalls three chaps lying in a narrow trench burrow, littered with greaseproof paper twists, idly and companionably chewing Mackintosh's toffees.

There is the same easy brotherliness when Sherston and

Captain Leake, the Company Commander, having marched all day, find they have just one small slice of ration bacon between them. 'I was frizzling my fragment,' Sassoon writes, 'when it fell off the fork and disappeared into the stove. Regardless of my unfortunate fingers I retrieved and ate it with great relish.'

The war artist Stanley Spencer, an ambulance man in Macedonia, fired no guns, laid no mines, sappered no tunnels. His contribution to the war was made in bacon breakfasts. Stationed with the 66th Field Ambulance in a camp at Karasuli, he cooked the bacon each day for sixty men – two rashers each. He once burnt the bacon, distracted by reading *Paradise Lost*. When he came to paint his war series for the Sandham Memorial Chapel in Hampshire in 1930, he turned these breakfasts into a great mess-tin mural running the length of the north wall. He called it a 'symphony in rashers of bacon'.

Once the rashers are suitably frizzled, Spencer paints them leaping like porpoises into the men's tins, lapping over the edges. Two orderlies swing a basin of tea, mud-brown, between them. The tea went in the tin first, then the bacon when the tea had been drunk. Never the other way around. The men who are waiting stick their cutlery in breast pockets (where Spencer kept his books of poetry) or into the tops of their puttees. They talk, stretch, shrug off greatcoats and clink their tins to say 'cheers!'.

If the food was hot, the men were lucky. Robert Graves writes of a stew which arrived warm from the field kitchen, but which had ice around the edge of the plate before he'd finished eating. When it came to the ration biscuits, as far as he was concerned their only use was as kindling for boiling up dixies of tea. I felt for the army dixy – 'an iron kettle or pot, used by soldiers for making tea or stew' – the same passion as for pottles and jorums.

Again and again, Graves and Sherston forego their own tea and breakfast to ensure the men have theirs. One of Sherston's small victories is getting his men their tea. 'Disconsolately they stood at the empty dixy – tired out by the long march and herded into a dirty van to be carried a bit nearer to hell. But I managed to get some hot tea for them. Alone I did it. Without me they would have got none. And for the moment the War seemed worthwhile!'

When I read those words, I had reached the age of twenty-six without ever having had a cup of tea. I'd had peppermint tea, of course, and nettle tea and chamomile tea. The kettle at home whistled to ginger and jasmine and dandelion and fennel. But never proper tea. Builders' Tea with milk and three sugars. English Breakfast under a cosy. Or one of the Empire teas, teas to make you stand up and sing the National Anthem: Ceylon, Assam, Lapsang Souchong, Earl and Empress Grey.

As children, Ed and I hadn't had tea. Too stimulating. Though we were cunning swipers of the froth and chocolate powder from the tops of grown-ups' cappuccinos. (Sticky-fingered, too, when it came to pocketing sugar cubes from the tables of museum cafés.) But we were too young for tea and then I was ill and tea became just one more thing to be hung up about.

Instead of counting sheep at night, I would count calories. How many could I save by not eating this or cutting out that? Tea with milk was a fixation. Let us say twenty calories a cup. Two cups a day makes forty calories. Fourteen cups a week is 280 calories. A year is 14,560 calories.

Over a lifetime, I worked out, by not drinking tea, I could save myself almost 875,000 calories. What did I gain by this mental arithmetic? It didn't help with sleeping. It only hardened my neurosis about tea-drinking. When friends had tea with milk, I'd think: there are 875,000 calories in that cup. Though I knew this wasn't, couldn't be right, the figure became fixed in my head and stopped me ever holding out a cup when the pot was poured.

The dixies of army tea, David Jones's char, were a turning point. What were twenty calories in the grand scheme of things? What was I so afraid of? That one cup would make me fat as a milch cow? Others in the office drank six cups a day. Some of the men, news-desk night-shifters, reporters dispatched to stand outside courts in the cold, had sugar and biscuits at every tea run. I had tried not to stare as they dunked Bourbons and Custard Creams at desks across the newsroom gangways.

The first cup of tea I drank wasn't a special one. I could have sought rare black tea leaves, a blend from the Himalayas, a porcelain cup, a silver tea strainer, an antique spoon. What I wanted, though, was to feel normal, to have the same cup of tea as everyone else, unthinking, every couple of hours, according to their inner tea-clock. A tea as run-of-the-mill as I could make it.

So, from the office canteen, I had a first cup of char in a polystyrene holder with a catering tea bag, hot water from a leaking dixy, and milk from a carton. Proper tea. Tea-tea. I had another the next day, and the day after that, and most days since. You'll think it's a little, unremarkable thing: a first cup of tea. But every splash of milk, every lone boiled egg was a quiet, private victory. No reason to hue and cry or tell the lads on the news desk, 'Look: tea!' They would have thought it very small beer when there were coups and riots and royal babies being born.

'Alone I did it.' But not alone, because Graves and Sherston had put me up to it and pushed me on. Now, when I cannot sleep, I count sheep, or books and their sequels, or stops on Tube lines, but not – I won't allow myself – the calories in tea cups.

Now, I anticipate some eye-rolling here. Is this girl about to tell us, I hear you wondering, that, having had her cup of char, she set her heart on Maconochie stew? That so mouth-watering were accounts of Sunshine sausages bolted while *Minenwerfer* screamed overhead, that she set out to recreate the recipes at home? Or worse: is she really going to equate anorexia with the hell of the trenches? No and no. Anorexia may make a hell of a sufferer's mind, but it is an internal sort of hell, sad and awful in its way, but not comparable to what Sassoon, Graves, Blunden, Jones and so many other men endured. And, no, my mouth did not water at Maconochie stew and burnt bacon. There was little in the trench diet to whet the appetite.

What I did find was that these passages made me think more gratefully of the ease with which we eat today, the abundance of choice, the bounty of year-round fruits. When Graves is shot in the lung and recuperating in a field hospital he begs the doctor for some fruit. The doctor shakes his head. He has seen none for days. 'Yet a few minutes later he returned with two rather unripe greengages. In whispers I promised him a whole orchard when I recovered.' I don't need to beg a doctor for a few plums, nor send my batman running stoop-shouldered along communication trenches in search of an orange. They can be had from the news-agent with my morning papers.

There have been times in my illness when I have been unnerved by the quantity of food in the shops. Even now there are days when, standing in the aisles of a super-market or in front of shelves of takeaway lunches, I feel overwhelmed by what is on offer. There is simply too much. Too many decisions to make about what is filling, what is fattening, what is healthy, what is not. I have often left empty-handed and gone hungry rather than make the choice.

A frizzled fragment of bacon is to me more manageable than the bloated BLTs, white with mayonnaise, sold in the lunchtime sandwich shops. It is more flavoursome for having been saved from the fire, more wanted for being the last one, and more warming for being cut in half and shared.

You hear it said that there is no anorexia outside the affluent West. That it is only in societies gorged on bumper-packs, grab-bags, tear-and-share portions, special offers, buy-one-get-one-free excess that women and men deliberately starve their bodies. Like many anorexics, I am spooked by canyon supermarket aisles and their infinite choice. Skimmed, semi-skimmed or full-fat milk? Cow, goat or sheep? Soya milk, almond milk, rice milk, oat milk, cashew milk, hazelnut milk, quinoa – for heaven's sake! – milk? I find myself wishing for a batman to bring milk in a dixy from the closest unshelled farm. No choice, no agonising, no drawing up a balance sheet of calories, fats and sugars.

But we have the shops we have, and while on bad days I may struggle with them, they represent unimaginable

abundance to much of the world and to any previous
generation. I found it encouraging to read of the joy with
which the Tommies greeted any relief from rations and it
made me more thankful for our supermarket shelves, the
wealth of choice, the cornucopia of fruits and treats. There
is no harm in Blunden's cakes or Graves's smoked salmon
or Sherston's bowl of strawberries, eaten as rare luxuries –
and no reason why I should not eat such things from time
to time and with the same pleasure.

If the soldier-poets write of their daily trench breakfasts with leaden familiarity – see David Jones's lament for
'grey-tepid coffee', 'gulped-down tea' and 'eked-out bacon'
– then their descriptions of food sent from home or eaten
on leave reach a pitch of ecstasy. Sherston has the knack of
timing his leave to coincide with the best of the summer
fruit crop. He is at home on sick leave in August for figs
at lunch – the best his Aunt Evelyn has had off the tree
that year. Then the following summer for a bowl of strawberries. No cream, alas. Wartime shortages. Aunt Evelyn
pulls out every stop: the smell of frying onions welcomes
him home, there is a steak (though it is tough) for dinner,
and not one, but two of his favourite puddings.

When Sherston is sent to Cork to attend an anti-gas
course, he cuts the exam on the last day and goes hunting
in County Limerick. It is worth it for Mrs O'Donnell's high
tea, which makes dining in the mess again unthinkable. 'It
had been a banquet. Cold salmon and snipe and unsur-
passable home-made bread and honey had indeed caused
us to forget that there was a war on.' But there is guilt in
this banqueting and he rebels against the cucumber sandwiches eaten at home when his men are under shellfire and
half under water.

He returns to the trenches with a bottle of brandy and a whole smoked salmon carried in his haversack from London to Amiens. Sherston worries that smoked salmon isn't much to men putting up with raids and rats and what Aunt Evelyn calls the enemy 'hell-hounds'. He is wrong. Smoked salmon from Piccadilly does cheer up Battalion Officer Barton. "'Gosh, if only this war would stop!" he exclaimed. "I'd be off to Scott's oyster-bar like a streak of light and you'd never get me away from it again!"' Barton – Harrow, Sandhurst, happily married, *pince-nez* – mourns not just the girl, but the plushly upholstered restaurants he has left behind. Returning from leave, he broods over a dinner three nights before at the Café Royal: 'It's too much of a bloody contrast, coming back to all this'.

When the men cannot shop for smoked salmon or dine at the Café Royal, Blighty must come to them. Hampers arrive from Fortnum & Mason. Both Graves's mother and Sherston's Aunt Evelyn send kippers from home – their safe arrival is of greater and more immediate concern than any bombardment. To the delight of the battalion, Aunt Evelyn also sends batches of especially good jams. The army jams come in tins, and of tins they taste. Sherston reports how Barton gazed at the cherry trees on the coloured jam label – 'a talisman which carried his mind safely to the home counties of England'.

The associative powers of food are such that Graves becomes almost crazed with longing for mince pies and the homeliness they promise. Waiting on the fire-step to go over the top, he finds himself lustily singing an advertising jingle, bayonet in hand:

My mind was a blank, except for the recurrence of *S'nice*

S'mince S'pie, S'nice S'mince S'pie . . . I don't like ham, lamb or jam, and I don't like roley-poley . . . The men laughed at my singing. The acting CSM said: 'It's murder, sir.' 'Of course it's murder you bloody fool,' I agreed. 'But there's nothing else for it, is there?' It was still raining. *But when I sees a S'nice S'mince S'pie, I asks for a helping twice . . .*

The attack is postponed until dawn, and then called off altogether. Graves lives to see another Christmas, and, one hopes, a S'nice S'mince S'pie.

Graves's eve-of-battle mince pies had the same galvanising effect on me as Mrs Cratchit's pudding. I had not had a mince pie since primary school. But I had once thrilled to the first tray coming golden from the oven in December announcing my birthday and the countdown to Christmas. The fruit would have been soaking in brandy since the summer holidays, the pastry flaked and rolled from scratch, and the pies lidded with marzipan stars. Our nanny Lorraine, who arrived Poppins-like when I was three and stayed for the next ten years, was an almost magical baker. The last mince pie I had eaten had been one of hers, its star curling and caramelised at the points, eaten the Christmas before she left to look after her own babies.

But with Graves's jingle playing in my head, in December 2013, a little over a century after its singer had stood on the fire-step, I had a mince pie – shop-bought and collapsing into crumbs – brought into the office by a colleague to cheer up a Christmas meeting. It couldn't hold a candle to Lorraine's stars – no mince pie could – but it was s'nice all the same.

*

The war turned the men into opportunists. When they were in rest billets and there was a farm and an *estaminet* and a Madame from whom to buy eggs and butter, they wasted no chance. David Jones came to look fondly at the grubby paste-boards outside cafés that promised

BIERE
EGG CHIP 3 FRANC
CAFÉ AU LAIT
ENGLISH SPOKE HEER

Blunden and his unit, billeted at the house of a farmer at Le Souich, are beside themselves when the old man shoots one of his geese for a roast dinner. While it cooks, they play cricket in the orchard with apples for balls. Blunden goes blackberrying in the woods on the road to Ypres, while Graves mounts a raid on the currant bushes in a garden at Vermelles. In one of Stanley Spencer's chapel scenes, the men lose themselves in a maze of bilberry bushes.

If the discovery of blackberry or currant bushes gives the men a lift, so too does a stolen hour with a book. Novels and poetry offer an escape from the most pressing and immediate horrors and books are as carefully husbanded as wire cutters and dry socks. Graves packs in his kit not just the usual waterproof boots and fourteen-day-battery pocket torch, but a Catullus and a Lucretius in Latin, a Shakespeare and a Bible, printed on India paper for lightness. Private Jones, who was small and slight, where officer Graves was 6 feet and strapping, regretted that he could only carry one book at a time. Graves complains of the lack of reading material in France and is elated when he spots *The Essays of Lionel Johnson* lying on a table. It is the first book he has

seen in the army that is not a military textbook or a trashy
novel. The name on the flyleaf? Siegfried Sassoon. They talk
of John Masefield poems over their cream buns.

Stanley Spencer wrote that he would go to war only 'if
I can have Milton, Donne, Shakespeare, a pencil and paper
in one pocket. Giotto, Raphael, Fra Angelico in the other'.
These pocket reproductions of the Italian masters came in
thin chapbooks with waxed-paper covers to withstand spilt
tea and bacon grease. Serving in Macedonia, he read *David
Copperfield*, *Pickwick Papers*, *Bleak House* and John Ruskin's
Modern Painters. He wrote home in April 1918 asking
his sister Florence to send more poetry: 'That's the sort
of thing I live on, along with army rations.' He thanked
her for the box of paints, the sketchbook and the biscuits,
which had all arrived undamaged.

Edmund Blunden is cast into a gloom when he discovers
that Kapp, formerly a satirical cartoonist and now second-
in-command of C Company, has nicked his John Clare.
He makes up for the loss of his own books by adopting
any he finds. At the mortared house of a French notary at
Mailly he tenderly recovers volumes bound in blue and red
morocco leather, and carries them trenchwards in a sandbag. He calls himself a 'rescuer' of books. Having lost his
volume of Clare, he turns to Edward Young, read in a pill-
box, to steady his mind and nerves. 'The mere amusement
of discovering lines applicable to our crisis kept me from
despair.' How many men were kept from despair by their
Everyman editions? And how many books were buried,
unfinished, in the mud with their readers?

During the worst period of my illness, between schools,
exhausted by a walk to the end of the road on matchstick

legs, reading gave shape to each day. Without the routine of buses, school and coursework, there was nothing else to mark the hours but embattled mealtimes. Each week's meal plans were written out on A4 paper and kept on Mum's desk. Checking the pad and discovering I would have to eat a bowl of natural yogurt after dinner on Friday would set me jittery all week. I railed against enforced bed-rest. Supervised mealtimes and no escape for exercise were monstrous after the discipline of hunger and the gym treadmill.

People talk about being scarred or marked by illness or depression. It's not something I recognise. For me there's no scar, no visible reminder. What I remember from the worst times is emptiness. A sense that life, the worthwhile living of it, had stopped and that there was nothing now but the cold closing-in of extreme hunger. Empty stomach, empty days, empty future. Emptiness today and emptiness tomorrow. The only way to bear it was to measure the days in books.

Monday didn't have to be the day I sat ashen over mashed potato, unable to eat a mouthful. It could be the day Linda Radlett, Nancy Mitford's Communist in a mink coat in *The Pursuit of Love*, arrived at Perpignan refugee camp, a copy of the *Tatler* under her arm. Propped up in bed and folded into the pages of the day's book, I could forget, briefly, wonderfully, the threat of dinner and its bowl of yogurt.

It didn't occur to me at the time, preoccupied as I was, but it strikes me forcibly in retrospect that I had entirely substituted one appetite for another. I had so suppressed normal bodily hunger, so strictly trained myself to deny all natural appetite and the painful spasms of an empty stomach, that I no longer really remembered what it was like to look forward to a meal, to feel peckish before it and full and sated after. Instead I had acquired something different: a trencherman's greed for books. Finishing one novel, I was on to the next. It was private gluttony, solitary banqueting, reading feasts for one. With no draw on my time except rest – no essays to write, no irregular verbs to chant, no equations to balance – I had days, weeks, months to read, indulgence I would never have permitted myself in eating.

What's strange is that in those initial months of bed-rest reading, I don't remember really taking in what was eaten on the page. That came much later. I was stony to descriptions of food and eating. Just as I could pass a choc-olate shop or patisserie without stopping in front of the windows but hurry on, thinking of a mint tea to warm me when I got home, so I read with a stubborn insensibility to cakes and scones.

While the weary routine of nursing fell to Mum, having an ill child in the house was as hard on Dad. He came up with a simple, practical, inspired way to help. He would try – and it was no easy thing – to make his patient laugh. He funnelled me books that had worked for him: Geoffrey Willans and Ronald Searle's *Compleet Molesworth*, an old *St Trinian's*, Evelyn Waugh's *Sword of Honour* trilogy, the first of Anthony Powell's *Dance to the Music of Time* series, Gerald Durrell's *My Family and Other Animals*, short stories by Stephen Leacock and Alexander McCall Smith, Miles Kington's *Let's Parlez Franglais!*, the Alan Coren omnibus, the collected Craig Brown. He went out to buy, on the morning it was published, Terry Pratchett's Discworld book *Monstrous Regiment*.

Chapter by chapter, spoof by lampoon, it started to work. I could smile at the *Sword of Honour* thunderbox, at Gerry Durrell's Magenpies, at Pratchett's cross-dressing recruits. The bad puns and silliness and slapstick lifted the oppressive, stifling confinement of bed-rest – but laughter seemed beyond me. Except it wasn't, not quite. Molesworth, my hero, my knight in rusting armour, the Curse of St Custard's, did it. Dad and I had read the books together when I was younger, turning quotes into shared jokes. I'd needed him to explain *'cave!'* and gerunds and beaks. Dad had all four books together in hardback – *Down with Skool! How to be Topp, Whizz for Atoms* and *Back in the Jug Agane* – with the dust jacket missing. He lent me his copy.

It was back-in-the-jug-agane familiar. Here was Molesworth as I'd remembered him, still un-spell-checked, still with his fringe in his eyes and blazer unbuttoned, drawn by Searle in blotched and spidering ink. At the first 'uterly wet and weedy' I felt a rush of the old feeling. At the entrance of Fotherington-Tomas 'skipping like a girlie . . . uterly wet and a sissie' my lips twitched. When I came to 'Hurra for the botany walk!' my eyes creased and my cheeks flushed. 'Boo to birds beasts crows trees grass flowers,' Molesworth roars, 'also cristopfer robin and wind in the wilows. Charge at the tinies and mow them down.' I hadn't done it for a long time, thought I had lost the trick of it, thought I might never manage it again, but I laughed and laughed – and was shocked by the strangeness of laughing.

As those months in bed went on – six of them in all – I made small gains. Laughing at Molesworth, eating a pear, drinking a glass of orange juice. I had stopped losing weight, but not put much on either. Even with the menu plan, I was eating sparely, still dry-mouthed before every meal. My table habits were monkish and fastidious – and a trial to Mum, who had to monitor them over drawn-out dinners. I would cut a chicken breast into ribbons and chew each one thirty, forty times before swallowing, as if I could grind it away before it reached my stomach. But, re-leased from the table and restored to my room, I read with the hungry, yomping enthusiasm of Sherston munching his sandwiches.

By the time he reaches Mametz Wood, scene of one of the worst battles of the Somme, Sherston is all for giving up. 'As for me,' Sassoon writes, 'I had more or less made up my mind to die because in the circumstances there didn't seem anything else to be done.' If any writer keeps him going, it is Thomas Hardy. Sherston survives Mametz and is marched to the lines in front of Fricourt Cemetery, where he finds a little dog kennel of a dug-out in which to read *Tess of the D'Urbervilles* as the shells go 'hurrooshing' overhead. 'I was meditating about England, visualising a grey day down in Sussex; dark green woodlands with pigeons circling above the tree-tops; dogs barking, cocks crowing and all the casual tappings and twinklings of the countryside . . . It was for all that, I supposed, that I was in the front-line with soaked feet, trench mouth, and feeling short of sleep.'

Tess and the langoustes at Amiens give him something to live for. Later, returning to Mametz, it is Hardy spur-ring him on. 'I didn't want to die – not before I'd finished reading *The Return of the Native* anyhow.' It is Hardy who just about keeps the shell-shocked Sherston upright when in April 1918 he is posted to Palestine. Reading Hardy's

Woodlanders at a camp near Ramallah is 'like going into a cool parlour with green reflections on wall and ceiling – after the dust and sweat of marching'.

My own Hardy moment came with *Tess*, pressed on me by both Sherston and Katy, my Hardy-mad friend. She'd been telling me for years to read Hardy, but Dickens had kept elbowing him out. When Sherston added his voice to Katy's I bought a copy of *Tess*, asking: 'Does it have a happy ending?' Katy shook her head. *Tess* changed one great thing for me. What was it that did it? Was it Tess's father's demand for lamb's fry, chitterlings and a noggin o' rum? Alec D'Urberville's strawberries? The trickle of dark treacle from Car's smashed pot? The black puddings with their 'marvellous herbal savours' that Angel Clare brings home to his reverend parents? It certainly wasn't Tess's crop of drab and desolate turnips.

Hardy did something wonderful. He painted milk in the sweetest, palest, colours, made it something quite lovely, a cool, marble-white balm for a dairymaid's soul. When Tess, very grieved, very wronged, comes to the dairy, it is on a day of low summer light. The sun throws shadows on the Blackmoor milchers 'with as much care over each contour as if it had been the profile of a Court beauty on a palace wall'. I could see the dairy cows in my mind's eye: rivals to the beauties painted by Lely and Kneller for the corridors of Windsor and Hampton Court. This one a duchess, that a countess; one a queen, another a lady. Between the stalls of these court beauties, Tess's prettiness is only one prettiness among many. She changes her bonnet for a milking hood and takes a stool. Here, she is serene, her pulse slows, and 'she appeared to feel that she really had laid a new foundation for her future'.

It is at the dairy, skimming milk, arms dabbled in curds, sleeping at night with the sound of the steady dripping of the whey, that she is most happy. The dairy chapters in *Tess* finally weaned me off soya, made me feel not that I *ought* to drink true, court-beauty milk, but that I wanted to. When I wavered in the dairy aisle – soya? quinoa? almond? – I was able to say to myself: think of Tess, think of Lely, Kneller, sun, painted beauties. Thanks to Hardy I drank proper milk – in first cups of tea and with my porridge in the morning – and laid new foundations.

When Sherston cannot have Hardy, he settles for Tolstoy. At Port Said he buys a copy of *War and Peace*, which he keeps with his other books in a Turkish bomb-box. He has the transport officer carry them from camp to camp under the pretence that the box contains mess kitchen utensils. He ends Easter Sunday's diary entry with a rallying cry: 'I should be in the soup without something to read!' And so should I.

For each of these men, as there has been for me, there is redemption in reading. It has the power to transport them from present horrors more swiftly and completely than any field ambulance or stretcher-bearer. In Hardy, Tolstoy, Clare and Shakespeare they find escape, solitude and a semblance of peace. When ration biscuits and char and the spoonful of rum fail, there is a book to be pulled from the haversack, promising deliverance, home and hope.

3

'Invincible hunger'

How did the war end? With langoustes and champagne? Oysters at Scott's and Piccadilly smoked salmon? Or with boiled eggs, cocoa and cold cherry tart? Not one of my war poets gives a word of it. After four years at the front, I wanted a triumphant cricket tea and one of Miriam's seed cakes, chilly though the village tent would have been in November.

I wanted, I suppose, my returning heroes to be restored to life as it was lived before the war. 'God in his heaven and sausages for breakfast!' was how Sassoon summed up his childhood. It was naivety on my part. A hangover from the happily-ever-after stories I'd grown up on and had never quite grown out of. I had, too, perhaps been spoilt by Dickens, who so neatly ties up his plots with an inheritance for the hero, church bells for the heroine, Madeira wine for the wedding guests and just deserts for the villain.

Sassoon, Blunden and Jones do not give us high tea or a victors' homecoming to Aunt Evelyn's roast chicken. Sherston is invalided out of the war in February 1918. In the final pages of his trilogy he is propped up in bed in London being brought tea by a nurse and railing against the 'war machine' and the bullet that had failed to finish

him off. At the close of *In Parenthesis*, David Jones's alter
ego Private Ball lies injured at Mametz Wood, crawling as
far as he is able, tin hat and rifle abandoned, to wait – 'But
why don't the bastards come' – for the stretcher-bearers.
Edmund Blunden we leave on the platform at Buire-sur-
l'Ancre waiting for a train to take him home. It is March
1918 – eight months still to go.

Robert Graves does give us the years after the war. It
is a ramshackle, wandering, hard-up decade: a failed turn
at shop-keeping, more children than he could reasonably
afford, poems published or unpublished, a spell as a lec-
turer at a university in Egypt where the breakfast eggs
always tasted of garlic. He abandons England – 'goodbye to all that' – and the book ends on a bathetic note of
retreat.

I was left hungrily unsatisfied and at a loss for what to
read next. I might have tried *All Quiet on the Western Front*
or *Journey's End*, but hadn't the stomach for another tour of
duty in the trenches. I had had my fill of rats and shrapnel
and tea that tasted of petrol. But after months embed-
ded with B Company, I couldn't easily return to civilian
reading.

When I explained my symptoms to the man in the
bookshop on Marylebone High Street, he nodded with a
pharmacist's sympathetic understanding before making
his prescription. I was sent away with a paperback copy
of J. L. Carr's *A Month in the Country*. I took my first dose
that afternoon.

Carr was not a soldier. Born in 1912, he was taking his
first steps when Sassoon, Blunden and Graves were marching through France. He was six when the war ended, too
young to remember much. *A Month in the Country* is fiction,

not memoir, but I believed in shell-shocked Tom Birkin as fervently as I did Blunden, Graves or any of the others.

Birkin arrives in Oxgodby in the North Riding with a neurasthenic stammer and a clicking facial twitch. His wife's gone off with another man, he hasn't any money and he wakes screaming in the night from remembered machine-gun fire. Before the war he had been a restorer of paintings. At Oxgodby church he is promised a Last Judgement which might, if the damp hasn't got to it, still be there under the whitewash. Fourteenth-century, he hopes.

His month in the church tower is one of ascetic simplicity. Graves and Sassoon convalesced at Craiglockhart hospital under the care of Dr Rivers. David Jones recovered from his Blighty wound at Shipston-on-Stour, where pretty nurse Elsie took him for strawberries and cream on her mother's lawn. (He felt quite queasy after.) Tom Birkin, in August 1920, recuperates at Oxgodby, sleeping in the bell chamber of the church, which smells noticeably, but not unpleasantly, of damp hassocks.

He is broke when he arrives and the vicar is in no hurry to advance him his twenty-five guinea fee. His food store is carefully husbanded: tea, marge, cocoa, rice, a loaf, a couple of rashers of bacon. He has brought a methylated Primus stove and reckons that with milk and vegetables from the village he can do well for himself. He hopes that a summer of Oxgodby hermitage will restore him. What he needs is: 'a new start, and, afterwards, maybe I won't be a casualty any more'.

But if he thinks the good people of Oxgodby are going to leave him alone to his rice and marge, he is mistaken. They see him come off the train with his kitbag. They see

the twitch and hear the stammer. They have framed photographs on their piano tops of sons who never came home.
The hospitable families of Oxgodby and of every village of
bicycling distance adopt the war-battered Birkin. While
he restores their church mural with verdigris, sinoper, red
ochre and malachite, they set about restoring him with the
best of their North Riding kitchens.

Before his stock of food, brought up on the train in a
fish-bass bag, has had time to spoil in the August heat,
offerings begin to arrive from Mrs Ellerbeck, the stationmaster's wife: a rabbit pie, currant teacakes, curd tarts.
'Dishes Mrs Ellerbeck had helped her mother bake, who
had helped her mother bake, who . . .' Mrs Ellerbeck, Tom
recalls, 'worked out how it was with me': that he has no
money, no home and no wife (at least no faithful wife) to
cook for him. The Ellerbecks' daughter is dispatched
to invite him to the house on Sunday. On the day there
are Yorkshire puddings, thick ones, in gravy and a fine
joint of sirloin steak. After an evening sing-a-long, Tom
discovers that Mrs Ellerbeck has smuggled a packet of beef
sandwiches into his coat pocket.

He joins the barley reapers getting in the harvest. At
midday, lunch is brought to the fields. There is rabbit
and potato pie to 'put fresh heart' into the men, and, at
four, greengage pie and scalding tea in a can. The tea is
always scalding in this part of the world – as it should be.
The next day Tom is nudged on the shoulder and a thick
beef sandwich appears. 'I had established a reputation for
invincible hunger.' Hard-boiled eggs are pressed on him,
ham off the hock, deep apple pie, more scalding tea, jam
tarts, tomato sandwiches (they have gone soggy) and batch
after batch of Mrs Ellerbeck's currant teacakes. When he

has to shift for himself he has loaf bread and a wedge of Wensleydale.

The Oxgodbers compete to feed Tom up, this poor bugger from London with his God-awful twitch. They can't ask what happened Over There, won't ask him to re-visit hell. They can only offer salvation in currant buns. It is an idea lovely in its simplicity. Tom cannot un-live Pass-chendaele: 'Bodies split, heads blown off, grovelling fear, shrieking fear, unspeakable fear!' But a buttered teacake from a shop in Ripon and a pot of tea, freshly made and scalding, and a first-rate seed cake are balm of an imme-diate sort. The twitch, the stammer, the nightmares will take longer to heal, but Tom will not go cold or hungry.

When I read Mrs Ellerbeck's feeding-up of Tom I saw the goodness, the generosity, the tenderness of her care. *A Month in the Country* shone new light, bright, August, barley-harvest light, on what Mum had been trying to do all those years, what she still, every time I go home for the weekend, wants to do.

As a teenager I spurned the instinct, however kindly intentioned, 'to feed me up'. Mum knew me and knew my mind's way of twisting words too well to use the phrase. But friends' mothers did not understand. 'We must feed you girls up!' was the jolly encouragement as spaghetti carbonara was heaped onto a plate. Nothing was more likely to make my jaw clamp and stomach turn. '*Fatten* you up' is what I heard. It was a threat. That creamy, eggy carbonara was an assault on my empty body.

Others saw what I did not: skinny legs, dark circles under my eyes, blue veins showing through cold skin. The natural maternal instinct, the Mrs Ellerbeck instinct, was to feed me up with second helpings, hot puddings and jam tarts. My mother, my brilliant, clever mother, who 'worked out how it was with me', knew that she must find some other way of persuading me to eat. She had to do it without me suspecting that I was being fed, or worse, fattened, up. I was wildly suspicious about just how much butter had gone onto my toast, how much cheese there was in a topping. The phrase she repeated again and again, hundreds of times in those months of bed-rest and many hundreds more in the years since, was that I had to eat enough 'to keep body and soul together'. She wasn't, she assured me, trying to make me fat. She wasn't conspiring or plotting. There was no plan to poison me with butter or olive oil or sugar in the apple compote. She wanted only for me to have enough energy to read books, go to school, then to university, to have friends, one day a boyfriend, to visit galleries, to sketch, to walk in the park, travel abroad, to have *a life worth living*. To be at home in bed, too hungry to sleep at night, cowering from every meal – that was no life.

She was right, of course. But I fought and resisted all the way, was ungrateful and unreasonable, tested her patience with tantrums and protests and bedroom doors barricaded with furniture as a defence against some new abomination – a banana, say – on the menu plan. Later, she would drive up to university several times a term with cold roast chicken wrapped in tin foil, portions of bolognaise in Tupperware, packets of muesli bars. I sulked. I *could* look after myself, there *were* shops here, I *was* eating. I can hear my own ungrateful student whinge even ten years on.

I didn't fully understand why Mum had persevered until I read *A Month in the Country.* She had been trying to do what the stationmaster's wife had done for Tom. She could no more right the mess in my anorexic mind than Mrs Ellerbeck could undo the damage of Tom's war, but she could give me the strength, whether it came from cold roast chicken or greengage pie, to keep body and soul together, until I was strong enough and ready to put my mind in order.

Mum, who had hated lacrosse and netball at school as fiercely as I had, never talked about eating for exercise. It was always eating for reading, writing, visiting churches, losing an afternoon in the Victoria and Albert Museum with a sketchbook and watercolour pencils. She saw that these were the incentives to offer, the things for which I would get better.

There's a glancing thought in *A Month in the Country* as Tom Birkin works on his Last Judgement. He is, for the first time in years, sleeping through the night. The bad dreams come less and less often. 'The work was tiring – I was on my feet most of the day, often eating whilst standing – and then, at night, up there in my loft high above the fields and away from the road, too far for voices to carry, there was nothing to disturb me.' Blink and you'd miss it. 'Often eating whilst standing.' So absorbed is Tom in his seraphic saints, St Michael's scales, the souls of the damned, he hardly notices what he is eating, cramming bread and Wensleydale into his mouth as he works, rapt by tempera paint. This is what Mum had tried to tell me. That eating would allow me to pursue the things I loved. I could do nothing worthwhile when bound up by hunger and illness.

My first real inkling of this promise of a better sort of life if only I would eat had come when I went to university. I was completely thrown by Freshers' Week and its

grisly round of curry house, pizza night, kebab shop, pub.
Each evening, sitting down, the hundred of us, to a meal
of sticky teriyaki chicken and egg-fried rice, my throat
narrowed to a pinhole. My mouth went dry. I felt sick and
feverish. I couldn't eat. In my room, maybe. Porridge, oatcakes, a bowl of vegetable bouillon powder in hot water
from the kettle. But not in public, not with strangers. Not
a curry.

Those first few days I was overtaken by a dizzying,
plummeting panic. I couldn't cope. I couldn't feed myself.
I would have to drop out. I would end up in bed again. I
sobbed on the floor of my room and called home four, five,
six times a day. On the fourth day, I was given a pre-term
essay. It was a dirty trick to set work in Freshers' Week, but
I seized on it. This was why I had come. Not to drink beer
or down shots or do forfeits over a curry. I wanted, as Tom
Birkin wanted, to look at paintings, sculpture, churches;
to see how they were made, who paid for them and why. I
went to the Fitzwilliam Museum, the college library, and
Heffers bookshop.

I had tea with the other art historian in my year, Hermione. She brought a chocolate cake, which was kind, though
it sat on the desk as if there was a bomb hidden under the
ganache. We looked through my books and I hoped she
wouldn't mind the untouched cake.

I wrote the essay, and, after a tearful, homesick first weekend, lectures started on the Monday. There was another
essay, another trip to the library and to Heffers. Hermione
invited me to dinner. It was a chance to redeem myself. She
made a vegetable stir-fry with prawns and glass noodles
on a two-plate electric hob in her draughty kitchen at the
top of a flight of uneven stairs. Others joined us. Dinner

sizzled out of the wok and onto unmatched plates. We sat on the floor, the edge of the bed, the sofa, the rotating desk chair, a dozen of us, wherever we could find a spot. The first-year architect in the room at the end of the corridor went running for a bottle of soy sauce. And I found, to my surprise and overwhelming relief, that in company and with these strangers who would become friends, I could eat.

The dish Mrs Ellerbeck is most famous for in Oxgodby is her tray of Yorkshire puddings. I don't think I had ever had a Yorkshire pudding before the anorexia, certainly never had one afterwards. They weren't the stuff of Freeman family Sunday lunches. My grandmother did roast chicken (and elixir-of-life chicken soup the next day) and rice pudding with nutmeg-freckled skin, but we were soft Southerners and didn't have Sunday Yorkshires.

Was there a toad in the hole on a family holiday near Fountains Abbey? Or did we just giggle over the name on a menu? I couldn't confidently have told you what went into Yorkshire puds. Butter, I could have guessed. Milk? Flour? Eggs? I knew people talked of the perfect mix for the batter. And batter I knew was bad. The thought that one might eat them *with* potatoes – two white starches in a meal! – was baffling. But Mrs Ellerbeck's Yorkshires did Tom Birkin the world of good. Mightn't they do me good too?

When the moment came, I wasn't in the right part of the world. I'd been walking with my boyfriend Andy on the Sussex Downs, three hours in the rain, with leaking boots, wet woollens, damp down the back of my neck. The pub that night offered a roast with All The Trimmings. Andy, with an invincible hunger to match Tom Birkin's, asked for his beef very rare. I eyed the vegetarian dish on the menu – pearl barley and roast squash – and the soup – pumpkin. I was very cold, my socks were wet and the walk had been a steep and brisk one. In the end, I ordered the roast.

The beef was wide as a saddle, slick and polished with gravy. There were roast potatoes as rolling as the South Downs Way. There were buttered carrots, playground-marble peas, and a bishop's mitre of creamed horseradish. What was left of the plate was given up to a great coracle of Yorkshire pudding. A Borrower could have crossed the River Ouse in it.

I thought briefly that I might have done better with the pumpkin soup. While I wavered, Andy had already started, talking cheerfully between mouthfuls of beef and potatoes. I ate my way round the pudding. Peas and carrots first. They were safe enough. Then the beef, cut small, and two of the potatoes. The coracle sailed in its gravy. There was nothing for it. The Sussex Yorkshire pudding on Andy's side of the table was already gone. I cut a section, thought of Mrs Ellerbeck, of Tom, of the peace and cool of the Oxgodby church, and tried my first Yorkshire. It was still scalding on the inside, buttery and soft. It was worth the three hours' walking, worth the rain, worth the socks drying on the radiator. Almost worth fighting a war for.

Tom Birkin wears his invincible hunger like a medal: a Victoria Cross for services to Mrs Ellerbeck's cooking. It seemed to me a funny thing to be proud of. Hunger was something to be quashed, suppressed, denied. Admitting to hunger was failure. 'Conquer your passions, boys, and don't be eager after vittles,' as Mr Squeers had it. But those were my rules. Others would have mutinied against them. For the man of appetite, hunger is something to be rallied and stoked, before eating and drinking until buttons protest.

The centenary of the war had led me to the trench memoirs; it also gave me Laurie Lee. On a Saturday morning in June, a hundred years after Laurie had been born in Stroud, I sat down in the sun – the first hot weekend of the year – with *Cider with Rosie*.

Tipped off a cart into a Gloucestershire lane on a parched June morning, the three-year-old Laurie takes one look at the Slad cottage and howls. His sisters, swooping on him like swallows, stop his tears. '"There, there," they fussed, "it's all right, don't you wail any more. Come down 'ome and we'll stuff you with currants."' And so they did. Later, Laurie would remember that first currant-stuffed afternoon. His sisters spent the day stripping the fruit bushes in the garden. 'They darted squawking from bush to bush, clawing the fruit like sparrows . . . Every so often one of them would dart into the kitchen, cram my great mouth with handfuls of squashed berries, and run out again. And the more I got, the more I called for more. It was like feeding a fat young cuckoo.'

That was how I read Lee: like a cuckoo, fatly and greedily over a long weekend in the country. *Cider with Rosie* on the Saturday, *As I Walked Out One Midsummer Morning* on the Sunday, *A Moment of War* on the Monday. Then *A Rose for Winter* in the evenings after the office. Still not sated, I read the Valerie Grove biography the following weekend. I was gorged on Laurie and dumbstruck by his cuckoo hunger.

When there is food, he eats himself into a drowsy torpor. When there is none, it saps his will to do anything other than scheme and dream of eating. The Lee family is too big – eight of them around the stew pot, mother Annie and seven children – and there is never enough to go around. Each child has their dollop of stew and seconds go to those who finish the first helping soonest. Laurie's brother Jack is the quickest. 'It left me marked', Laurie later wrote, 'with an ugly scar, a twisted, food-crazed nature, so that still I am calling for whole rice puddings and big pots of stew in the night.'

Annie's kitchen is a place of alchemy. There, muddied vegetables become great stews, steaming and squabbled-over: chopped carrots like copper pennies, radishes, chives, potatoes dipped in a bowl of cold water to take off the mud. Once cooked, though, this bounty – cauldrons of stew, coloured with Oxo – boiled away to never quite enough. The children are gannets: 'we grabbed and dodged and passed and snatched, and packed our mouths like pelicans'. On high days and holidays and summers of plenty, they eat until they are sick. When the blackberries are in season, they pluck and gobble until their lips are purple and their hands stained up to the wrists.

There are summer picnics with cakes and buns and macaroons and treacle and fresh-made jellies and slices of bread as wide as soup plates. At the Parochial Church Tea and Annual Entertainment, the spread is 'an orgy of communal gluttony' and the children set out to get their money's worth. The guests may all go home groaning, but it is only the village boys who return the following morning to inspect the leftovers – half-eaten buns, ham coated with cake crumbs – and guzzle the lot.

With spare pennies, the boys descend on the sweet shop for sherbet, sucked up with liquorice straws, and at Christmas they accept treasures finer than gold, frankincense and myrrh while out carol-singing: nuts, cakes, figs, preserved ginger, dates and, suitably for the season, cough drops. Mother tortures the children with stories of her time in service, describing meals at the Big House, while they grimly eat their greens and bacon, grinding their teeth and swallowing their hunger. 'There'd be river-trout,' Annie rhapsodises, 'or fresh salmon lightly sprinkled with herbs and sauces. Then some woodcock perhaps, or a guinea-fowl – oh, yes, and a joint as well. And a cold ham on the sideboard, too, if you wished . . . Then Cook would send in some violet cakes, and there'd be walnuts and fruit in brandy.'

I read all this in a sort of delirium. It wasn't so much the woodcock and guinea fowl, the walnuts and jellies, as the plucking and gobbling, the purple lips, the stained wrists, the illicit scrumping, the truffling in cupboards, the Christmas hoarding, the pelican snatching. Laurie positively pets his hunger. He revels in it. It is a necessary fast before the rapture of Gloucestershire ham, buttered potatoes and marrowfat peas. I read the family's Sunday breakfast of a pound of large sausages, 'dripping fat' and dipped into pepper, with amazement. How could anyone celebrate the dripping fat of burnt sausages, boast of it, recall it decades later? My immediate reaction was one of revulsion. How horrible. But Lee's peckishness was catching.

I *wanted* a sausage. I had not wanted a sausage since the Halloweens and Bonfire Nights of primary school. Not only that. I wanted the fresh boiled egg that 'tasted of

sun-warmed manna', the bread and butter cut into trian-
gles, and 'cocoa frothed and steamed'. I wanted the treacle
biscuits Laurie takes when he sets off from the cottage at
the beginning of *When I Walked Out One Midsummer Morning*. I even wanted – can I admit it? – the suet pies which
await him in London.

It is only when he takes a room above an eating-house in
Richmond that he has, for the first time in his life, enough
to eat each day. The landlady is another Mrs Ellerbeck.
She brings him sandwiches in bed, as if fattening him for
a prize. The steam of boiling meat comes up through the
floorboards and he writes a giddy extended encomium to
the suet pies made by his landlady:

> The blackboard menu, propped on the pavement
> outside, offered a list as immutable as the elements:
> 'Bubble. Squeak. Liver and B. Toad-in-the-Hole. Meat
> Pudding or Pie.'
>   My favourite was the pie – a little basin of meat
> wrapped in a caul of suety dough which was kept boil-
> ing all day in a copper cauldron in a cupboard under the
> stairs . . . There must have been over a pound of meat
> in each separate pie – a complete working-man's meal,
> for sixpence. And remembering the thin days at home,
> when meat was only for Sundays, I ate at least one of
> them every day.

There is pudding, too. Winter or summer, the house serves
a cold sweet of custard and prunes.

I wanted it all. Bubble and squeak, liver and bacon, beef
suet pudding, custard and prunes. I hardly trusted myself
to read on, afraid of being so overpowered by Laurie's hot

gravy and cold custard that I'd rush out to a cook shop and succumb to a steaming suet and beef pie. I dealt with it firmly: with a two-hour walk. It had rained the night before, a summer storm, and the verges were thick with bloated slugs. They, too, had been at the suet puddings. I walked off the cravings that had rattled me and came back to the book calm. I might manage the prunes, but suet was a leap too far.

From Tilbury docks Laurie sails to Vigo, on the north-west coast of Spain. He changes his shillings for pesetas, buys bread and fruit, and walks out into open country. What follows is a period of hunger, deeper and more prolonged than anything experienced in childhood. At the cottage the food had not been plentiful, it had been monotonous, but there had always been *something*. Bread, at least, and even in winter fresh milk beneath the ice on the pail.

In Spain, on the arid stretches between towns and villages, after the bread and dates from his pockets are gone, there is nothing. 'All I remember of those first days from Vigo', Laurie writes, 'is a deliriously sharpening hunger, an appetite so keen it seemed almost a pity to satisfy it, so voluptuous it was.' He finds a handful of wild grapes and eats them green and unripe. He scavenges a patch of beans.

The word he uses to describe his eating each time he reaches a village is 'gorged'. He is gorged on bread and stew and 'warmed to idiocy' by wine in a mountain tavern. He is gorged in Zamora on roast kid and beans, the meat coming off the bone like rose petals. In a farmhouse above the Zamora wheat plain he takes pleasure even in the sounds of cooking. He lies with his head on his arms, too thirsty and famished to speak, listening 'voluptuously'

– that word again – to the sounds of a woman cooking: the rattle of the pan, the crackle of the fire, an eggshell breaking against a bowl, the hiss of frying oil. This mouth-watering concert climaxes with a clatter as a plate of two fried eggs is put down on the table and a glug as purple wine is poured into a glass.

Weeks go by when he survives on plums, figs, ears of wheat and goat's cheese as hard as a stone. Madrid is a miracle. The fish markets and restaurants are like the visions of a starving anchorite who has wandered too long in the desert: craggy oysters, calamari in golden rings, lobsters still twitching, bowls of mussels, 'feathery' shrimps, saucers of sizzling kidneys, roasted sparrows, snails, fried squid, hot prawns in garlic, stewed pork, belly of lamb. He eats as much as the pesetas he earns from his fiddle will buy him. What a thing to be ravenous, then to eat until bursting. I only knew how to eat enough to take the edge off hunger, not to silence it completely.

When Laurie returns to Spain a year later, it is to a country made desperate by war. If the hunger of *As I Walked Out One Midsummer Morning* had a sort of romance – the wandering troubadour sustained by music and sunlight alone – the hunger described in *A Moment of War* is a terrible one. The soups that he and the Republican fighters warm their hands on are made from hare bones boiled up and boiled up so many times that there is not a scrap of nourishment in them. The men dust soot and plaster from hunks of stale bread and dip them in melted snow to moisten the crumbs.

In one village, where the farms are hard with frost, the fighters come across two widows, who work the same magic that Annie used to in her Gloucestershire kitchen.

Presented with three bony chickens – bought by the men for over a thousand war-inflated pesetas – the sisters simmer the birds in a pot over the fire with tomatoes, dried beans and garlic sausage. 'How the widows had done it', writes Lee, 'seemed a miracle. We stood there in a swoon of hunger.'

When he is arrested, there is one sandwich each day, passed through the bars of the cell by a local church sister. It prompts another 'voluptuous' – a word used even more often than 'gorged' – reverie. 'In twenty-four hours it was all we got, and how we longed for noon. But that sandwich . . . what a feast it was to our shackled appetite and hungers. And how voluptuously remembered since.' Laurie's voluptuous hunger, his gorging whenever opportunity allows, left me in a state of confusion close to torment. My stomach keened for the café counters of Madrid: the feathery shrimps, the sizzling saucers of garlicky kidneys and prawns. I rarely drank alcohol, had never had it when ill as a teenager and never developed a taste – or head – for it since, but in my fantasy those dishes of spitting prawns came, as Lee's did, with goblets of cold, amber sherry.

While my stomach made its demands, my mind fought for its old dominance. Broth from bones and unripe grapes: that was my entitlement. But the more I tried to convince myself of the superiority of sooty, stale bread and 'wolf-like' hunger, the more visions of crab, calamari and lobsters on ice danced and tempted. I took myself out for another very long, stern walk.

As I walked I felt cross and jealous of Laurie. Why was it so easy for him and so difficult for me? How did he manage it with such evenness: going hungry when there is no food and bolting it, gorging on it when it is there. He is never fussy, never refuses the breakfast coffee floating with fatty gobs of goat's milk. Down the hatch, and off across the Iberian plains. He is an easy, unconcerned travel-ler. Apart from the treacle biscuits, the only possessions he takes with him are his violin, a rolled-up tent, a blanket, a change of clothes and some cheese. Meanwhile, I, even for a night away – and apprehensive for a week before – travelled with porridge oats, pressed fruit bars, packets of almonds and dried apricots, carrot sticks, apples and an emergency banana – all of it insurance against the seizure that came with being away from home and familiar foods.

In the worst years after my diagnosis, I rarely travelled. At most for a few nights in England with Mum to look after me and armed with oats and a carton of soya milk, but never further afield and generally with clamp-mouthed misery if others wanted a pub lunch. When a friend from sixth form invited me to stay with her family, her mother – and I am grateful to her still – agreed to make me a grilled chicken breast and salad for lunch each day and pasta with tomato sauce each evening. That was all I could eat and she was a marvel to make allowances. It built my confidence and made other trips possible.

In the year between A-levels and university, I went to Italy on an art history tour, visiting in six weeks enough church frescoes to keep Tom Birkin in work for a lifetime. Before I went, Mum repeated again and again, as if it were a protective charm: 'You can eat pasta. You know you can eat pasta. Eat enough to keep you going.'

On the first day in Verona there was the choice of pasta at lunch and I could not eat it. At dinner there was pasta and I could not eat it. I came back to the hostel head-achey with hunger and took a cereal bar from my suitcase.

In the morning I had a cereal bar for breakfast, another for lunch, another again for dinner. That got me up to around 600 calories a day, enough – just – to stagger around on. By the time we arrived in Florence, I was down to my last bar. They were supposed to be a pick-me-up snack if a train was delayed; they were not meant to be my entire diet. There was a desperate phone call home. The next day six boxes of cereal bars arrived by overnight courier from London. They kept me going until Rome.

The great triumph of that trip wasn't the Sistine Chapel, the Birth of Venus or the Villa Rotunda, but a small private victory. In Mantua, at a *gelateria* opposite the round church of San Lorenzo, I bought a single scoop of ice cream – *mela*, sweet apple – in a wafer cone. I was absorbed by the day's visits, to the Palazzo Te with its painted bacchanals, to Alberti's Basilica di Sant'Andrea, to the statue of Virgil, and carried away with *dolce vita* spirit. I couldn't have done it under other circumstances, not in London, not in the drizzle, not from a supermarket tub.

In Mantua, in the sun, it was possible. It would have to substitute for both lunch and dinner and I wasn't sure I could ever manage it again, but I had my *gelato* in the sunshine with a photograph to prove it. From an internet café I sent the picture home. It is framed on Mum's desk.

I was nineteen when I went to Italy; by the time I got to Laurie Lee at twenty-six, I still couldn't eat with any assurance away from home. I did a disservice to any country I visited with my reliance on cereal bars and packets of nuts and seeds. The ruins of Mycenae, the slender saints of Chartres, the Ponte Vecchio in Florence do not for me conjure the taste of stuffed vine leaves, sugared crêpes or

smoked, peppered, papered salamis so much as the crackle
of cereal bar plastic.

It was – and I knew it – a limping, limited way to
travel. At best, I could fix on one simple, local dish – a
pesto pasta or plum tomatoes with filo-thin ham – and eat
that each day for a week, but if any waiter had lifted the lid
from a crock and revealed a whole roast kid and beans, I'd
have run yowling for the first boat home. Couldn't I rouse
myself to adopt Laurie's eating at least in part? His diet
of dates and figs, grapes and olives, beechnuts and raisins,
sunflower seeds, bread and bags of plums? No more rum-
maging in rucksacks for hay-manger cereal bars.

Laurie's hasty, stolen meals eaten while on the road are
fondly remembered. He cannot walk through a village
without a Sussex housewife or Spanish *abuela* dashing down
the road after him with a 'screw' or 'twist' of tea or sugar,
or a small cake wrapped in tissue paper. In Madrid there
are prawns in more screws of paper and, later, during the
war, a ration of grey bread and a screwed paper of olives.
At Puerta del Sol there are little paper packets of bitter
sweets.

I listened to the rustling of all these twisted paper packets as keenly as Laurie had heard the voluptuous hiss of
frying eggs. They had an appeal that the plastic of shop-
bought cereal bars did not. Screws and twists of unfamiliar
foods seemed possible. The words suggested just a little,
just a taste, nothing so alarming as a great goat stew pot
lifted from the woodsmoke.

In September 2014, after the June of Laurie Lee, I went
away for a weekend to St Ives. We set off one morning,
Andy and I, to walk along the coast to Zennor. On the way
we stopped at a bakery for bottles of water and the local

saffron buns. The baker – and she was a true Mrs Bun, with floured forearms and hot cheeks – put the buns in a paper bag and flipped the bag somersaulting over and over itself so that the top sealed in a neat, cylindrical twist. It crinkled when she handed it across the counter.

The walk, which we had thought would take two hours, took five. Our plimsolls slipped on the rocks and I was pilchard-sunburnt. At midday we sat on a boulder high on the cliffs, ankles scratched by the gorse and very lost. I untwisted the paper and shared out the crumbling, saffron-dyed buns. They gave us new heart for the cliff path and it was cheerful to sit there, passing the water bottle and wondering if the rescue party would be able to find us. If, indeed, we wanted rescuing from this empty, beautiful place, spotted with petticoat mushrooms.

We found our way to Zennor at teatime, parched and burnt. The apple juice and beer in the pub garden were sweeter and cooler than Amiens champagne. There was a ploughman's sandwich each in the sun with truckles of cheddar and pots of piccalilli. 'Truckle' joined jorum, pottle and dixy in my diary-dictionary. I ate the lot, down to the last pickled onion. After, there was a slice of carrot cake, more crumbling and buttery than the buns, with frosting.

I hadn't eaten so much in a sitting in years. But I hadn't before had the stamina to walk for five hours. I left Zennor – in a cab, we were neither of us fit to walk back – in a happy stupor. Some of it was sunstroke, some of it the company, but much more was the elation of conquering saffron buns, ploughman's sandwiches and carrot cake. In London two days later, I found the paper bag crushed at the bottom of my rucksack, the last of the bun crumbs flattened to saffron discs.

*

Laurie's minstrel walk across Spain inspired a keen armchair wanderlust. I didn't hanker after sleeping outdoors,
certainly couldn't have played a fiddle for my supper, but
his writing, walking and eating had a propulsive, infectious energy.

Mum set me on the road again with her copy of Patrick
Leigh Fermor's *A Time of Gifts*. Six months separate the
wandering tours of Paddy and Laurie. Paddy dodges the
clubmen of Pall Mall, rushing for their hot China tea and
anchovy toasts, and hails a cab for the docks. He leaves a
damp, blowy, streaming London in December 1933 on a
steamer from Irongate Wharf to Rotterdam. Laurie was
to sail from Tilbury to Vigo the following June. Paddy
reaches Rotterdam, under a hush of snow, the following
morning and orders fried eggs and coffee at a seamen's
tavern. An appetite quickened by adventure makes it the
best breakfast he has ever eaten.

From the Hook of Holland he walks to Dordrecht,
Brabant, Arnhem, Cologne, Heidelberg, Stuttgart, Ulm,
Augsburg and Munich, where he takes against Lucas
Cranach's cat's-eyed minxes on the gallery walls. He stops
in Vienna, then walks to Bratislava, into Hungary, to
Prague and Slovakia. Then through the unpronounceables:
Kövecsespuszta, Diosegh, Sala-nad-Vahom, Kissújfalu,
Köbölkút. We leave him, at the end of *A Time of Gifts*, on
a bridge above the Danube between Slovakia and Hungary.

Between the Woods and the Water takes up again in Esz-
tergom before passing through swineherd country on the
way to Visegrád. Then Budapest, and across the Hun-
garian plain, the Hortobágy desert, the Transylvania
Marches. There is a rest cure at Kápolnásfalu, then it is on

to Romania – Dracula country – and along the shelves of the Carpathians, picking wild strawberries and watching in the night for wolves. He reaches Orşova and the Iron Gates gorge. I am out of puff just writing it.

In *The Broken Road*, the third of his walking memoirs, posthumously published, Paddy arrives in Sofia, and walks south across the central plateau of Bulgaria. He visits the Balkans before returning to Rustchuk. He crosses the Danube into Wallachia and walks to Bucharest, to Varna on the Black Sea, to Burgas and, finally, arrives by boat in Constantinople. Paddy is away for thirteen months and not once in all that time does he send home for a cereal bar.

There is a phrase he has to describe a particular sort of shy, dainty, feminine behaviour: 'niminy-piminy'. He uses it in *The Broken Road* about Bulgarian girls who will only sip at their tumblers of wine, rather than throwing them back as the boys do. That is what my eating abroad had been: fearful, niminy-piminy slivers of prosciutto and single olives. Paddy, once he leaves England, abandons himself to inns, *Schlösser*, beer gardens, coffee-houses, *châteaux*, *kastélyok* and shepherds' huts. He eats whatever his hosts' larders can give, whether fine wine from a castle cellar or wild mushrooms gathered in a bandana scarf and watercress pulled from a stream.

His epic walk is sustained by foot-long loaves of black *Butterbrot*; spiced bacon; boiled *Eier im Glas*; carp soup stained scarlet with paprika; poppyseed and caraway pretzels; smoked pork and pears; salami and pumpernickel bread; rose-petal jam; coffee and croissants; oily courgettes and ladies' fingers from bronze pans; young cucumbers cooked over thorns; parcels of sweet halva made from sesame paste; yellow kashkaval goat's cheese; and quinces, crab apples and walnuts, shelled and crunched on the move.

So much of Paddy's eating is done in motion. He sets off from Heidelberg with a rucksack heavy with *Gebäck*: buttered shortbread biscuits. These, he writes, were 'munched as I loped along the over the snow'. Like Sherston, Paddy is an incorrigible muncher. He is later to be found in a transept of Augsburg cathedral 'munching bread and cheese and an onion'. When he can stock up, he does. In Hungary, a day after leaving a *kastély*, he pulls a whole roast chicken from his rucksack – 'a tramp's dream'.

All of this was glorious. A loping, picnicking, munching freedom. Not the awful sense of confinement at a table. Paddy has his leftovers in the hollow of a willow trunk, or buttered rolls on top of a hayrick, or lentils and sizzling mackerel – 'I had thought I was beyond eating; but these delicious fish were demolished in no time' – on a pebble beach near Varna. It seemed to me a liberation from my old, captive ways: supervised at dinner, following a menu plan, compelled to stay at the table until I had at least tried what was on the plate.

Paddy's happy, effortless eating is perfected in *Mani: Travels in the Southern Peloponnese*. At Kalamata in midsummer, with his girlfriend Joan and friend Xan Fielding, Paddy sits down to dinner above quayside flagstones that throw back the heat like a casserole with the lid off. They step fully dressed into the sea and carry their table a few yards out, then three chairs. They sit up to their waists in cool water:

The waiter, arriving a moment later, gazed with surprise at the empty space on the quay; then, observing us with a quickly-masked flicker of pleasure, he stepped unhesitatingly into the sea, advanced waist deep with a butler's gravity, and, saying nothing more than 'Dinner-time', placed our meal before us – three beautifully grilled kephali, piping hot, and with their golden brown scales sparkling. To enjoy their marine flavour to the utmost, we dipped each by its tail for a second into the sea at our elbow.

What a performance! I was carried away by the impetuousness of it, the careless spirit of eating not just *al fresco* but *al mare*. This was what I wanted: to eat with the unselfconscious cheer of Paddy and his Kalamata guests, untroubled by the goggling crowd on the quay who send can after can of retsina out to the eccentric half-mariners. The thought of being stared at while eating and not minding, of basking in the attention, was new and compelling.

I haven't yet contrived to take my dinner in the Messenian Gulf, but if I ever do find myself in the Peloponnese, I will be straight out into the sea with menu, plate and cutlery. So far I have had to satisfy myself with Paddy's favourite discovery from his months in Bulgaria: yaourt.

It seems in retrospect that I almost lived on this stuff, sprinkling sugar on the dimpled crust and then spooning away. I had yet to learn how to squeeze lemon on top until the sugar is soaked, in the manner of some cunning Athenians. I was further still from the delicious Cretan method: pouring in a circular helping of honey from a rotating spoon-tip and then scattering the chryselephantine whorls with fragments of peeled walnut.

It is the purplest of passages. Can we really let him get
away with 'chryselephantine whorls' for the gold of honey
and ivory of yogurt? Yes, I think that under the circumstances we can.

Ever since yogurt and honey and nuts had made their
first appearance on the menu plan, I had been frightened
of them. At first, I had bargained and pleaded. Could it be
soya yogurt, not Greek? Could I have it without honey?
Without nuts? Could I not have an apple instead? Over the
years, I'd come round to eating the stuff. *Tess* had helped,
by reconciling me to milk. The calcium, I knew, would
mend my damaged spine and I was nervous of one day
being bowed and hunchbacked, as my doctor had warned.
But my bowls of yogurt were always eaten with glum duty
and taken like bitter medicine.

Now here was Paddy in the cool of a village dairy, somewhere between Tirnovo and Rustchuk, sharing with a
party of itinerant beekeepers – their honey is manna, if not
from heaven, then from the Balkans – earthenware bowls of
'indescribably good' yogurt. The Bulgarians call it *kissolo
mleko*, which is prettier than the translation: 'sour milk'.
Before I read Paddy, yogurt had meant brittle bones, defi-
cient calcium, the dread menu plan. After *The Broken Road*
a bowl of yogurt had the effect of one of Paddy's 'lantern
slides', calling up a traveller's snapshot of the clean dairy,
the earthenware dishes, the honeycombs folded in muslin
and the quiet beekeepers in their plaited osier hats.

Paddy finds in every inn, every castle, every fisherman's
cabin willing guardian angels. Whenever he is most woe-
begone, chilled, lonely, footsore, thirsty and unfed, some
saviour will appear with a tray of buttered rolls and soup

–'Sit up, drink it while it's hot' – brought to him in bed. When he loses his way among cliffs and rock pools and ledges slippery with bladderwrack one freezing night by the Black Sea, he staggers, desperate and certain he will die, on to a lighted cave, a hideout of fishermen and goatherds. He crouches, teeth chattering, by the fire while they nurse him with fish, lentils and tumblers of tea, two inches deep with sugar. Bottles of raki do the rounds. 'I began,' he recalls, 'as the food and drink piled up inside, to feel marvellous.'

How easily he settles at the tables of his hosts, whether they are counts, char ladies or Greek soldiers with ouzo in their packs. He never refuses what is offered him, not even the cured camel meat *pastourma*, dried in a paste of garlic, which makes his breath as violent as a blowtorch. He is a fearless eater. His motto might be 'eat first, ask later'. In his travel book *Roumeli* he eagerly spoons *avogaraho*: grey mullet's roes from Missolonghi sealed under yellow wax. He is a great mucker-inner. I, on the other hand, was a confirmed not-for-me-er.

So when my chance came to out-Paddy Paddy, I took it. A girlfriend, Camilla, had invited me to Morocco with her family. This was a greater challenge than a weekend in St Ives or the South Downs. I steeled my nerves, filled my suitcase with cereal bars and boarded the plane from Gatwick.

On the first morning, I borrowed a book from Camilla's father, the books on other people's bedside tables being so much more interesting than one's own. It was Richard Hughes's *In the Lap of Atlas*. Hughes was a willing eater. In his first long vacation from Oxford in 1919 he made straight for London, where he had Chinese chop suey in the

East India Docks, later remembering it as 'white stringy stuff, soaked in yellow gravy, chopped dog or cat on top'. This early encounter with exoticism set a pattern of experimental eating: coffee stiff with clotted cream in Hungary; cold fried steaks on icy mornings in Connecticut; truffles eaten propped on embroidered cushions in Morocco; a lunch of Turkish Delight and cucumber salad on Mount Athos; sea urchins and brown bread for breakfast on the deserted island of Psathoura.

In one lyrical, musing passage he pays tribute to the tagines and couscous of Moroccan cooking:

> Now how many Christian cooks, I wonder, could roast a sheep (or even a chicken) so tenderly that you could pinch off a mouthful without difficulty between finger and thumb? Yet that is what the Moorish cooks do. I have eaten meat in Morocco at expensive European hotels which needed knife, forks, and then almost a shark's triple denture to dissever it . . . but without exception in the houses of natives I found it as tender as butter.

With the meat comes the Moroccans' famous couscous: 'This is a tall cone of something white and mealy (flour steamed over broth, I believe), in consistency like milled chestnuts, generally sprinkled with powdered cinnamon and sugar, and with roast quails or some other pleasant surprise hidden at the centre.'

That night, there was a couscous at dinner. It came to the table in a tall, glazed terracotta cone painted with chevrons. The man who carried it was a Berber. He had grown up in the Atlas and had come down, in the best storybook tradition, to seek his fortune as a guide and *consigliere*. Like many of the Berber he was slight, narrow-backed and wiry. Lifting the glazed clay pot above his head was a feat worthy of Atlas himself. The cone came off a diadem of steaming couscous, set with crescents of caramelised onion, roast pumpkin, toasted hazelnuts, pine nuts and almonds. There were no quails hiding under the grain, but lamb tender as butter, as Hughes had promised. On the very top of the crown of couscous, quite improbably, were slices of grilled, honeyed banana.

Fired with the spirit of Paddy and readied by Hughes, I helped myself to the collapsing couscous. From where we sat, at an outside table, we could see the mountains, in outline against the dark sky. Next to Camilla, my oldest friend, who had stood by me through the worst of my illness, when I was starved and unhappy and no company for her at all, who had coaxed me to eat when I was most frightened to do so, I spooned a first, second and third mouthful of the sweet, steaming couscous. And when our Atlas came round with the dish again, the couscous much fallen in now, I did what I had not done since the illness first took hold. I had a second helping.

There's a coda, a final flourish to Richard Hughes's couscous. When the dish and cone are cleared away, the servant returns with a basin and ewer of hot water. A traditional couscous is eaten, Hughes tells us, with the fingers. The meal is rolled into a ball in the palm of the hand, then flicked, neatly, or as neatly as an unpractised Westerner can manage, into the mouth with a thumb. Regrettably, Hughes writes, it more often than not ends up down the back of your neck or – thwump! – in a neighbour's eye.

The basin of water, then, is for washing the couscous's stickiness from your hands. But not only that. 'If you have a fine long white beard,' writes Hughes, 'you may now shampoo it, and comb it out, all shiny and fluffy and soft. At least, I once saw this done by the City Fathers at a dinner party given by the Caliph of Safi: and very nice they all looked.' I had no long white beard to wash, but I smiled when the mint tea was poured from a silver kettle after dinner, and thought of the Caliph and City Fathers whiskered in soap suds and bubbles.

I'm far from a Phileas Fogg. No plans to fly the world in eighty days. No bucket lists of countries to visit or maps covered with drawing pins. After a week, I am ready for my own bed and books. But my four travellers – Tom Birkin, Laurie Lee, Paddy Leigh Fermor and Richard Hughes – have made me less fearful. When Paddy writes of Bulgaria or Lee of Zamora or Hughes of Morocco and Jamaica there's a part of me that thinks: 'Take me with you!' A week away. Two weeks. Could I go as long as three? I want to put myself in their hands, pass them the menu and say: 'You do the order.'

What they share is an untroubled hunger. Hunger for new places, new tastes and savours. They have the camel-like power of going days without eating, certain that when the great leg of lamb, cloves of garlic, thyme and rosemary pressed down between the folds, is lifted blistering from the fire, they will eat until the bones gleam. Theirs was a marvellous hunger, a voluptuous hunger, a swooning, insatiate, invincible hunger.

4

'A frabjous dish'

Of all my heroes, all those lopers and munchers, those public schoolboys and cricketers, soldiers and wandering minstrels, did any one of them ever cook a meal? Rarely. There is always an Aunt Evelyn, a Mrs Ellerbeck, a quartermaster, a Moroccan manservant, a pretty girl at the *Schloss* to lay the table with good things. It is the same for Dickens's title boys Davey Copperfield, Nicholas Nickleby, Oliver Twist, Martin Chuzzlewit and Pip of *Great Expectations*. Rarely do they shift for themselves. They can rely on a Peggotty, an Aunt Trotwood, a Newman Noggs, a Mrs Bedwin hovering in the wings with nourishing beef tea.

And they are all definitely *heroes*. Without really meaning to, I had been reading almost entirely about men. Men with uncomplicated, unashamed appetites. What about Little Dorrit? Doesn't she cook and eat? Only in mouse-like bites, saving the lion's share to warm on the Marshalsea gridiron and serve to her father at a table set with a clean cloth, a phial of cayenne pepper and a pennyworth of pickles. I hadn't excluded women deliberately. I had been reading in a grazing way, without much plan, but I had successfully dodged any heroine, any leading lady with even the faintest rumble of appetite.

What's more, nothing I had read had been strictly food writing. Where food came into a book it was incidental, giving colour and savour to the story. The meals I had read dropped like plums, unexpectedly, undesignedly, into my lap. I'd been ambushed by Rotterdam breakfasts and Kalamata picnics and found, to my great surprise, that I quite welcomed the ambush. I was eating more widely, more easily, more cheerfully. When faced with a quivering fruit jelly, turned from its mould, or a sharp, white sheep's cheese, I thought of their originals on the trestle tables at Slad or in the Mani tavernas and ate them with Laurie and Paddy over my shoulder, urging me on. And if I was strong enough for Yorkshire puddings, couldn't I brave food writing proper?

The week before the trip to Morocco I had walked to Marylebone for my holiday books. I came away with George Orwell's *Keep the Aspidistra Flying*, a short story by Will Self and a slim pocket Penguin edition of M. F. K. Fisher's kitchen essays collected under the title *Love in a Dish*. The cover – a blue soup tureen among vine and acanthus leaves – caught my eye against the shop's William Morris shelf papers. Its littleness and pastel cover gave it the feel of a sweet – a humbug or a mint imperial – picked from a jar.

It wasn't at all the right book for the destination. It was perverse, really, to sit in the bowl of the Atlas, reading about the Francophile American Mary Frances Kennedy Fisher in the markets of Dijon, Vevey and Aix-en-Provence or shucking oysters on the beach in California. While we had our hard-boiled eggs and baked flatbreads, an approximation of a Berber breakfast, she had café au lait and fresh, flaking croissants.

I read the eleven short essays on the first morning, light-headed with her milky pastis, pale rosé and marc. I was smitten: by the man with the tiny donkey selling mint drops from the Pyrenees; the beans as long and thin as hairpins; the white onions in a crochet bag; the butter in its crock on top of the old piano; the loose, trip-you-up red tiles of the kitchen floor; the butcher who drove right up to the door in his jeep, sounding his horn to sell cut meats, black and green olives and marbled cooking fats.

In one essay, 'I Was Really Very Hungry', Fisher, on one of her walking-reading-writing-shopping-cooking-eating tours through France, stops at an old mill, now a restaurant, in northern Burgundy. She is there out of season and the only guest. The young servant girl and Monsieur Paul, the unseen chef, have her captive. She fears, as dish after perfect dish streams from the kitchen, she may never escape.

First are the hors d'oeuvres: pickled herrings, the best she has ever eaten, mild and pungent; a sizzling plate of scorched endives; and green lentils with minced fresh herbs, tarragon vinegar and walnut oil. The servant girl hovers. 'Madame should be eating the little baked onions while they are hot.' Madame does. 'I ate several more than I had meant to. They were delicious, simmered first in strong meat broth, I think, and then drained and broiled with olive oil and new-ground pepper.'

The servant girl brings Monsieur Paul's pâté: unctuous goose breast, the finest pork, a suspicion of nutmeg. The main course, meanwhile, is still diving and curling in clean, river-drawn water. The serving girl brings in the bucket for inspection. 'Your trout, Madame.' It is *very* fresh. It disappears into the kitchen still swimming and reappears a few minutes later as *truite au bleu* with tiny boiled potatoes and a sauce of chopped chives, hot, sweet butter and a tablespoon of thick cream.

Then there is Monsieur Paul's special terrine, more special even than the pâté, of wild duck, spices and wines, followed by one of his special cheeses, a special filter of coffee and the most beautiful apple tart the now quietly moaning Fisher has ever seen. 'But this pastry is like feathers – it is like snow,' sing-songs the serving girl. 'It is in fact good for you, a digestive!' It takes determination, but Fisher, trembling with exhaustion, refuses a second slice.

I was poleaxed. How had she done it? How had she found the space for it? Not to mention the sherry, the Chablis 1929, the vast glass of marc. Why hadn't she begged for mercy after the pickled herrings? Because, as she explains, in another essay, 'G is for Gluttony', she was caught up in the sheer, thrilling greed of it, and the incomparable cooking of a master. She might never have the chance to eat such a meal, such trout, such apple tart again:

> I cannot believe that there exists a single coherent human being who will not confess, at least to himself, that once or twice he has stuffed himself to the bursting point, on anything from *quail financière* to flapjacks, for no other reason than the beastlike satisfaction of his belly. In fact I pity anyone who has not permitted himself this sensual experience, if only to determine what his own private limitations are, and where, for himself alone, gourmandism ends and gluttony begins.

She would have pitied me. Neither gourmand nor glutton, but teetotal and niminy-piminy fearful of pâté, terrine,

cheese, cream and pastry. Monsieur Paul would have had
me thrown in the millpond. But if I could not stuff myself
to bursting with *quail financière* or flapjacks, I could amply
do so with books.

Back in London, I had my own Burgundian feast. The
London Library was my Monsieur Paul, a second-hand
online bookseller my serving girl. I had hors d'oeuvres of
Fisher's *With Bold Knife and Fork* and *Consider the Oyster*, a
pâté of *Long Ago in France*, a *truite au bleu* of *As They Were*
and a terrine of *A Cordiall Water*. To prove I still had room
for more, I read Joan Reardon's biography *Poet of the Appetites: The Lives and Loves of M. F. K. Fisher* as my apple tart.

For a month I read nothing but rich, winy, gamey
dinners, eight or nine courses long, at the *Trois Faisans*
restaurant; Hershey's chocolates and potato chips; roast
beef with *foie gras* and *soufflés de Gruyère*; sweetbreads in
white wine and galantine of veal; *truffes au chocolat* and caramel tarts; candied fruits and sugared almonds; painted
ovals of marzipan and sweet rum omelettes with 'F' for
Fisher branded across their tops in burnt sugar; little rich
decadent tins of lark pâté and escargots drowned in their
butter . . . and . . . and . . . and . . . And I could only cry:
'Non!' It was too much. I was out-faced, out-buttered,
out-gluttoned. When Mary Frances wrote that she had
probably breakfasted on sufficient croissants and French
bread to make a delicious pile as high as the Eiffel Tower,
I whimpered my defeat.

Once I had recovered from my reading feast and had
several very long walks, my initial alarm settled. I may
not have been up to lark pâté, but I was spellbound by her
writing and wanted to try something, if only smally and
haltingly, of her cooking.

I had felt myself with her in Dijon, Marseilles, Avignon and Provence picking over radishes 'as fresh and delicate as dewdrops' and cherries crisp as new almonds. I warmed to the lunch she gave under the fig tree at St Helena in Napa County, California, where she served her guests cold crab bisque with iced cucumber, and hot peaches and new-picked strawberries for dessert. I would have begged an invitation to tea with Mary Frances and her sister Norah in their Dijon garret with a pitcher of milk, a pot of honey, sweet, fresh butter, spiced gingerbread, grapes and pears, all from the markets and patisseries that morning.

I liked her bubbling, boiling-over, irrepressible way of writing. Her 'snippets' of salt pork, 'sippets' of toast and 'soppets' of wafer tart to eat with a birthday fruit punch. I smiled at her homey, down-on-the-ranch description of black tea 'strong enough to trot a mouse on', and at the family tradition of sitting on a ham baguette to squash it flat before a picnic. Only certain bottoms were up to the task: it needn't be a large one but the person attached to it must be able to sit still and not squirm for twenty minutes so that the butter melted, but the baguette didn't lose its shape. I liked her habit of bestowing human traits on her dishes: a 'lusty ratatouille', a 'dainty omelette', the ripe, firm tomatoes philosophically 'ruminating' in basil and olive oil. I liked her unfamiliar words. She writes of 'skirling' a nut of butter in a skillet. It is just right for that steady turning of a pan on its axes as butter melts over heat.

When I had first started cooking for myself at university on the two-hob top of a Baby Belling oven, I had refused to use any fats. I used to lay a chicken breast in an inch of vegetable stock made up from bouillon powder and half-fry, half-steam it with frozen peas. The stock would boil dry and I would prise the breast from the pan, leaving behind a deposit like dried white glue. The chicken tasted of nothing very much, but this was a virtue, I thought. The less appetising a meal was, the less of it I would want to eat.

As I gained in confidence (and tired of scrubbing stuck chicken flesh from the pan) I allowed myself a drop of olive oil, which I would dab, dab and dab again with kitchen paper until the barest film remained. Still, it was an improvement on the evaporated shallows of stock. Mary Frances wouldn't have tolerated such fuss-dabbing. In Provence she discovers a wonderful olive oil from an unctuous vat that she would not mind being shipped home in like the Duke of Clarence, drowned in his barrel of malmsey. Her malmsey-wish came back to me when, soon after my discovery of Mary Frances, a friend, Andrew, back from a holiday in Greece, came to dinner bringing with him a bottle of olive oil. It was a gift in lieu of wine and I was glad of a change from elderflower pressé.

This oil, from a southerly island, had the almost transubstantial quality of making even the limpest rocket salad from a plastic bag taste of sun and sea and the silvered light of olive groves. I eked it out over weeks and months and it has ruined all olive oils since. No oil bought from the shops is as virginal as that bottle from Greece. Others are tinny and bitter, corrupted where my bottle was Artemis-pure. The island olive oil would have been wasted on skirling the pan. I saved it for dressings and for a last trickling over pasta.

Mary Frances, having reconciled me to olive oil, did something greater still: she won me over to butter. It was

her skirling that did it. Now, when I make eggs, I cut
my measure of butter (Mary Frances would probably still
think me very stingy) and skirl it in the base of the pan,
making it figure-skate over the surface. And I think of her
skirling in the kitchen at Marseilles in bare feet on the red-
tiled floor, with pots of geraniums on the window ledges
and the mistral blowing outside.

It wasn't all fair winds. Each time I thought I was
catching up with Mary Frances she had a maddening habit
of dashing ahead, leaving me stuck on some impossible
recipe. Yes, I was with her on the virtues of eggs and of
skirling a slice of butter before scrambling them. But then
she would go and do something unspeakable like pour half
a pint of rich cream into her scramblies before topping
them with chopped chicken livers. At this, I would have to
throw up my hands and admit that I was beat.

I was with her on her recipe for trifle. The fruits –
peaches, apricots, plums, cherries, mandarin sections,
whatever is in season – were to be marinated in brandy.
Yes, I could do that. Someone in the family, she continues,
with a steady hand and peaceable disposition then lines the
bowl with the fruits until the colours are like the patterns
of stained glass. Yes, I had a steady hand. I remembered
an undergraduate visit to the Sainte Chapelle in Paris and
I imagined my trifle bowl looking like the glowing windows on that afternoon of slanting sun. But then Fisher
walloped me with not one, but two sorts of little biscuits,
langues de chat and small sugar cookies, followed by a *crème
anglaise* folded with more whipped sweet cream and a topping of brandied raisins, silvered ginger, slices of hazelnut
. . . and so on and so forth. I was gazumped again.

She has a knack, bewildering to me, of adulterating

every dish she touches with butter, cream or cheese, often all three. When I reached her section on celery, I was sure I was on safe ground. And then, blast the woman, she came up with a recipe for Christmas Celery: celery baked in butter, Béchamel sauce, Gruyère cheese and breadcrumbs. I was doing my best to be an attentive pupil, but she didn't make it easy.

I really did want to learn to cook, and to cook with pride and skill. I could do the odd dish – a puttanesca sauce, a tray of roast vegetables, a stir-fry of prawns and beansprouts – but I tended to fixate on particular recipes. If I had found a meal I could eat calmly, I would cook it night after night, for months on end until I was sick of the sight, smell and taste of it. It was a guarded, faint-hearted way of cooking and I didn't want to carry on with it for ever. The same meal eaten over and over couldn't help but lose its flavour. When out and abroad I could now rise to the occasion with couscous or saffron buns, but my home repertoire was tried, tested and stale. I wanted Fisher to be my guide; if only she would meet me halfway on the cream.

The Christmas Celery recipe appears in an essay framed by what she calls her 'vegetable love'. This was more like it. I was good at vegetables. I could crunch through celery and carrots and cucumber and radishes, pop punnets of cherry tomatoes as if they were praline truffles, and bite into little gem lettuces whole like cream buns. I had tried to jolly my eating along by telling myself that while all other foods were still rationed to small portions, I could eat my rabbity fill of vegetables. And they were very rabbity vegetables: raw and, apart from those heady few weeks of the Greek olive oil, undressed. Tomatoes might get a splash of balsamic vinegar and a grinding of black pepper, but spinach came just as it was, wilted in water and chewed like cud.

Mary Frances wouldn't have stood for it. What one needed were vinaigrettes, home-made mayonnaise, salt, melted sweet butter, lemon juice, basil, tarragon, dill, mint, parsley, nutmeg for the spinach and dry white wine for the mushrooms. And, of course, there is not one of her vegetable dishes that cannot be improved by being smothered under a blanket of double cream and parmesan. She reserves a special affection for zucchini – courgettes – which light her up with 'inner glee' when cooked into a 'mishmash' with celery, parsley, spring onions and butter, to be eaten after a quiet bath and before getting into bed with an old *Inspector Maigret*.

Reading Mary Frances, I began to experiment. Some of the recipes were hers, some cut from the newspapers at my desk in the morning. I made vinaigrettes for sliced beetroot: red wine vinegar one day, cider vinegar the next, this mustard or that, a little more or a little less olive oil, black pepper, and, if I had them, chopped parsley or chives. I took ribbons from a courgette with a vegetable peeler and left them ruminating, covered by a second plate, under olive oil, mint, lemon juice and zest, salt, black pepper and toasted pine nuts. I made ratatouilles, which aspired to lustiness. I got the hang of blanching florets of broccoli so they kept their bite and tossed them with soy sauce, sesame oil, mirin, chilli and ginger. I cut heads of celeriac into matchsticks for remoulade, substituting the mayonnaise – in the same enemy camp as double cream – for a tablespoon of natural yogurt, lemon juice and the russet and dun of a Dijon mustard.

Having tutored me in vegetable love, Fisher then did something marvellous: she had me buying, boiling and buttering new potatoes. It was these words that did it: 'Perhaps the most subtle I ever ate were in Sweden, when they were steamed quickly, right from the garden, on a bed of fresh dill, and lifted out like fragile eggs and served on hot plates with more chopped dill and sweet butter.' Each one, she writes, was as round and plump as a cherub's cheek.

I did what she told me. I bought miniature new potatoes, small and round as ball bearings, from the Saturday market, steamed them and skirled them in butter and chopped dill. Buoyed by the success of it, I had more the next day, this time with butter-softened spring onions and grain mustard. And the next day: with chopped anchovies, mint, lemon and capers. Fisher concludes her thoughts on new potatoes with this: 'Plenty of butter, freshly ground pepper, chopped herbs if one wishes, and there is a frabjous dish indeed.' The day, the three days, that Fisher helped me over my fear of potatoes done in butter were frabjous ones. Callooh! Callay! A Jabberwock slain.

Fisher is a keen Carroller. She hums and hymns him as she cooks. She cannot start sautéing an onion for a soup without crooning the Mock Turtle's song from *Alice's Adventures in Wonderland*. As the onion softens, the Mock Turtle sounds in her ears:

> 'Soo—oop of the e—e—evening.
> Beautiful, beautiful Soup!'

'That is exactly how I feel about it', she writes, 'when I am tired and cold and hungry, poor or rich, I would rather

drink a bowl of hot broth than confront any meal ever de-
vised.' I am in sympathy with her on soups as I never could
be when she is singing little love songs to *pâté de foie gras*.
I have adopted her Mock Turtle, and when I am skimming
stocks call on him for a kitchen duet:

> 'Beautiful Soup, so rich and green,
> Waiting in a hot tureen!'

He and Fisher have kept me company as I've made
misos with steamed purple sprouting broccoli and soy
sauce; beetroot borschts that stained fingers, apron, tea
towels, kitchen tiles and teeth; a soup of fennel, celery, carrots, onion, tomatoes and white beans for an unexpectedly
chilly summer evening; a gazpacho with chopped egg for
an even more unexpectedly balmy one; a porcini and portobello mushroom soup for September; a celeriac, bacon
and thyme soup for a Sunday night in January, supped up
while reading the weekend book reviews:

> 'Soo—oop of the e—e—evening,
> Beautiful, beauti—FUL SOUP!'

Soup is an ally. When I am having a bad day, a bad patch,
when the old compulsions come simmering and bubbling
to the surface and my throat tightens because I must not
eat, because I don't deserve to eat, when the thought of
a square meal is impossible, I can, unless things are very
bad, manage a bowl of soup. If there is chicken stock in a
jug in the fridge – I left the gritty bouillon behind with
the Baby Belling in university gyp-rooms – a tablespoon
of barley, a carrot and an onion, and if I can have it hot

from a deep bowl and go to bed early, then I have some hope of waking up the next morning calmer, quieter and with my mind's book room in better order.

For Mary Frances, the most beautiful of beautiful soups is beef broth. One beef broth in particular, brought to her in bed when ill with flu in May 1921 when she was twelve. On the fifth day of lonely quarantine (there were three younger siblings at home) and on a diet of watered fruit juices, a wonderful, scented breeze comes through the open window from the kitchen: beef broth in the making. The breeze is followed soon after by her mother with a little tray and a big bowl – the biggest bowl, a kitchen bowl, of beautiful soup, clear and coloured like strong tea, with a pearly vapour of steam rising from the surface. 'It filled me with bliss. I drank all the dark, heady broth – slowly, no doubt noisily, and very voluptuously.' She tips it back, down to the last drop, then shuffles down on the pillows for a long, sweet nap.

Mary Frances is right, of course, that your own soups, however much you peer into the cauldron, however much you call on the Mock Turtle to advise on the seasoning, are never as good as your mother's. My chicken soup – whitish and lily-livered – is nothing to Mum's rich, restorative one. It is always chicken soup rather than beef broth that is ladled into bowls to nurse ailing Freemans. It is chicken soup that comes up the six flights of stairs to my flat in a flask to cure a chest cold. These days I am too old really for soups made in Mum's kitchen and carried across London. But it does seem to be what mothers do and, if I ever have children, I hope they will feel the same affection for my chicken, ginger and noodle soup, gulped from the deepest kitchen bowl.

Some mothers take it too far. Mrs Sassoon, hearing that the schoolboy Siegfried is unwell, descends on Marlborough College and, having tasted the sanatorium beef broth, marches off to the Ailesbury Arms, orders beefsteaks, hijacks the kitchen and brews the strongest beef tea the school has ever tasted. 'To this day I don't know for certain how many steaks she got the goodness out of,' Sassoon writes in his childhood memoir *The Old Century*, 'but I imagine that the feeding bottles from which I dreamily imbibed contained the essence of about half an ox.'

It is the detail of Mary Frances's beef broth that makes it so appealing: the little tray, the biggest bowl, the clear, strong colour and the spoon she is given to eat it with: the Irish pattern, which is usually saved for Occasions.

Fisher has a liking for the equipment of eating. That soup would not have tasted as it did, or worked the same curative magic, if it had been eaten with a plastic spoon or a bent or tarnished one. In Marseilles, cooking in a poky kitchen-bathroom, she cheers herself up by shopping for Provençal pottery, plates and bowls, and two sturdy wine glasses that make everything taste better. Staying near Lake Lugano in Switzerland she buys *boccalini* – little pitchers with handles for clear, turtle-beautiful soups. In Dijon, at the Grey-Poupon shop, she admires the old faience mustard jars in the window and leaves with a *moutardier* and a 'darling' wooden spoon with a blue ball on the end. Her lusty ratatouilles are cooked in an earthenware casserole in a low oven for five or six hours and stirred every two hours with a long wooden spoon.

When she is served whole écrivisses at a smart luncheon, the crayfish arrive with the correct complement of silver pliers, claw-crackers, gouges and forceps. Her Dijon landlords the Rigoulets introduce Mary Frances to *escargots d'or*, scrubbed with little curved brushes made in Paris. Only when the snails are scrubbed does Monsieur Rigoulet make the extra trip to the market for the parsley, garlic and sweet butter.

What splendid paraphernalia she accumulates: claw-crackers and little snail brushes, *moutardiers* and darling spoons – and everything tasting the better for them. Mary Frances, armed with woven baskets and crochet bags, comes home from the market staggering under the weight of her loot. For her, there is pleasure in every part of cooking and food: the shopping for it, the scrubbing of it, the careful covering of it with wire cloches (this, before refrigerators reached Provence), the polishing of the silver pliers, the carrying of the clay casserole from counter to table, the right sort of jug for the right sort of clear *consommé*.

It helped if I thought of eating as just the last line of a recipe, the postscript scribbled at the end. Eating was the difficult bit. If I could enjoy all the parts that came before – the shopping and scrubbing and soup bowls – I stood a better chance with the meal itself.

I have described my aversion to canyon supermarkets and their shelves stocked to surfeit. Faced with two hundred different yogurts, I flounder and leave without. It is easier for me at a market stall that sells only one yogurt, from a herd in Kent, from a farmer who knows each cow by name. If the farmer is chatty, and if the sun is shining, and if there are sweet peas to be bought at the next stall, and courgettes at the one next to that, and cherries in brown paper bags, and butter for skirling and eggs for scrambling, then I am really very content pottering and filling my canvas bags, and later scrubbing my vegetables clean in the sink at home with a stiff-bristled brush.

Then there are Mum's summer courgettes, yellow and green, with blowsy flowers. She contrives to have a glut of them every year, no matter how hot or cold, wet or dry, bad or good the weather, grocers' dozens of them, galumphing out of their beds and across the paths, ballooning into marrows if they are not pulled from their plants every morning. We confer; what do we do with them all? A salad, a soup, a tian, a quiche, a frittata. A gratin, a risotto, a cake, a muffin, a chutney. A ratatouille to sate the lusts of Pan and Priapus. At the end of the season we are desperate. Courgette meringues? A courgette fool? Courgettes cut into rounds in a jug of late summer Pimms?

Courgettes, picked clean of their caterpillars, are better for being garden-grown or bought at a market, and better still when eaten from a particular Mason's Ironstone china plate: a 'Bamboo' pattern of pale celadon and madder pink, bought on a morning's antique-shopping with Dad. The same shop – but a different trip – also gave up four shallow soup bowls with handles and matching saucers in Mason's 'Indian Grasshopper' livery. They are the best thing for summer soups of peas and podded broad beans.

When I first started boiling eggs for supper, my friend Adam, knowing that I was newly partial to them, but not knowing what a thing it had been for me to eat eggs for the first time in years, gave me a present of two stoneware eggcups in darkest blue. The eggcups I'd been practising on were mimsy white porcelain ones that tended to topple over and – Humpty Dumpty – spill the yolk. The new eggcups are as indestructible as Prussian soldiers in their blue jackets. A pair of soft-boiled eggs served in them is

a fine supper. I think of our friendship each time I take
the cups from the cupboard, as I think of Dad when I lay
the table with Bamboo plates and Indian Grasshopper
bowls.

I was lucky to live for two years – the two years I was
reading Sherston, Laurie, Paddy and Mary Frances – with
a girlfriend, Olivia, who is a keen market-shopper. She
can be relied on to go into raptures in the shop on the
Edgware Road that sells Tupperware boxes in infinite
shapes and sizes, and in another hung with vast, tied,
feather-duster-brushes of parsley; to walk to the weekend market for rhubarb in February sleet; and to dither
over stacks of enamel baking dishes under the Brixton
arches.

One damp January weekend in the first year we lived
together, Olivia and I walked to Chinatown. We were both
tired and winter-glum and a wet, crowded West End did
little to lift our spirits. But the back room and basement of
a Chinese grocer was quiet and warm and we spent an hour
marvelling at durian fruits and smiling 'Luck Fish' shaped
out of tapioca. We left with a bamboo steamer, two shallow jade dishes for soy sauce, pak choi, water chestnuts,
lotus roots and frozen vegetable dumplings. At home we
unwrapped our new toy, setting the steamer over a pan of
water. The dumplings, little drawstring purses of shitake
and oyster mushrooms, went into the bamboo basin and
were left to steam under its lattice hat. They came out hot
and translucent, to be dipped into soy sauce from the jade
bowls. We both felt, after a round of dumplings, and then
another, a great deal less damp and gloomy.

The bamboo steamer lives next to the pan I use
for porridge, and although Olivia is no longer at hand for

Saturday marketing – she moved to Stockwell, south of the river, where the shops are Portuguese and West African – I think of her each morning at breakfast, and miss her constant presence and her experimental beetroot cakes baked in a tin from our shop on the Edgware Road.

I was with Mary Frances on so much of it: the market-going, the plates and bowls and favourite Irish pattern spoons, the skirling, the vegetable love and beautiful soups. I was with her on the niceness of flowers on the table: snowdrops and dark, bruise-purple cyclamen for the lunch at Monsieur Paul's mill; wild narcissus with 'celestial' fillets of fish, their tails crisp, at an inn near Lausanne; fresh lavender from the man with the tiny donkey in the market in Provence. As a little girl she had been entrusted with making the nasturtium-flower sandwiches for her mother's Californian afternoon tea parties.

Where she leaves me behind is in her luscious, voluptuous, confessional gluttony. It is there from childhood, eating mussels on Lauguna Beach with messy 'drippings, slurpings, moans of pleasure, animal sighs of repletion'. It is honed at boarding school with chocolate bars: 'borrowing, hoarding, begging and otherwise collecting about seven or eight of these noxious sweets and eating them alone upon a pile of pillows'.

At twenty-one, in Germany, she eats a bowl of exquisite potato chips, so many of them she cannot then face the dinner she has ordered. She writes that she was ashamed of her greed, but you know it is a fib and she would gladly do it again. At twenty-three she discovers caviar in Strasbourg and realises she 'cannot possibly, *ever*, eat enough of it to satisfy my hunger, my unreasonable lust'. At the *Trois*

Faisans in Dijon the dinner is a 'gluttonous orgy'. Never before or since has she eaten so much.

In *Long Ago in France* she remembers, 'I was wildly hungry and happy in those days, and could eat and did eat not one horse but several.' Who could begrudge her such happiness? She is newly married, abroad in Burgundy and seated in 'introspective and alcoved sensuality' in a restaurant in front of oysters, snails, ripe cheese from a Cistercian abbey and a soufflé of kirsch and glacé fruits. Her heroes are Brillat-Savarin, Lucullus, Nero and Rabelais. Her appetite is Gargantuan and 'husky-gutted'.

If any reader now accuses me of double standards, I am guilty as charged. Why is Laurie Lee allowed to be voluptuous and gluttonous and gorged, but Mary Frances not? Why is Laurie's insatiable hunger charming and boyish, to be indulged and praised, while in Mary Francis's case I disapprove? I had let Paddy lope across Europe eating whatever he chose and only once winced at his eating. It was in the Munich beer garden where he eats ham, salami, frankfurters, *Krenwurst*, *Blutwurst*, *Schweinebraten*, potatoes, sauerkraut, red cabbage, dumplings and colossal joints of meat that might have been elephant steaks. He drinks beer, and more beer, and more beer still. It leaves him in a well-deserved state of 'hoggish catalepsy'.

The truth is that I was forgiving of Laurie and Paddy and unjust to Mary Frances. When I first became ill, I was thirteen. I have lived with anorexia all of my adolescent and adult life. My entire experience of being a woman is a state of self-denial and self-loathing and dismal daily quarrels between body, mind and appetite. When I purse my lips at Mary Frances's hungry, happy years in Dijon and the 'prodigal bounty' of her table, it is only partly disapproval. Mostly it is envy.

For all the progress I have made, there is a block. I can and do eat, I shop, cook, wash and spin lettuces and water the herbs on the windowsill. But I still eat very little. I like those Indian Grasshopper bowls partly because they are small. You can fill them to the rim and the portion will be a doll's one. I cannot imagine ever eating eight chocolate bars in a sitting or managing a lunch like Monsieur Paul's. On hopeful days, I wonder if I will prove myself wrong. At fifteen I'd never have believed I would one day eat roast beef and Yorkshire pudding. In another fifteen years, I may match Mary Frances course for course. It seems unlikely now.

It is shameful to admit it, but I took the Joan Reardon biography from the library partly because I wanted to see the photographs. I thought Mary Frances must have been as plump and round as a mustard jar. Yet here was Fisher, slender at Vevey market, carrying her woven basket and choosing lettuces from pallets. Here again, fresh and summery, in an appliqué sundress on a lawn at San Jacinto. And again, trim and lively, perched on a kitchen counter in a white blouse and striped apron, with a saucepan on her lap. There was perhaps a thickening of the waist in later years, but in photograph after photograph she is slim and chic, lips painted red and eyebrows plucked into high arches. The brows, alas, she later lost when a kitchen gas oven blew up in California. 'Nevermore any eyebrows or lashes,' she wrote, 'but it's fun to put on new ones.'

I had done well enough, I thought, for now. I had a repertoire of soups and salads and had conquered, vorpal sword in hand, new potatoes and butter. I returned the

Fishers I had borrowed to the library and shelved the ones I had bought. I didn't beat myself up too much for failing at her trifle and her Christmas Celery. I thought of her often when I went to markets, and tied my apron, and stood at the hob with her Mock Turtle.

A year after I had first picked up *Love in a Dish*, an exhibition opened at the National Gallery. The paintings came from the collection of Paul Durand-Ruel, an early champion of the Impressionists. There were the expected Degas ballet girls, in white tulle and ribbons; Renoir's pretty sitters in pretty hats in pretty gardens; and Manet's still-life 'Le Saumon', a *tableau* of sour lemons and a salmon with a tail as crisp as the celestial one Mary Frances had eaten at Lausanne.

There was a complement of Monets: a sun-shaded reader in a pleated bonnet; rivers and windmills; trains in the snow; boats in a harbour. Then something not at all like familiar Monet: a close-up, tablescape painting of two *galettes des pommes* on raffia mats. The slices of apple, as Monet paints them, are golden, cooked in sugar and calvados and arranged in a Catherine Wheel pattern. The pastry is scored like a shell and a sharp knife waits on the tablecloth. In the summer of 1882, the painter had decamped to a hotel in Pourville-sur-Mer where the *spécialité de la maison* was a *galette* of caramelised apples with a frangipane almond filling.

I was sure I'd come across them somewhere before: *galettes* as neat and golden and devoutly arranged as Monsieur Monet's. On the walk back across town to Paddington it came to me. At home, I took Mary Frances from her shelf and skipped through *Long Ago in France*. Here it was. While she is lodging with the Rigoulets, Papazi, the father of Madame Rigoulet and the owner of the little snail-scrubbing brushes from Paris, offers to instruct Mary Frances in The Making Of The Tart.

First, there is the mixing and rolling and flipping of the dough into a wide, flat baking tin, two feet across, brought from Alsace. Then, the chilling of the pastry in the wine cellar. Then, the apples from Normandy, peeled and cut into thin, even half-moons and tossed into a bowl of white wine to keep them bright. Then, the beating of the eggs and cream and nutmeg into a custard, to be poured into the cool pastry:

> He took the apple slices from the bowl one by one, almost faster than we could see, and shook off the wine and laid them in a great, beautiful whorl, from the out-side to the center, as perfect as a snail shell . . . Papazi shuffled the thin pieces of fruit like a wizard or a little fat god, and they seemed to fall out from his hands and fall rightly into place. He did it as effortlessly as a spider spins a web.

It was, Mary Frances declares after the baking, 'the most delicious tart in a whole land famous for them'.

For a week after seeing the exhibition, I had the cat-alogue open on my desk at the Monet *galettes* with the Fisher book next to it. I called Mum about the calvados. No, there was none in the cupboard at home. I Googled 'Tarte Tatin recipe' and frowned at the ingredients: 50g butter, 50g caster sugar, ready-rolled puff pastry (Papazi would have winced), half a teaspoon of cinnamon, six Cox's apples, *crème fraiche*, icing sugar and calvados. Well, I could dispense with the last three for a start. Calvados cream was asking too much. Butter, sugar, pastry, cinnamon, apples. I took a breath and tied my apron.

My pastry, ready-rolled, was nothing to Monsieur Paul's. It was not snow or feathers, but it did crisp and puff as the packet promised it would. My apples were not fine half-moons or crescents but bulging and gibbous, and when turned from the pan onto a plate my Catherine Wheel came out as a marmalade jumble. I had no two-foot tin from Alsace, but a non-stick saucepan made a *galette* just right for a Mason's Bamboo plate. It was little and lop-sided, a *galette* even Monet couldn't have made becoming, but for a first attempt it wasn't bad, and it was mine.

I let it cool by the window. No mistral here, just a dusty breeze blowing the seed heads from Paddington's plane trees. After a deliberately light supper of courgettes and lentils I washed my plate, cutlery and pan. I dried and put them away. I wiped the kitchen work surfaces. I fluffed and folded the tea towels. I could put it off no longer. I took a photograph – proof to be sent to Mum later – and eased a slice, a sliver of *galette*, onto my plate with a knife. At my table by the window, level with the tops of the trees, parched and hot in an unseasonably warm spring, I had a mouthful of apple and butter pastry. And another. It was the most delicious tart in all of England.

The California childhood Mary Frances describes in her books was not at all like my childhood. Her memories are of mussels steamed over sea grass and hot coals on Laguna Beach and of swimming like dolphins with her sisters and brother in the coves before collapsing onto the sand to eat hot, salted crisp breads, hair and bodies drying in the sun.

My holidays were, like those of most English children, damp and chilly – very much like the ones described here by Elizabeth David:

> North Cornwall and its leafy lanes dripping, dripping; the walk in a dressing gown and gum boots through long squelching grass to the stream at the end of the field to fetch water for our breakfast coffee . . . A loaned bungalow on the West coast of Scotland. Rain drumming on the corrugated iron roof . . . On with our Wellingtons and sou'westers.

What charm is there in mussels on Laguna Beach when you might have pilchards in soggy Penzance? While we did have some blessedly sunny summer holidays in France as children, our half-terms and Easters were always Blighty ones. We went to Yorkshire, where we were tickled by the thought of toad in the hole, and where it rained. To Cornwall, where we collected bucket after bucket of limpet shells, day after day, until they covered the bottom of the bath, and where it rained. To Turnberry in Ayrshire. Rain. To Wales. Rain. Wales again. Rain and sausages. Wales a third time. Rain. More sausages. There was no dolphin swimming – we would have had pneumonia – and no basking on the beach eating crisp breads. It was Wellingtons and sou'westers, as it was for Elizabeth David.

I had admired Mary Fisher, been chivvied along by her, shaken out of many of my old frets and fears. But with Elizabeth David I found something different: a fellow feeling, a familiarity and sense of kinship. Mary Frances was bombastic in her writing, bullish even, possessed of an unshakeable confidence. She didn't seem to suffer the humiliations of the Englishwoman abroad in France, convinced at every moment that she is too dumpy, too frumpy, and not at all sure what to do with her silver écrivisses crackers. Mary Frances is a self-possessed, admirably certain American and mercifully unafflicted with the very English, very embarrassed feeling that one is never quite up to snuff, never quite at home in unfamiliar places or company. Mary Frances cracks her crayfish with complete assurance.

I knew Elizabeth David's England in a way I couldn't know Mary Frances's Californian beaches, ranches, vineyards, West Coast boarding schools and Hershey's bars. The England of Elizabeth David, though separated by seventy years from the one I grew up in, was recognisably my England: an England of nannies, Wellington boots, Regent's Park, Primrose Hill, expeditions to see the windows at Selfridges (where Elizabeth ran up bills for roast chicken, cream and coffee); the Tate Gallery; the *Sunday Times*; Scotch eggs for picnics; fish at school on Fridays with custard and tinned fruit cocktail (the staples of Godstowe in the 1920s, and of my London primary school in the 1990s); Agas; 'hellish' summer weather and Woolworths. Ed and I belong to the last generation of children who went to Woolworths for our pick'n'mix. Outings to the branch on the Edgware Road were red-letter days.

More than anything, though, it was her books that drew me in. Mary Frances had been a reader, certainly, of Lewis Carroll and *Inspector Maigret* and others. But Elizabeth was in a league and library of her own. We know a little of her desert island books from the titles she took when she sailed in 1939 from Port Hamble for Cap Le Havre, the first stop on the two-year voyage that she would later distil into her first book, *Mediterranean Food*. The man she sailed with was Charles Gibson Cowan, an East End actor, Grub Street hack, vagabond and sometime down-and-out. When they met, he was thirty-one; she twenty-two. He had a wife and child. Her family did not approve. None of it stopped them.

Charles bought a boat and made her seaworthy. Elizabeth bought china, casserole dishes, a potato peeler, malted milk tablets and Oxo cubes at Woolworths. He packed a compass and a copy of *Visual Signalling Part I*. Together, they argued about the ship's library. In *The Voyage of the Evelyn Hope*, his memoir of their Mediterranean odyssey, Charles explains that between them they had narrowed the books they needed down to about 400, with shelf space for only a third. They jointly decided on *Pears' Cyclopaedia*, a *Complete Shakespeare*, a Bible, Marlowe, Gibbon's *Decline and Fall of the Roman Empire*, Milton's *Paradise Lost* and one of the two *Alice* books. Was it *Wonderland* with its Mock Turtle or *Looking-Glass* and the Jabberwock?

Charles chose Rupert Brooke, Byron, Ambrose Bierce, H. G. Wells, *Jude the Obscure*, Aldous Huxley's *Antic Hay*, Rabelais, the plays of George Bernard Shaw, Anatole France, a couple of dozen Greek dramas and the Lonsdale Library's *Cruising and Ocean Racing*. Elizabeth packed *The Seven Pillars of Wisdom*, the collected Joseph Conrad, a *Golden Treasury*, a second Marlowe (in case Charles's was not complete), the *Arabian Nights*, a Chekhov, more Anatole France, the *Odyssey* and *Iliad*, several Baedekers, *Robinson Crusoe*, the *Barchester Chronicles*, G. K. Chesterton's *Short History of England*, Mark Twain, Beatrix Potter's *Tailor of Gloucester* (a china-fancier's delight) and a hundred cheap paperback thrillers to be thrown overboard as they were read.

How could I not adore such a woman? When I am away, any space in my suitcase not taken by cereal bars is given up to books. Seven of them for a weekend. Twelve for a week. I was imaginatively carried away by Elizabeth David's bunk cupboards stacked with paperbacks as I had been by Sherston's boyhood book room.

It wasn't only her books. She has an art historian's eye. She remembers the barrow boy at Chinon who arranged his bunched radishes and salad greens into a 'little spectacle as fresh and gay as a Dufy painting'; the dressed salmon that might have been a Chardin still life. She notes that John Constable's windmills seem convincingly to turn, while the sails of lesser artists stand still, because his father was a miller and Constable, alone of landscape painters, understood how the grain was milled and ground. She invokes the Dutchman Jan Davidsz de Heem for his painted lemons, their rinds peeled in a single helter-skelter strip, and Diego Velázquez for his eggs spitting in oil. In an essay on nutmegs she tells the story of the sculptor Joseph Nollekens, whose penny-pinching was such that he used to pocket the nutmegs from the table at the Royal Academy for his evening glass of hot spiced negus. When she wrote that the Victoria and Albert had a large collection of silver nutmeg graters, I was off across the park to see them with my sketchbook.

There is a pleasing precision to her writing, every meal painted with the fine brushes of a miniaturist. How lovely are her candied walnuts on the confectionary counters of Turin, like 'nuggets of some marvellous quartz'; her bronze and copper pork noisettes with rows of black, rich, wine-soaked prunes in a long white dish; her mornings at market day at Uzès, where even in February there were 'little

round crisp, bronze-flecked, frilly lettuces, baskets of mes-
clin or mixed salad greens, great floppy bunches of chard,
leaf artichokes, trombone-shaped pumpkins'; her dish
of *oeufs à la neige*, as 'frail and pale as a narcissus'; her
garnet-bright Jamaican guava jelly; her soups, 'delicately
coloured like summer dresses, coral, ivory and pale green'.

Her recipes may be done in the most delicate of watercolours, but they are never weak-washed or insipid. Her
manifesto for cooking and eating calls for 'life', 'guts',
'bite' and 'a certain amount of dash'. Dash! That is what I
lacked in the kitchen, and in my cautious eating. Dash and
'sumptuous simplicity' are the key to her cooking. If 'voluptuous' is Mary Frances's most commonly written word,
'simplicity' is Elizabeth's. The most sumptuous of her
simple dishes are omelettes. These were my next challenge
after Sherston's boiled eggs and Mary Frances's scrambled
ones. Elizabeth writes:

> What one wants is the taste of the fresh eggs and the
> fresh butter and, visually, a soft bright golden roll plump
> and spilling out a little at the edges. It should not be a
> busy, important urban dish but something gentle and
> pastoral, with the clean scent of the dairy, the kitchen
> garden, the basket of early morning mushrooms or the
> sharp tang of freshly picked herbs, sorrel, chives and
> tarragon.

Her measure of perfection is the omelette of Madame
Poulard of Mont-St-Michel. Visitors to her hotel kitchen
speculate wildly about those omelettes. Did she add cream
to the eggs? Did she have a special pan cast by the black-
smith? Was there a fabled breed of hens laying golden

eggs each morning? Did she sneak *foie gras* into the beaten whites and yolks? Madame Poulard's secret recipe, as quoted by Elizabeth, is simple to the point of abstraction: 'I break some good eggs in a bowl, I beat them well, I put a good piece of butter in the pan, I throw the eggs into it, and I shake it constantly.'

Trusting to Mesdames Poulard and David, that is what I did. Break, beat, butter, shake. It was, as they had promised, 'a golden bolster of an omelette', eaten with one of Elizabeth's frilly lettuces, sharply dressed in lemon juice and olive oil, on a Mason's Bamboo plate. I have made many more since. Break, beat, butter, shake. Sumptuous simplicity.

I wish now, I wish fervently, I had made a resolution then, after that first shaken omelette, never to read any recipe except those written by Mary Frances Fisher and Elizabeth David. Each is so prolific, each so curious in both intellect and appetite, that I would never have been bored, never have exhausted their books and essays. I would have been quite happy and well and sane with beautiful soups and golden omelettes. I wish I had devoted myself to them and no others. I wish I had been spared what I read next.

That summer, as I stockpiled *Loves in Dishes* and *Books of Mediterranean Food* on the shelves at home, a very different sort of food writing began to appear in the newspapers and magazines that crossed my desk each morning. Here, there were no omelettes, no boiled eggs, no scramblies, with or without cream and chicken livers. No eggs at all. No lamb as tender as butter. No roast beef or suet pies. No celestial fish. No trout, no pickled herrings, no beautiful grilled *kephali* with sparkling scales. No frabjous new potatoes.

No delicate potato chips. No pastry, no butter, no sugar,
no wheat, no dairy. No *galettes des pommes*. No Cratchit
Christmas pudding. No saffron buns. No scalding tea, no
coffee stiff with clotted cream. No life, no guts, no bite,
no dash. No daring, no adventure. No joy.

This was clean eating, green eating, lean eating. Food
from a Scrabble board: kale and quinoa, chia and avocado,
agave and baobab, goji and amaranth. Eggs? You got no
points for those. If it wasn't Scrabble, it was an absurd
parlour game of substitutions: courgette spaghetti, cauli-
flower rice, coconut yogurt, cashew cream, buckwheat
porridge, almond milk, hazelnut milk, hemp milk, a lurid
cheesecake of avocado flesh.

What started on blogs and photo-sharing websites
spread to the newspapers. First on the lifestyle pages, first
as a joke, later in earnest. Then on the recipe pages, the
health pages, the retail pages, the book pages. Every
bookshop promised wellness with wheatgrass juice. Glow.
Detox. Nourish. Delicious. Good. Simple. Meat-free,
gluten-free, dairy-free, sugar-free. It was inescapable. Even
the doughtiest of supermarkets climbed onto the band-
wagon with nut milks, coconut oils and chia pots. Friends
who had resisted every former dietary fad and fashion now
declared themselves intolerant, allergic, hysterically sensitive to even a grain of wheat, a thimble of milk.

I should have beaten it back, this clean-eating creed
and crusade, built myself a fortress of books: a Dickens
barbican, a Sherston palisade, ramparts of Laurie Lee and
battlements of Paddy Leigh Fermor. I should have called
on Mrs Ellerbeck to brandish her rolling pin from the
drawbridge. I didn't. I let it take over. This disgust of food
dressed up as an almost religious virtue. Those monstrous

voices that I had battled with for years, those voices spitting against the filthiness of eating, the shame of appetite,
those bullies and demons came roaring back. What had
once existed only in my unhappy mind – disgust for food,
an obsession with a clean, pure, empty stomach – was now
bodied forth by siren-beauties and 'wellness' bloggers in
books and newspapers, on restaurant menus and in shopping baskets.

But this wasn't pure or good or well. This was a trembling, frit way of eating. Believers were told that for a
holiday they must pack their bags with goji bars, cartons
of almond milk and tamari nuts. At a restaurant, diners
must order only side dishes: brown rice, steamed greens,
hummus. This was what I had rebelled against, this restric-
tive, choked eating, which despised spontaneity, which
never dared to try something new: not the local cheese,
not the smoke-house salmon, not the couscous and tender
Berber lamb.

I knew in my rational moments that this was all wrong.
Inwardly I screamed at the voices to leave me be, to let
me have my health, my sanity, my hard-won relish for
market-shopping, cooking, eating. I gathered my Elizabeth Davids, some bought, some borrowed, like amulets.
She would protect me, she would ward them off.

When the sirens sang the dangers of fruit – bananas
bad as chocolate bars, grapes like sugar bullets, raisins as
tooth-rotting as candy – I searched in Elizabeth's books
for recipes with which to stop my ears. At Malta she
writes of ripe figs and delicious oranges, and small, sweet
melons stuffed with wild strawberries and peeled white
grapes. At Elche in Valencia she eats fresh dates, the first
of the season, 'small, treacle-sticky . . . in tortoiseshell-cat

colours: black, acorn brown, peeled-chestnut beige'. She recommends, in season, the dark, juicy summer cherries that English fruiterers call 'bigaroons'. She describes a present of ripe mulberries given to her each year from a magnificent tree in the grounds of Rainham Hall in Essex and the summer puddings and mulberry-syrup water ices she makes with them.

I thought back to an afternoon I had spent with my fellow art historian, Hermione, at Gainsborough's house in Sudbury. It was a weekday, cool and overcast, and we were among the very few visitors. In the garden, a mulberry tree was jam-ripe and dropping. Might we? The gallery guard almost begged us to. In another day the fruit would be over, lost to wasps. You did not have to pluck them, barely touch them for the berries to come away, bursting and staining. We ate until our hands were crimson.

Must I give up pasta too? And play their game of 'spiralised' substitutions? Courgette spaghetti, celeriac gnocchi, asparagus linguine, carrot tagliolini? Certainly it would help use up the summer glut. But couldn't I have my courgettes softened in butter and rosemary and tossed through real linguine? Not some pale courgine, courgetti, courgetelle imitation. Must I snub the little raviolis filled with cream cheese and parsley Elizabeth David had bought at the market at Uzès? I read and re-read her catalogue of pastas, unknown to post-war England:

All the varieties such as bows and butterflies, shells, knots and wheels, melon seeds, stars, ox-eyes and wolf-eyes, rings, ribbed tubes and smooth tubes, cannelloni, little hats, marguerites, beads, miniature mushrooms, quills and horse's teeth, green lasagne and tagliatelle, twists and twirls and whirls and all the other ingenious inventions which turn an Italian pasta shop into a place of such entrancing fantasy.

I was recommended a book – *The Geometry of Pasta* – by friends, Natalie and Ollie, who made their own pasta, laying out lasagne sheets like bed linen to be pressed and folded. It was a glossary of *gnocchi* and *gomiti* with drawings and etymologies of pasta names: *busiati* – reeds; *campanelle* – bell flowers; *canestrini* – little baskets; *capelli d'angelo* – angel's hair; *cavatappi* – pig's tails; *conchiglie* – conch shells; *ditali* – thimbles; *farfalle* – butterflies, these our favourites as children.

I might have had *fazzoletti di seta* – silk handkerchiefs; *fettucine* – ribbons; *fusilli* – spindles; *gramigne* – weeds; *lumache* – snails; *orecchiette* – little ears; *pappardelle* – gobble-uppers; *strozzapreti* – priest stranglers; and *avemarie* – the tiniest of pastas, sometimes shaped liked stars – *stelline* – which need only as long in salted boiling water as it takes to say one 'Hail Mary'. Were these not more entrancing than limp strings of courgette?

The sirens would never have allowed me the saffron buns – gluten! sugar! butter! – I had eaten on the path to Zennor under a matching saffron sun. Elizabeth David would have applauded the buns and called for more. It is near Córdoba that she first sees purple meadows of autumn-flowering crocuses. She watches a local farmer prepare the saffron, picking the orange stigmas from the flowers one by one and heaping them in a shoebox by his side. The fallen crocus petals are like pools of quicksilver. She has saffron buns in Cornwall, at St Just in Roseland, dazzling-yellow, though the dye is synthetic annatto, not crocus saffron. I suspect ours were annatto, too, but on the day I believed them true saffron and imagined distant fields of purple crocus flowers.

If I had been a different person, a more resilient one, I might have read the sirens and scorned them. Let them have their parlour games and spiralisers, I would have my omelette. But I am not resilient, I am nothing if not susceptible, and the enchantresses of clean eating stirred the old thoughts. How beguiling they were, the sirens, their figures so slender, their skin so golden. Did I not want to be, like them, deliciously well, deliciously free, deliciously clean, lissom and lovely, and purged and pure?

Over that late summer and autumn, I stopped eating red meat, then chicken, then fish, then eggs. I stopped pasta, potatoes, bread and white rice. I stopped eggs, cheese, butter, yogurt and milk. Tess's dairy, Paddy's gold and ivory whorls might never have existed. I stopped eating sugar, dried fruit, fresh fruit. Sugar, any sugar was arsenic, hemlock, deadly nightshade. It was so sweet, so addictive, so perilous – so the sirens said. A menace to health. An opiate. A hobgoblin.

Instead, there was quinoa, avocado, amaranth, buckwheat, almond milk, kale, edamame, aduki, kelp and coconuts, and the fear, the returning fifteen-year fear, of eating anything that wasn't on this narrow list, anything that wasn't 'clean'. This wasn't like the difficulties I had got myself into walking at night in the cold and not eating enough to keep me on my feet. This was more acute, more like my worst, adolescent days of shivering hunger.

How did I let it happen, and so rapidly? I was tired, I think, and worn out by four years of late nights in a newsroom. Not only late nights, but early starts, and working

Sundays, Bank Holidays, Christmas and Easter. The more tired I was, the less I wanted to eat. I was sleeping badly, awake for hours in the night, hungry, allowing myself an inch of almond milk diluted with hot water from the kettle. Tossing and turning with ravenous emptiness. The less I slept, the more taxing the next day in the office. The more demanding the day, the less I ate, and so the less I slept. But exhaustion alone – nor the thwarted, frustrated feeling that I wanted now to be writing, not editing, not tied to a desk in a newsroom – wasn't enough to send me into such a spiral.

I think it was more inward than that. Did the illness, half-dormant while I read my way through Dickens, the war poets, the loping Paddy, the voluptuous Laurie, sense that I was winning? Did it return, vengeful and furious, to punish me for *galettes* and honeyed yogurt? Anorexia has so often seemed to me something demonic, something foul squatting on my chest like the demon in Henry Fuseli's *Nightmare* or a raging Jabberwock.

I thought I had got away, shaken it off, driven it out, but it came howling back. Jaws that bite, claws that catch! I had lowered my guard and, fanned and flamed by the sirens, the monster bit and caught me. When I tried to wrestle free, to shut myself in my mind's library, I found – how had I not seen and stopped it sooner? – the cases once more smashed, the shelves scattered, and the old, terrible chaos.

5

'Some way of composing my mind'

When Alice first reads *Jabberwocky* in Looking-Glass House she can make neither head nor serpent's tail of it. It is only by holding the poem up to the mirror that she puzzles out the words. 'Twas brillig, and the slithy toves . . .'

The Jabberwock of the John Tenniel illustration is a dragon with waxed whiskers. Its claws are furred, its feet are talons, its tail trails in the darkness of the tulgey wood. How small Tenniel's beamish boy (who might, with his long, fair hair, be Alice in armour) seems as he swings his sword back, almost toppling over with the weight of it. I have called my illness a Jabberwock. Is that right? Is it a demon of the imagination? A 'something', as Alice calls it, not real, distorted in the looking-glass, but filling the head with frightening conviction. Something only I can see and hear, always beyond grasp.

Anorexia is very like a Jabberwock. You share your head with a monster whiffling malice and nonsense, burbling that you are fat, foul, snivelling, worthless. In the library of your mind, it tears its claws through pages, stamps dirt across covers, lashes at pen pots and ink stands with its tail and beats its high-domed head and scaled shoulders against the door when you try to shut it out. It is a shape-shifting illness. Too many times I have pulled across the bolts, sunk to the floor, thought I had quieted it, only to find it slithering under the door like a flat-nosed snake. I have watched as it has transformed itself back into a monster and seated itself, gloating, in my chair, in my book room, my head. At other times the illness has been a swarm of flies, filling my mind from bookshelf to bookshelf. In the worst of the illness, I would see lips moving – a doctor speaking, Mum reasoning – and hear only a deafening drone.

At such times I do not think: this is anorexia. I do not think: these are the delusions and hallucinations of the illness and if I were to open a medical textbook, a dictionary of psychiatry, now, at *anorexia nervosa*, I would find my symptoms numbered in clear bullet points for the benefit of the student. I do not think: it is all there, in twelve-point font, quite plain, quite fitting the diagnosis. I think only: I am losing my mind. And then: I am mad. This is madness.

There is a loneliness to any madness. How do you tell people: I hear voices that I know, I *know* cannot be real. But they are louder, closer, more pressing, more persuasive than the real voices of family and friends and doctors. How do I explain that I see things that aren't there, that I know can't be there, but there they are as clear as that window, as solid as that lamp-post. That I look in the mirror and see another person, my body grossly swollen and vast. That my mind is not my own.

People would say: but the girl's mad. It would make them uneasy. In another, less compassionate age they would have said: put her away somewhere. So of course you say 'anorexia' because that has a doctorly, academic ring to it. Others are reassured that if the madness has a suitable name, there will be a suitable cure. Ah, it is only 'anorexia'. This pill, this menu plan, that therapist will right it. But to the anorexic, the diagnosis is small comfort. Cowering from Jabberwock voices, unable to eat, sleep, think for chattering, screaming, murderous noise, you nurse the thought: I am mad.

There have been three times since the illness first took hold when I have felt this madness. First, in those two years at school when I pared back and pared back my eating and in the year of bed-rest that followed. Second, in the year of university interviews and A Level exams when stress brought on the clattering and clamouring. And a third time in the late summer, autumn and winter that I became obsessed with purging and scouring myself 'clean'. All three have brought with them debilitating insomnia. Hunger and sleep deprivation are enough to play tricks on anyone's mind, even those who are otherwise quite well and sane. Starving, exhausted and plagued by Jabberwock noise, I was both frantically lonely and never alone.

During those first two periods of acute illness, I could not have written this. I could not have coolly listed symptoms, or said: it is a Jabberwock, or: I am mad. When it came the third time, I had something new in my arsenal. More than a vorpal sword: a wolf on my shield.

'The merest schoolgirl,' writes Virginia Woolf in her essay *On Being Ill*, 'when she falls in love, has Shakespeare and Keats to speak her mind for her; but let a sufferer try to describe a pain in his head to a doctor and language at once runs dry. There is nothing ready made for him.'

When I read Woolf's essays and diaries it was with sobbing relief and recognition. Here was what I knew of mental illness and its distress. Here, written clearly and surely, were tocsin noise and shadow-shapes in mirrors and the certainty that one cannot go on with such drumming and beating in one's head. Here – and what a deliverance it was to discover her – was a writer who allowed me to say, not that I was not mad, for I felt very mad indeed at the time, but that I was not the only one.

I don't know whether Woolf's malaise was anorexia. Her husband Leonard Woolf described it as manic depression: periods of soaring creativity, elation when she was writing, then months of glooms and despairs. Her doctors called it neurasthenia – a disorder of the nerves. Leonard complained that this was just a name: 'a label, like neuralgia or rheumatism, which covered a multitude of sins, symptoms, and miseries'. They, the doctors of nervous disorders, had not the slightest idea about the state of his wife's mind. Woolf called it simply her madness. 'I find', she wrote, 'that unless I weigh 9 ½ stones I hear voices and see visions and can neither write nor sleep.'

Since her death, her suicide, hounded by mind's squall and madness that could not be quieted, some Woolf scholars have read anorexia in her diaries and letters. Once they have settled on a name, Woolf's armchair doctors argue about what caused it, her mad-manic-neurasthenia-nervosa. Was it the deaths in sad succession of her mother Julia, her half-sister Stella, her father Sir Leslie Stephen, her brother Thoby? Was it childhood sexual interference by her half-brother George? Did all this contrive to hurry a sensitive and nervy child into starvation and madness?

Leonard Woolf's descriptions of these periods of madness are very awful. When I read them, it was almost through my fingers. He catalogues the stages of Virginia's illness each time it returned. Severe physical, mental or emotional strain. A peculiar headache low down at the back of the head. Insomnia. A tendency for the thoughts to race. A 'passing across the border' of sanity into insanity. Delusions. Voices. Melancholia and despair. Unwillingness to speak. Fatigue, needing not just a night's rest to right, but a week's. Living for months in a nightmare world of frenzy. In the worst of her depressions she refused to eat. Leonard writes:

> For weeks almost at every meal one had to sit, often for an hour or more, trying to induce her to eat a few mouthfuls. What made one despair was that by not eating and weakening herself she was doing precisely the things calculated to prolong the breakdown ... Deep down this refusal to eat was connected with some strange feeling of guilt: she would maintain that she was not ill, that her mental condition was due to her own fault – laziness, inanition, gluttony.

It was a battle, as it must have been for my mother with me, to persuade his wife to eat. She knew later how infuriating, how unreasonable she must have been. In a letter, written some years after the meals Leonard describes, she admits to 'disgusting scenes over food'. I, too, regret my former scenes. I wish I had not thrown that slice of fruitcake on the floor, shedding crumbs and currants on the tiles.

Leonard wrote his diary in code so Virginia would not be upset if she found his notes: 'V n. v. w. b. n.' was 'Virginia not very well bad night'. Reading Leonard's notes was a stark, jolting lesson in the toll illness takes on the person doing the looking after – and how thankless the task. Leonard is valiant in trying to make sense of madness:

> Superficially I suppose it might have been said that she had a (quite unnecessary) fear of becoming fat; but there was something deeper than that, at the back of her mind or in the pit of her stomach a taboo against eating. Pervading her insanity generally there was always a sense of some guilt, the origin and exact nature of which I could never discover; but it was attached in some peculiar way to food and eating.

In this, Leonard is clear-sighted. He knows that the fear of being fat is a sham for something more difficult to pin down. Some taboo or terror or guilt. That is the thing. One isn't really frightened of being fat, but of something else: a loss of control, a chink in the armour, a breaking of some unspoken rule. I still don't know where it comes from, this strange guilt and its bludgeoning punishments. I have never completely discovered its origins, even after fifteen years. Leonard continues:

> This excruciating business of food, among other things, taught me a lesson about insanity which I found very difficult to learn – it is useless to argue with an insane person. What tends to break one down, to reduce one to gibbering despair when one is dealing with mental illness, is the terrible sanity of the insane ... All Virginia's actions and conclusions were logical and rational; and her power of arguing conclusively from false premises were terrific. It was still more useless to argue with her about what you wanted her to do, e.g. eat her breakfast, because if her premises were true, she could

prove and did prove conclusively to you that she ought
not to eat her breakfast.

This all sounded very like what I knew. The hours spent
over meals, coaxing spoon to mouth, the powerful sense
of guilt at laziness and greed, even when over-worked,
sleepless and starved, the grim logic of the 'good breakfast'
before school, the wild paranoia and rage when sat at a
table and told to eat. There are differences, too, of course.
I have never suffered her sort of headache, low down in the
back of the head. I have never heard London's sparrows
sing in Greek as she did. But I have heard voices – an 'odd
whirr of wings in the head' – and seen spirits in mirrors.

In 'A Sketch of the Past', a rag-tag memoir of her
childhood at Hyde Park Gate and St Ives, she writes of a
looking-glass dream. 'I dreamt that I was looking in a glass
when a horrible face – the face of an animal – suddenly
showed over my shoulder.' She was never sure afterwards
if it was a dream or if it had really happened. But she
always remembered the other face in the glass and that it
had frightened her. I have never seen a face in the glass:
nothing so solid. But often, in my worst moments, I have
looked in a mirror and seen not only my own distorted,
swollen reflection, but something like a black hood behind
me, seeming, even without a face, to leer and mock.

Leonard remembers Virginia's morbid horror of being
looked at, of being photographed, of sitting to the sculptor Stephen Tomlin. It was 'Chinese torture' to her. 'The
sittings ended only just in time; if they had gone on much
longer, they would have made Virginia seriously ill.' This,
too, is familiar. I have more than once left a hairdresser,
only half dried because I could not sit in front of a brightly

lit mirror watching my reflection shift and swell. Two twenty-pound notes left on the reception desk and out into the street, grateful for air, one side of my head still damp and dripping.

She proved herself braver than I am in the hall of mirrors at the Earl's Court Exhibition Centre with her brother Adrian. 'We grew long – & lopsided & gigantic & dwarfed.' The hall made her laugh and she and Adrian felt they had had their money's worth. The only time since childhood that I have been to a hall of mirrors, at the Hyde Park winter fair, it was to me something from a nightmare and set my head rattling with sick-making noise and panic.

But should we call her madness anorexia? For all that it sounds like what I know of the illness, it is a presumption, an intrusion, to knock on the skull of a woman I have never known, to shine a surgeon's lamp in her ear and say: I have found the worm in your brain, I know what ails you. If she knew her illness as madness, not as anorexia or mania or neurasthenia, I will use her word and not impose any other.

You might reasonably ask: was it sensible to read Woolf? To surround myself with the devils of her depression, 'hairy black ones', and her intolerable fits of the fidgets? Mightn't I have been better off with Wodehouse, bedfellow to Woolf on the shelves? Surely Bertie would have been a better tonic for a tired and fractured mind? But prize pigs and country weekends were not the medicine I needed. Something had gone wrong with my mind, the third crisis of my long illness, and I needed to take the measure of my madness and find some new method to right my thoughts. 'I feel my brains, like a pear,' Virginia wrote to her sister Vanessa, while convalescing from a breakdown, 'to see if its ripe; it will be exquisite by September.'

*

To tell the truth, I had never got on with Woolf before. I had read a handful of the *Common Reader* essays at university in a week when I was supposed to be writing about German woodcuts and engravings. I had picked her up in protest because I did not take to Hans Baldung Grien, thought him weird, and did not like either the grinning, capering skeletons of Michael Wolgemut's *danse macabre*. So I read Woolf on George Eliot and Jane Austen and Thomas Hardy, the names I recognised, wrote a slapdash essay and shut my books on the skeletons.

Later I read *A Room of One's Own*, which was galvanising, and *Mrs Dalloway*, which was head-scratching. Then I gave up. But I had a nagging feeling that I was missing something. I had tried Woolf's criticism, polemic and fiction. When I returned it was to her diary. At the Persephone bookshop on Lamb's Conduit Street in Bloomsbury, Woolf territory, I bought a copy of *A Writer's Diary*, filleted by Leonard from Virginia's many diary notebooks. It came in a pale-grey slipcover. I was hooked, caught and reeled in. I read in a rush, not wanting to do anything but read, then ordered the full five volumes of her diary, edited by her niece-in-law Anne Olivier Bell. It took six months, on and off, to read the diaries' 1,750 pages.

Reading the diaries coincided with my last months at the newspaper. I gave my notice between volumes two and three, edited my last features while reading volume four, and in my fledgling weeks as a freelance writer I started volume five.

The diaries also followed the falling-apart of my eating. Buckwheat porridge and almond milk in the morning. Amaranth and quinoa soup at lunch. Aduki bean soup for dinner. The soups were warmed in the office microwave. Those last few months were dismal. I had lost my way. I was acutely cold, hungry and tired to the marrow.

For a month after I left the newsroom at the end of February 2015, I slept: twelve hours at night, a nap before lunch, to bed again in the afternoon. By April I was feeling more sensible, the clatter in my mind was quieter, and I never wanted to see another quinoa soup – or office microwave – again. My leaving present had been a cast-iron casserole dish. I christened it with a ratatouille. It was lusty and warming. I was beginning, with rest, and beautiful stove-simmered soups, to rally.

I woke up each morning, took two steps from the foot of the bed to my desk, opened my laptop and started writing. I was absorbed by new projects and commissions. I found that when I was writing, the voices dimmed to whispers; still there, still agitating, but not as insistent.

Woolf had been a consoling presence through it all. She had been mad, once, twice, three times and had quieted her madness. 'And so here I am,' she was able to write in November 1919, 'sitting after Saturday tea, a large warm meal, full of currants and sugar and hot tea cake, after a long cold walk.' That was how it felt as I wrote my first freelance reviews at home: like coming in to a fire after a long cold walk for hot tea and currant teacakes.

It took six months to feel less skittered. In September I went away to Sussex where Andy and I walked from Monk's House, Virginia's cottage at Rodmell, to Charleston, where her sister Vanessa Bell made a home for her children Julian, Quentin and Angelica, and on to Berwick Church, where Vanessa and her partner Duncan Grant had painted the murals and decorated the pulpit with vases of flowers. It was where, socks sodden, I had had roast beef and York-shire pudding, sirens be damned. I read the 1,750 pages of the Woolf diaries devotedly and never once does she eat a chia seed or a goji berry. Not when there was roast beef and plum tart waiting on the table at Monk's House.

I found in her diaries, and then her letters, a corrective to clean eating. Meals may not always have been easy for her, as they so sybaritically were for Mary Frances Fisher and Elizabeth David, but Woolf struck a balance between not wanting to eat and knowing she must eat. In her writing there is a spring-like pleasure, pinking and blossoming, cautious and gradual, in food and in her attempts, often haphazard, to cook.

'I caused some slight argument (with L[eonard].) this morning,' she wrote on 13 January 1915, not long after a period of severe illness, 'by trying to cook my breakfast in bed. I believe, however, that the good sense of the pro-ceeding will make it prevail; that is, if I can dispose of the eggshells.' She has her breakfast in bed – more usually safely cooked in the kitchen first – at home and abroad. In Sussex, there are mushrooms from Asheham Hill, col-lected the day before, with bacon, toast and hot coffee. In Paris, bacon and eggs and the morning's letters on a tray on her lap.

At Monk's House she and Leonard shared a passion for mushrooming – 'I must go out and pick 'shrooms, the sun being out' – blackberrying, apple-sorting and watching hares on the Downs. In the orchard are plum trees crowded with fruit, well-kept rows of pears, artichokes and potatoes, raspberry bushes piled with pyramids of fruit, and a great many apple trees. To stop the children from the village school stripping the branches, the Woolfs share them out, with a strict compact that the children must respect the orchard and not scrump its trees.

'Our way of life here – cooking messes, cutting fresh asparagus from the earth seems to me almost divine,' she wrote. Coming home from long, cold walks with her dogs Grizzle and Pinka, she has muffins with honey, or hot tea-cakes full of currants and sugar, or a long slab of fruitcake. Taking tea with Thomas Hardy, there are cake stands and a chocolate roll on a round table – 'what is called a good tea' – and she is disappointed when Hardy eats nothing of the spread. He was eighty-six, so perhaps he can be forgiven. His maid Nellie reported that at this great age he was mostly fond of 'kettle broth': finely chopped parsley, onions and bread cooked in hot water.

> 'Soo–oop of the e–e-evening,
> Beautiful, beauti–FUL SOUP!'

At dinner, when at home, Woolf has omelettes and good coffee. Luncheon might be rissoles and chocolate custard. And 'shrooms, 'shrooms, 'shrooms every year when it was their season, carried home in a large white pocket handkerchief. I started looking, on my morning walks in the park, intently at mushrooms. Could I? Dare I? With a little butter? I did not dare. Unless some sensible market man or grocer has inspected them for me, I am not bold enough to roll my dice on a pert, pushing Hyde Park mushroom. But Woolf had me buying them in mixed bags: portobellos and chestnuts, buttons and chanterelles, and skirling them in butter and thyme, and eating them on toast with a Sassoon soft-boiled egg tipped out of its shell over the top.

When a restaurant menu offered a chicken-of-the-forest and horn-of-plenty risotto, and after I had asked and been told that these were both mushrooms, and liking the names very much, I ordered the dish. The mushrooms were earthy and sweet and mellow and odd.

Only once have I been out mushroom-hunting with friends who knew what they were doing, or claimed to, though the squabbling and skirmishing over the French handbook – 'I'm sure it's a chanterelle. Look at the picture: identical!' – did not inspire confidence. I enjoyed the search at any rate, bent from the waist, scouting head-first and eyes down through the woods near Poitiers, keen for yellow-white flutes. But it was our last morning and we were flying home at teatime, leaving our hosts to dare a mushroom supper.

When I think of the 'shrooms laid out on a handkerchief in the kitchen at Monk's House, I see them as painted by William Nicholson. He was a keen forager and painted four still-lives of mushrooms collected on trips over twenty years. The one that is closest to my idea of Woolf's mushrooms is a 'shroomscape painted in 1940. Nicholson and his wife Marguerite had been bombed out of their home and studio in St James's and had moved to the White Hart Hotel at Nettlebed in Oxfordshire. Their October exile coincided with the mushroom season and they briefly forgot the war with a hunt for horse and button mushrooms. These Nicholson painted on a pewter dish, higgledy-piggledy, tumbling like acrobats, their gills still pink.

Woolf, when she wasn't truffling mushrooms or shaking omelettes, had her meals cooked for her. In January 1920, she and Leonard were getting their meals from Mrs Dedman in the village: 'stews & mashes & deep many coloured dishes swimming in gravy thick with carrots and onions'. Mabel and Louie, her cooks of the 1930s, worked together topping and tailing vast basins of blackcurrants and gooseberries for jam.

New cooks were taught to make bread. Baking was the only cooking Woolf did well and without mishap. Louie remembers her breaking off from work three or four times in a morning to knead her dough. Woolf's experience of bread-making gives colour and crust to Susan's kitchen-dreaming in *The Waves*: 'I knead; I stretch; I pull, plunging my hands in the warm inwards of the dough. I let the cold water stream fanwise through my fingers. The fire roars . . .' This is baking as kneading, stretching meditation.

She is quietly pleased with the new oil stove, installed at Monk's House in September 1929:

> At this moment it is cooking my dinner in the glass dishes perfectly I hope, without smell, waste, or confusion: one turns handles, there is a thermometer. And so I see myself freer, more independent – & all one's life is a struggle for freedom – able to come down here with a chop in a bag & live on my own. I go over the dishes I shall cook – the rich stews, the sauces. The adventurous strange dishes with dashes of wine in them.

Is that not a manifesto? Freedom with a new oil stove, glass dishes, a butcher's chop, dashes of wine. A year later, mistress of the new oil stove, Woolf is able to say: 'I walk; I read; I write, without terrors & constrictions. I make bread. I cook mushrooms. I wander in & out of the kitchen.'

Freedom for me was writing at home, warming a lunch of Sunday leftovers in the orange casserole, putting stock

on to simmer while I raced a deadline. With book reviews
on my slate, I was free to read all day, in office hours, and
then into the evening. And this was work!

In the summer of 1926, at the height of her infatua-
tion with Vita Sackville-West, Woolf writes an invitation:
'Will you dine with me off radishes alone in the kitchen?' I
cannot now eat a radish without it seeming conspiratorial,
something to be done in cahoots with a friend or fellow
plotter. Vita, in turn, is a great giver of picnic dinners.
At Sissinghurst they have cold salmon and raspberries
and cream and chocolates given by Vita's mother Lady
Sackville. On another night Vita magics up a basket of
peaches and half a bottle of Château d'Yquem from Lady
Sackville's cellar.

A hare hangs in the Monk's House kitchen for a pie and
Woolf comes home off the Downs or across the garden
from her writing lodge to a supper of roast chicken and
apple amber (a baked sweet apple, lemon, meringue
and shortcrust pastry pie) in February, and roast beef and
apple tart in October. Angelica Bell's January birthday is
celebrated at Charleston with ham and chicken and ices
and rolls and pâté sandwiches. Quentin's August birthday
is marked each year by roast grouse for dinner and a brace
more to take back to London.

The city has its own spoils. A 'most scrumptious' Charbonnel tea and iced coffee at the chocolatiers on Bond
Street. A visit to the National Gallery with ices at Gunter's
to follow. Cold roast chicken before a Bloomsbury party at
Gordon Square. Hot soup, cold meat, coffee and biscuits
after a lecture by the art critic Roger Fry. A night on the
town with the composer Ethel Smyth and home late to dine
off sandwiches in a state of 'highest glee'. In January 1933

there is a trip to Sadler's Wells to see the ballet *Pomona*, for which Vanessa had designed the sets and costumes. At Vanessa's studio on Fitzroy Street they are warmed by large dishes of hot, writhing, indecent-looking sausages.

As Woolf owls across the city, she admires the 'carnal splendour of the butcher's shops with their yellow flanks and purple steaks', and meets the confiding haulers and traders on the docks, who beckon her closer and say: 'Would you like to see what sort of thing we sometimes find in sacks of cinnamon? Look at this snake!' There was a trip, too, to Billingsgate fish market: 'the most smelly place I have ever been to'.

It was companionable to walk with her in London, to keep in swinging step with her down Oxford Street and around the Serpentine. Not just, now that I was loosed from the office, at night as I had with Dickens, but in the early morning and the afternoons on my way to and from the library. Here at last was a woman who walked. Elizabeth David, for all her affection for Primrose Hill and Regent's Park, had not been a walker. She admitted as much: never further than an inch if she could possibly help it.

If Woolf could power her walks with teas and ices then so would I. Salt-beef and mustard bagels from Brick Lane to put me on my mettle for Whitechapel and the Limehouse canal. Tea and toast and rubber-band eggs for the river – Pimlico to Southwark, Tate to Tate – on a blue and freezing March morning. Kippers and buttered rolls for losing my way in Clerkenwell. These were Woolf's gifts to me: to walk and be warm, to have something in my stomach as I sketched and photographed and turned the A-Z upside-down.

Walking and reading, reading and walking, keep
Woolf calm, keep the 'galloping' horses tied and bridled.
She finds, in the periods when she is well, schemes and
methods to ease her head, her racing heart, the dry, bitter
taste in her throat. Ways, when her mind's horses start
to gallop, setting off pounding, shaking headaches, to
'dandle' her brain until she is well again. There is rest and
quiet at Monk's House and games of boules, and baths,
and her gramophone, and walking miles over the Downs,
and reading – Cowper, Gilbert White, Ruskin ('that old
fraud'), Madame de Sévigné, John Donne, *Romeo and Juliet*.

Having no good book to read brings on an attack of
the 'fidgets'. This is the remedy: down to the river, to the
stationer's for a new notebook, along the Strand, to a bookshop to buy a Penguin, home to read an Elizabethan, tea at
a table set with flowers, a cake baked, a new essay dreamt
up.

When she is bad, when the 'gnats settle', she walks herself calm, imagines herself stamping them underfoot. As a
young penny-scraping book reviewer she dreams of having
£3 for rubber-soled boots. Later, a literary lioness with
money to spend, she shops for a green linen waterproof.
Leonard buys a new mackintosh. Walking with Leonard in
the afternoons is 'an enormous balance at the bank: solid
happiness'. She walks the marshes in her nightdress in a
September heatwave.

In my case, walking is not a stamping of gnats. I have
squashed no Jabberwocks under my boots. What I do find
when I walk is that any blood, any rushing, any noise in
my head is diverted. Feet and legs steal all energy away. As
I walk, my mind, screwed tight with anxiety, loosens. The
noise dims. My soles take the load. However jiggered and

apprehensive I am, an hour's walk, two hours' better, will unjigger me. Then home, clear-headed, to read or write.

'So divine it is,' writes Woolf of her method, 'coming in from a walk to have tea by the fire and to read and read – say *Othello* – say anything. It doesn't seem to matter what.' To relax, it is *Little Dorrit*. To revive a tired mind, a 'good hard rather rocky book', such as Herbert Fisher's *History of Europe* in three volumes. To counter a frosted Easter, colder than Christmas, she reads Mandeville's *Fable of the Bees*. Wordsworth's *Prelude* is so good and so 'succulent' that she hoards it 'as a child keeps a crumb of cake'. When she is distracted and wants soothing, it is the Elizabethan poets. 'Chaucer', she writes, 'I take at need,' as if he were an aspirin or stomach settler.

She is bitter about doctors and their work. Leonard's antipathy did not come from nowhere: it came boiling first from Virginia. In *Mrs Dalloway*, Doctor Holmes is a buck-up-man! bully. 'So you're in a funk,' he tells the trench-haunted Septimus Warren Smith. Sir William Bradshaw, expert in psychiatric disorders, watches the clock and thinks of sending his bill. What can any doctor, Woolf asks, even a 'Sir Somebody Something', know of a man, his health, his mind in forty-five minutes and not a minute longer? If Septimus would only put on weight, his doctors insist, if only he could get himself from seven stone six to twelve stone, he would be hearty and well. But that it is only the body. Would it help his mind? Would it stop him seeing dead men – among them his fallen comrade Evans – behind the railings in Regent's Park?

The doctors in *Orlando* are no better. They counsel rest and exercise, starvation and nourishment, society and solitude, bed-rest and forty-mile rides, sedatives and irritants. They prescribe, as the mood takes them, 'possets of newt's slobber on rising, and draughts of peacock's gall on going to bed'. 'Doctors know very little about the body; absolutely nothing about the mind,' says Peggy, herself a doctor, in *The Years*. 'I always said they were humbugs!', crows her brother North.

I have more sympathy than Woolf does for doctors presented with a disorder of the mind. How do you treat what isn't visible, what won't show up on any scan? You cannot tap your fingertips on stomach, sternum and scalp and say: 'Tell me where it hurts.' There is no blister to lance, no wound to suture, no muscle to ice. You don't catch it like a virus. It is not a germ that gets into a paper cut. There is no warning rash or temperature. Woolf called it 'the depression . . . which does not come from something definite, but from nothing'.

Not all doctors are *Orlando* charlatans or *Dalloway* barrackers. My own doctors worked miracles. They saved my life. They took a body, a starved shell, weeks from death and would not let it die. When all I could hear were Jabberwock voices telling me I could not live, the doctors talked, and Mum talked, and they kept their voices level until their words began to make sense of nonsense. They asked what the Jabberwock said and challenged its looking-glass gibberish. They countered madness with reason: the voices were not real, they were not right, and I would never be rid of them so long as I starved. If I could only eat a little, that little would start to quiet them.

In those early years of my recovery I depended not just on Mum, but on a GP and therapist who had seen devils and Jabberwocks before, as Mum had not, and who knew their tricks and mischiefs. I also saw what harm a bad doctor can do. Soon after my diagnosis, the health insurers sent me for an assessment with one of their men to decide whether I qualified. As I sat in his office, this doctor looked me up and down and said, quite chipper and careless: 'Well, you're not as thin as some of the girls I see.' It set me back months. Still, he judged me ill enough to satisfy the insurers, and I was returned to the care of my GP and therapist. Though they had no pill, no panacea, no potion, they were willing to listen to what sounded like madness and believe it and take it gravely and seriously.

I have come to think, though, that with any collapse of the mind, there is only so much doctors and therapists can do. Talking, and much more than talking, being listened to, does help. It helps enormously. But there comes a time, after the very worst is over, when counselling becomes a chain. It holds you back. Therapy asks you to examine and re-examine your patterns of thought. 'And how did that make you feel?' is the endlessly repeated question. After a certain point, therapy and its talking made me feel trapped. I needed to find something that would take me *out* of my thoughts, not that asked me to return to them time and again.

At eighteen, I asked to stop going to therapy sessions. After an alarming, jittery year when there wasn't anything else to fall back on, my thoughts slowly turned from inside to out, from past illness and unhappiness to light and recovery. There were the first excitements of churches, sketching, libraries and essays, later the discovery of nerve-steadying walking and reading. I am better when not coiled in on myself, not going over the past, when I am on my feet and out across the park, along the river, or to St James's Square to collect more library books.

It helps too sometimes, to laugh at myself, my irrational fears. I know it is absurd to quail at a lavender macaroon. Who is frightened of sugar, egg whites, butter and almonds? In a pale-pistachio box? Tied with a satin garter ribbon? Have you ever heard anything so feeble, so niminy-piminy? 'Oh ridiculous crumpled petal,' Woolf chastises herself when she is being excessively sensitive. I am getting better, when I quaver at some dish or pudding, at teasing myself. Am I really so frightened of a meringue? Is it so very menacing? I give myself a good kick for such milquetoast carry-on. Oh ridiculous. *Kick*. Crumpled. *Kick*. Petal. *Kick. Kick. Kick*.

Woolf has a phrase, and she, too, is teasing when she writes it: 'Life is a hard business – one needs a rhinirocerous [her spelling] skin – & that one has not got.' I have not got it either. No protective rhinirocerous hide. I find some simple matters of life not at all easy. One of those is eating, the other is sleeping. Not being able to do them does make life a hard business.

If you know yourself to be subject to irrational glooms and torments, if your mind cannot be trusted to be even and sensible, it is critical, it is life-saving to find some ruse, some sympathetic medicine to keep you going. When I read, when I walk, when I am taken out of myself I am quiet, my mind is steady. When I am walking, when I am reading, I do not feel that I am mad.

A walk is best when it finishes in Marylebone. Through the stucco squares of Bayswater, across the Edgware Road, Crawford Place, Crawford Street, down Paddington Square Gardens, Moxon Street, Marylebone High Street. Then back the same way, this time lopsided, weighed down with book-shopping. If I am walking to the British Museum I keep on, along New Cavendish Street, crossing Wimpole Street, and here I can almost hear the echo of a spaniel's bark.

Spurred by finishing the diaries, I tried the novels again. I started with *Flush*, Woolf's biography of Elizabeth Barrett Browning's lady's-lapdog, installed in splendour at 50 Wimpole Street. I read *Flush* at a spaniel-dash, not outfoxed and lost as I had been with *Mrs Dalloway*, but keenly sniffing the air. I bought a second-hand copy of *The Haunted House*, a collection of Woolf's short stories, and read *Lappin and Lapinova*, which has a husband and wife playing at rabbits and feeding each other lettuces and hard-boiled eggs on a honeymoon picnic.

Her story *The Shooting Party* made me hungry for game, never having had pheasant or grouse or partridge or pigeon before. The bird served at the party of the title is revealed under a silver cover: 'And there was the pheasant, feather-less, gleaming; the thighs tightly pressed to its side; and little mounds of breadcrumbs were heaped at either end.' Not many weeks after reading those words, I was invited to a lunch at which grouse was promised; I remembered Woolf and braved myself for the bird. But it was such a small thing, so fine-boned, with pin-cushion breast and sewing-scissor legs, that it seemed very rum to have shot it for barely a morsel-mouthful of meat.

I read *Mrs Dalloway* again, this time with boot-to-pavement excitement. I wanted to be out walking in town, to Bloomsbury and to Bond Street with its flags flying, its shops, its pearls, its salmon on an ice block. There are pearls in the Bond Street windows still today, and choc-olates at Charbonnel, where Woolf had her scrumptious

tea, but no fish shops with salmon on ice. Then I wanted
to read everything – novels, stories and journalism. I read
in no planned order. *To the Lighthouse, Jacob's Room. Between
the Acts. Orlando, The Voyage Out, Night and Day. The Waves.
The Years.*

When there is food in her writing, it is done in glorious
polychromy: dots and darts of bright colour. There is in *A
Room of One's Own* a dinner at a men's college at Cambridge
where the sole are sunk in a deep dish, under a counterpane
of the whitest cream, branded with brown spots like the
flanks of a doe. After that, a course of partridges: 'many
and various . . . with all their retinue of sauces and salads,
the sharp and the sweet, each in its order; their potatoes,
thin as coins but not so hard, their sprouts, foliated as rose-
buds but more succulent'. Then a pudding, wreathed in
napkins, a Birth-of-Venus pudding, rising 'all sugar from
the waves'.

In *To the Lighthouse*, a bowl of fruit – grapes, pears, bananas – arranged in a pink-lined shell reminds Mrs Ramsay
of 'a trophy fetched from the bottom of the sea, of Neptune's banquet, of the bunch that hangs with vine leaves
over the shoulder of the Bacchus (in some picture), among
the leopard skins and the torches lolloping red and gold'.
When she is not dreaming of Neptune and Bacchus, Mrs
Ramsay is a stickler for 'real butter and clean milk'. No
place for almond milk in her kitchen. (Place, though, for
an earwig, which falls into Mr Ramsay's milk glass.) She
stands one evening, her face lit up by blue light, among
shelves of blue-and-white china dishes. Willow pattern,
perhaps, with a blue Chinese junk sailing not to a lighthouse, but a porcelain pagoda.

When the Ramsays' rowboat is finally launched to the

lighthouse, there are sandwiches in paper, cheese to be sliced with a penknife and a hard-boiled egg for peeling. Mr Ramsay unwraps gingerbread nuts and offers them to his daughter Cam, 'as if he were a great Spanish gentleman, she thought, handing a flower to a lady at a window so courteous his manner was'. And I thought: why be dashed on the rocks by siren singing when I might sail by Woolf's lighthouse lamp? I imagined a rowboat and a flashing light and steered a course for it. I would have real butter and milk and penknife-cheese sandwiches and hard-boiled eggs and courtly gingerbread. I would have, if anyone cared to serve it, *Boeuf en Daube* – 'Mildred's masterpiece . . . the beef, the bayleaf, and the wine' – on a blue china dish and Neptune's pears to follow.

Woolf shook me from my fruit fear. I would have cherries, and drop the stalks from a boat into a river as Jacob does at Cambridge, and count the stones to tell my fortune – 'Tinker, tailor, soldier, sailor, apothecary, ploughboy . . .' – with Mrs Manresa in *Between the Acts*, and eat dates from a long box, and white and purple grapes from a greenhouse, and pick at saucers of red fruit, and cut up huge pineapples such as Leonard brings home for Virginia. And, I told myself, when the courgettes came 'scrolloping' out of their beds in August, as the cucumbers do out of theirs in *Orlando*, I would have them, not spiralised, but with butter and garlic and rosemary and crisp parings of fennel.

I wanted to do as Mary Datchet does in *Night and Day* and go to a chophouse, upholstered in red plush, for my lunch, and have a steak, two inches thick, swimming in a pewter dish before ambling a lunch hour away in the British Museum under the Elgin marbles, the engraved obelisks and winged Assyrian bulls.

I admired the neatness of Mary's pyramids of little
pink biscuits assembled before one of her bed-sitting-
room salons. Were they Crawford's Pink Wafers? I hadn't
had one since children's tea party days when girls in grey
school pinafores ate any biscuit so long as it was pink. That
meant Pink Wafers and pink Fox's Party Rings on pink
paper plates. We used, with solemn seriousness, to propose
marriage with our pastel biscuits and wear them on our
ring fingers and nibble round their edges until – snap! –
scattering pink biscuit shrapnel over the paper tablecloth,
in the jelly, in cups of apple juice, where they sank and
went soggy.

I haven't managed a Pink Wafer or a Party Ring yet, but
I did buy a packet of Rich Teas, after reading Mrs Paley in
The Voyage Out waking hungry and summoning her maid
to find the biscuit box. I was so tickled by the idea of the
small-hours biscuit box that I began to allow myself one
Rich Tea when I woke in the night empty and grumbling.
Woolf gave me permission to eat, not to lie awake hungry
until breakfast at five.

In *The Years*, Eleanor Pargiter stays with her brother and
sister-in-law at Wittering where, in a china box on the
bedside table in the guest room, she finds 'four biscuits
and a pale piece of chocolate', as a protective against midnight hunger. There are also copies of George and Weedon
Grossmith's *Diary of Nobody*, *Ruff's Tour in Northumberland*
and a volume of Dante with which to read herself back to
sleep.

It was *The Voyage Out* that nudged me to try crystallised
ginger, pressed on Rachel Vinrace by the forthright Miss
Allen. 'You've never tried? . . . Then I consider that it is
your sacred duty to try now. Why, you may add a new

pleasure to life . . . I make it a rule to try everything.' She fishes a lump of ginger from the jar and offers it to Rachel, who takes it, tastes it, spits it out and throws it from the window. I had better luck. I paired my crystallised ginger with yogurt – Paddy and Woolf in one bowl – and liked it and added a new pleasure to life. I made gingerbread biscuits – singed at the edges and raw at the centre, but good – and crowned each one with an amber bead of ginger from the jar.

There is a memorable teatime conversation in the early chapters of *The Voyage Out*, on board the *Euphrosyne* as it steams towards South America. Richard Dalloway has surfaced after a bout of seasickness and is meditating a slice of yellow cake and smooth bread and butter. 'There are three stages of convalescence,' says the hearty shipowner Willoughby, father of the ginger-spitting Rachel, 'the milk-stage, the bread-and-butter stage, and the roast-beef stage. I should say you were at the bread-and-butter stage.' Willoughby passes the plate. 'Now, I should advise a hearty tea, then a brisk walk on deck; and by dinner-time you'll be clamouring for beef, eh?'

I, too, was at the bread-and-butter stage. A few months after going freelance I was sleeping better, my mind was quieter, I was eating again, not quinoa and coconut but soda bread and market honey, chicken soup and ratatouille. Bread, butter and brisk walks had set me on an even keel. Another month, I thought, and I'll be clamouring for beef.

How much richer meals tasted after hunger. Real milk, even semi-skimmed, was overwhelmingly creamy after almond milk; roast chicken crisp-skinned and gorgeous after beans and lentils; porridge oats flapjack-sweet after chia seeds. I recognised and shared Flush's nose-twitching on his first visit to the Barretts' house in Wimpole Street, trotting up the stairs behind the butler and smelling from the kitchen below 'warm whiffs of joints roasting, of fowls basting, of soups simmering – ravishing almost as food itself to nostrils used to the meagre savour of Kerenhappock's penurious fries and hashes'.

Writing this now, eighteen months after leaving the newspaper job, I have read almost to the end of Woolf. There are still some *Common Reader* essays, and *Three Guineas* and much journalism. I have read only the milk-top cream of her letters, in a paperback edition. There are six volumes of collected letters in the library when I am ready for them.

I have played a game of sorts, of keeping Woolf alive. I have told myself: there is still *Night and Day* to read and she is alive. Still *The Years* and she is alive. Still *The Waves* and she is alive and watching hares on the Downs. I have read all the novels now and I have had to reconcile myself to the knowledge that she did not live, that in the end she did not get better. That her madness took her over and that she could no longer read or walk herself calm. Her last two letters were to Leonard and Vanessa. I should share her words here, for any reader who does not know them, but I cannot go back and read the letters again. Nor can I easily re-read the last pages of the diary. It is too sad and rattles me too badly.

While Woolf has been the most extraordinary consolation – and no other writer has so helped me make sense of my own mind, nor offered such a rubric for how I might mend it – she is also a writer who frightens me. For long periods she succeeded in reining in and stabling her gal-loping horses, tied them, kept them in hay. For years, she managed it. Then, with the upheaval of the Second World War, the death of her nephew Julian, her apprehension about her last books *Between the Acts* and the biography of Roger Fry, they came loose.

I don't need to read the letter to Leonard again because I read it over and over the first time, could not let it alone. I remember this: 'I feel certain I am going mad again . . . I begin to hear voices, and I can't concentrate . . . I can't fight any longer.' It is dreadful and it makes me sick, makes me dig my nails into my palms. To have fought and fought – and been beaten. It was an unjust end, to drown with stones in her pockets because nothing else would drown out the noise.

But her last two letters also made me want to fight for life and health all the more fiercely. I cannot be certain of my mind, I cannot be confident I will never lose my wits and reason again, I cannot know that the Jabberwock voices will ever be entirely silenced, but I do resolve to fight. I will walk them away, and read them away, and write them away, and slash and feint and parry with vorpal sword and redouble my attack and drive them back.

If Carroll gave me a sword, Woolf has given me a shield. I imagine it blazoned with a wolf's head, like the wolf Vanessa cut and printed from a woodblock as an emblem for Leonard and Virginia's Hogarth Press. Is a wolf a match for a Jabberwock? For my sake, it must be.

There are two other lines of Woolf that have printed themselves like woodblocks on my memory. I say them to myself to counter the words in the last two letters. The

first is this, from her New Year's Day 1898 diary entry,
a few weeks before her eighteenth birthday. She worries
about the year and years ahead: 'And another & another &
another yet to come. Oh dear they are very long, & I seem
cowardly throughout when I look at them. Still, courage
and plod on.' And this from her 1935 diary, January again,
when she was fifty-two: 'I wish I could find some way of
composing my mind – it's absurd to let it be ravaged by
scenes . . . On the contrary, it is better to pull on my galoshes & go through the gale to lunch off scrambled eggs
& sausages.'

That is the remedy to: 'I can't fight any longer.' That is
what I hold tight from Virginia Woolf. Galoshes. Courage.
On.

In Woolf I have found not just a manifesto for freedom –
freedom through walking, reading, writing, through an
oil stove and glass dishes – but a powerful exposition of
happiness. For she is not incurably gloomy Although there
are moments when the books, the letters and diaries are
difficult to read – the madness of Septimus in *Mrs Dalloway*, the last two letters – there was much more that urged
me on to life and happiness.

There is often in her writing a sole-springing giddiness.
A wind-up-toy energy and will to be up and writing, up
and reading, up and gallery-going, chit-chatting, feud-
stoking, book-binding, boules-playing and walking,
walking, walking and making up as she walks, a story,
an essay, a review, a 'thoughts on Walter Sickert', a word
game for her nephews. There is a new pencil to be bought,
a new pen, new nibs. There is Vita's Rolls-Royce for rattling through Kent. There are visits, trips and excursions

to Kew Gardens, to Hampton Court, to Hampstead Heath, to Keats's house, Carlyle's house, to the Royal Academy to see the Summer Show, to Chartres, Corinth and Constantinople, where she keeps notes of her spending – Champagne: 30 drachmas, Turkish Delight: 1 shilling and 4 pence – to Florence, with its roofs like 'a great basket of white & brown eggs', to a party with Bertrand Russell, and home after to drink cocoa with Leonard, already back and smoking shag tobacco in the kitchen.

'What a lark! What a plunge!' is Mrs Dalloway's spring-morning cry. And what a lark, what a plunge it was to be loosed from an office, to write and walk in London – not at night, but early in the morning, with the park to myself – to feel a lovely, late-blooming, late-twenties rush of happiness. There is an image in *Mrs Dalloway* of a match burning inside a crocus. It describes the glowing, illumi-nated feeling of desire or love or attraction, burning very bright, if only very briefly. Feeling happy was something like that, a striking of a match, a flaring of light after dark-ness. This was happiness that must be caught and bottled and held up to a lamp, as the Stephen children did with the moths they captured with glass jars and cotton wool soaked in rum and sugar on summer nights in St Ives. If I didn't catch it and seal it, it would be lost. Happiness seemed so slight, so elusive a thing.

There was a morning in October, six months after I left the newspaper, when I was out walking very early in Kens-ington Gardens, before the runners and dog walkers and park gardeners. I must have taken some of the same paths that Virginia, Vanessa, Thoby and Adrian were marched along on their daily walks from Hyde Park Gate. I passed the Round Pond where Virginia's boat, the *Fairy*, was sunk, and the lawns where the siblings had broken penny slabs of chocolate into four quarters. We had had weeks of late Indian sun after a wet summer. The parks were lushly green and the trees cut from jade. The light was blue-white and I felt that morning an extraordinary, unfamiliar, spinning-top happiness.

There had been flashes of it before. At university, in my third year, I had gone with others from the student paper to see the last issue of term come off the press. Our paper, our words, our photographs, our edits and sub-edits, the last paper not just of the term, but of the decade – December 2009 – hot off the press and bleeding ink onto our hands. Overnight it would be delivered to every porters' lodge.

On the way back into town we stopped in Market Square and, standing under the eaves sheltering from Michaelmas rain, four of us shared a polystyrene tray of chips from a van. Chips! My first in many years, doused in vinegar, thirsty with salt, dipped in ketchup. Happiness.

I was happy, too, on the walk to Zennor tearing the saffron buns in half to share, sitting on our rock and look-ing for seals in the water. Woolf had been there too and had seen the seals, as we did not. Happy, too, sitting on the headland the next day looking out across at Godrevy lighthouse on the sort of white-bright, breezy, sailing day James Ramsay crossed his fingers and prayed for.

But that Kensington Gardens morning was something new. I felt not just happy, but quiet. That October there had been hours, whole days, weeks with no clamour. If I had listened, I am sure I would have heard the Jabber-wock, distant and angry, furling and unfurling its wings, scratching a claw against scales, scheming. But I wasn't

listening for it. I was reading, writing, walking, sketching, butter-skirling, omelette-shaking, mock-turtling,
ginger-biscuiting. There was sun, day after day after day.
And I heard no Jabberwock.

6

'How does tha' like thysel'?'

O nce upon a time, because that is how stories start, there was a little girl, not in a red riding hood, but a yellow mackintosh, who spent weekends and holidays at her grandmother's cottage. There was no deep, dark wood; this was Henley, and though the walls were made of pebbledash, not gingerbread, it was a sweet-shop cottage inside.

There were Iced Gems before breakfast and Smarties for tea. Wine Gums in the playroom and Pringles in bed. In the car, Smith Kendon travel sweets were offered from a Carmen Miranda box and sucked on the back seat in tutti-frutti silence. There were elevenses milkshakes whizzed in the blender and poured into glass tumblers with curly-wurly straws. The grandmother, with stern words about not telling parents, taught how to blow bubbles in the milk. There were tiny wild strawberries by the front door, perfect as cowrie shells, and a vegetable patch, netted against birds, for raspberries. These were eaten with double cream or single cream or ice cream or any cream or tipped into the milkshake mix for a banana-choco-raspberry swirl. Breakfast was Alpen with raisins and white sugar.

Did I really used to eat like this? Dizzy with sugar on Hansel and Gretel weekends? The little girl in the yellow mackintosh seems to belong to another person. Could she have been me? Was I ever so free, so childishly hungry for sugar and cream and treats? I remember it. I can taste on the tip of my tongue the sugar peaks of Iced Gems eaten in bed in the morning: the icicle tops bitten off first, the biscuit pennies eaten after. Yes, there were roast chickens and chicken soups and parsley salads cut from the garden, but what has stayed with me are the larder's glass jars of sweets, chocolates and tooth-gluing gums.

I used to eat without a thought. A year could be measured out in sugar. January was lean. Christmas chocolates finished, no family birthdays. If we could keep going until February there would be Valentine's chocolates wrapped in red foil, and at the end of the month pancakes mottled as papyrus with brown sugar and lemon juice. In March it was Ed's birthday. A cake, a party, Coco Pops for breakfast. Then Easter: a chocolate egg each, big as any laid by an ostrich, Creme Eggs at school, hunts for Mini Eggs in the flowerbeds. A bit soily? A quick dust and good as new, eaten one after the other, small and speckled and pastel-pretty – a little girl's dream of a quail's egg.

In the summer holidays: ice creams. Mini Milks from the corner shop. Calippos in the car, Cornettos on the beach. Then, September: back to school, a fallow month. October: not much better, until Halloween, a spooks' blaze of sugar: jelly worms, pumpkin gums, iced bat biscuits, cobweb candyfloss and Trick or Treat hauls. For years, until I saw it written down, I thought it was 'Trickle Treat', because that's what it was: a trickling stream of late-October goodies. November was scorched marshmallows on a bonfire or on the hob at home if it rained.

December was almost too much. A chocolate every day

after school from behind advent calendar doors, Lorraine's mince pies with marzipan stars, and boxes of Marks & Spencer *Lebkuchen*. These were impossible to sneak from the box. We were always caught by incriminating trails of cinnamon dust on the kitchen counters. Then my birthday: a cake, more mince pies, marzipan fruits, peppermint creams, gingerbread snowmen and shivering green and red jellies pitted with silver balls. On Christmas morning: a windfall of chocolate coins, a candy-cane shepherd's crook, chocolate raisins, sherbet dippers, fudge squares in cellophane, and at the foot of the stockings clementines, which rolled under the bed and were forgotten.

I look at it all fondly now. I don't frown at that Laura, that other Laura, for pouring custard over chocolate truffles – another grandmother-approved experiment – and enjoying herself very much indeed. To the Laura I have been since the illness, such a pairing is impossible. It is strange to feel yourself divided into two people: one allowed licence and leniency, sugar-greed and cream-lust; the other bound by cheerless discipline, hunger and restraint.

It was striking, reading Virginia Woolf's childhood memoirs and her early diaries, how affectionately she writes of nursery eating. At Talland House in St Ives, the Stephen children would lower a basket on a string for titbits from the kitchen. When the cook was in a sulk, she would snip the string. Every day there was a great dish of Cornish cream, with yellow skin, passed around the table with brown sugar. The children had 'splits' for tea – buns split down the middle and filled with cream and jam.

In London she and Vanessa bought Bath Buns and shortbreads and ate them travelling down Oxford Street on the top of a bus. Their mother Julia Stephen made up stories about children who had roast turkey and raspberry puffs on their birthdays and toasted chestnuts on the hob. Virginia's half-sister Stella took her to teashops for glasses of milk and biscuits sprinkled with sugar at marble tables. Aunts and elderly relatives sent presents of jams and Californian honey. When Woolf writes, in *The Waves*, of 'plates upon plates of innocent bread and butter' shared in the nursery, is there a note of regret for the loss of innocent eating?

I don't remember being a particularly fussy eater. I had my superstitions – Smarties eaten in a certain colour order, the blues last, and fetishes for this spoon and not that with my breakfast cereal – but no more or less anxiety about food than most children. There was one nursery teatime when, in fit of spoilt madamism, I asked for my grapes to be peeled. Lorraine gave me a choice: I could eat my grapes unpeeled or I could sit on the stairs. I sat, a cross Sheba in a knitted cardigan on the bottom step, crying myself into a tantrum. After ten minutes' exile I was allowed back, contrite, to eat my grapes unpeeled. I never asked again. But Lorraine did make an exception at Halloween, peeling grapes for 'witches' eyeballs', which we ate with a gruesome smacking of lips.

I relished new foods. On a family holiday, Ed and I were given biltong sticks from a tiffin tin, while others had sundowner cocktails. We gnawed our biltong sitting on the bonnet of a Jeep like a pair of cub hyenas. Over a half-term in France we had *citrons pressés* in tall glasses with long silver stirring spoons and sugar cubes from a bowl to sweeten the lemon juice. In went cube after cube of white sugar until the juice was so thick the spoons stood upright in the glass. *'Citron presseé! Citron pressé!'* we sang at every café, and it is a miracle we have a tooth between us.

I was never sporty, and netball, rounders and later lacrosse were a humiliation of missed balls, failed swings and dropped catches. It was no good on annual summer sports days to have more 'I-Have-Read-Twenty-Five-Books' badges than the gold, silver and bronze medallists. But I was not couchbound. I jumped elastics and skipped ropes and hung from monkey bars. When we went for tea with school friends – a sister and brother of the same age – we bounced with Zebedee glee on the trampoline in the back garden. Zebedee, Zebedee, Zebedee from half past four until supper at half past five – spaghetti, meatballs, vanilla ice cream – then Zebedee, Zebedee, Zebedee until we were picked up at half past seven. Why weren't we sick? We must have had stoneware stomachs.

At our near neighbours' house – a sister and brother again – we had hot sleepover popcorn with butter and white sugar in front of *The Crystal Maze*. The mother of another set of friends allowed us Sunny Delight, absolutely forbidden at home, in pint glasses jingling with melon-wedge ice cubes. At weekends we rode bikes, built dens, swung swings, scaled rope ladders and ran squealing through sprinklers. Taken swimming, we stayed in the water until we were two blue prunes, chattering with cold. In the digestive hour after lunch, when swimming was banned, we would sit on the edge of the pool, watching an inflatable plastic whale bump from pool-side to pool-side, our legs dangling in the water, the sooner to be back in when the hour was up.

Mary Frances Fisher, writing of her California childhood, remembers the oatmeal cookies 'loaded with raisins' that powered the Fisher children out and into the garden. 'Given a couple of them as we raced out of the back door after supper, which we usually ate early so that Father could get to a meeting, we were set for hours of Run, Sheep, Run through the orchards of young apple trees and old walnuts.'

So it was with us. We never had sweets and snacks in the week. Pudding was yogurt and fruit, pith, peel and all, and how we cursed school playtime snacks of carrot sticks and hot Ribena in a flask when others had Skips and Magic Stars. But on high days and holidays, weekends and at friends' houses, we were Sugar Mice, Honey Monsters, Milky Bar kids. We had Bounty bars after swimming, kept tubes of Rolos in our bike baskets, drank gallons of sickly Yoplait, thick as house paint, after a day's canoeing. We had a good trick for the Rolos. You were supposed to give the last one away – always a wrench. So Ed would give me his last and I would give him my last and we both would feel the honourable thing had been done. On Saturdays we cycled to the shop for paper swag bags of pink shrimp, sherbet saucers, dolly gems, cola bottles, gummy eggs, sour rings and white mice.

A boy at my sixth-form college, knowing I had been ill, once asked: 'Well, were you fat? Did you need to lose the weight?' He might have put it less baldly, but I answered honestly. The galling answer is no. Galling because, what a farce, what a waste to have starved a body that was skinny enough to begin with. For all our Bountys and Rolos, we were neither of us, Ed nor I, fat. Quite the opposite. 'Ooof, bony bottom!' Lorraine would protest when one of us sat on her lap. And: 'Ouch, bony knees!' as we clambered off.

My pre-teenage relationship with food wasn't good or bad, it was simply unthinking. I knew from evening tooth-brushings that sugar would rot my teeth. I learnt, later, that too much food would make me fat. But it didn't apply to me. I was not fat, I was thin, and that was that. Besides, fat wasn't then something bad. Comic, yes, in a roly-poly, Tweedledee and Tweedledum way, but not grotesque, not something to be feared. We had read André Maurois's *Fattypuffs and Thinifers* at school. The Fattypuffs are a profiterole people; the Thinifers thin and dry as water biscuits. The Fattypuffs are fond of hot cocoa, chocolate éclairs and cream buns like bath sponges. They have a nap every hour in feather-cushioned armchairs.

The Thinifers, across the sea channel, are vigorous gymnasts. They eat little but boiled spaghetti, drink nothing but water, work six days a week, are punctual to the half-second and find satisfaction in mental arithmetic and the counting of small change. The two peoples are, naturally enough, sworn enemies and the story huffs, puffs and pole-vaults towards its inevitable Waterloo.

When I read this book, with its line drawings of Fatty-port – umbrella domes, onion minarets, Tunnock's-teacake rotundas – and Thinniville – Rapunzel towers, gothic spires, spindly crockets, fiddly ironwork – I did not sneer at the Puffs with their light snacks of woodcock and champagne, nor particularly admire the lean, academic Thinnies. I knew that temperamentally I was more a tidy, book-worm Thinifer than a sprawling, lounging Puff, but I could see that there were merits to each.

Naturally, that is how the story ends, with a peace treaty and the opening of patisseries and confectionary counters in Thinniville, where the Ministry of Slimming is abolished and new clinics promise: 'Two pounds gained every week. A Fattypuff in three months.' Fatness becomes the fashion and those Thinifer ladies who cannot manage it adopt wide, hooped crinolines.

Thinifer soldiers marry Fattypuff girls and one hopes they have babies that are neither one thing nor the other. Because the best thing is to be ThiniPuff, with the punctiliousness and ambition of the former, and the gaiety and good humour of the latter; to have one's books and crisply folded newspaper, but also cake and Turkish Delight. So I was a ThiniPuff child, bookish and self-contained, but eager enough for hot chocolate and biscuits when they came.

I would say I was a happy child. A worrier, certainly. A bad sleeper, definitely, even then dependent on audiobooks on a Fisher Price cassette player. Shy, yes, and tending to solitude, but happy. Happy with my bike, happy with Swiss Cottage library books, happy playing Monopoly, Risk, Cluedo, Slam, Cheat and Snap! with Ed, happy with holiday scrapbooks and Mini Milk ice creams eaten in the back of the car on summer days out, melting over our hands and sunburnt legs. Something went wrong in the move from primary to secondary school. I suspect it does for many children. Somehow I lost the knack of happiness, and with it any joy in eating

If I think back to the ThiniPuff child reading *Harry Potter* in the holidays, breaking off ski-slope prisms of Toblerone, I want to say to her: 'Enjoy it! Cherish it! This is freedom! You will never have it again.' But that would break the spell. It's no good my going back, a melancholic ghost of summers future, to shatter the contented toothcrunching of chocolate and almond nougat. If I intervened,

I'd ruin it, the innocence before fats and calories and hunger and illness.

After months of reading Virginia Woolf I wanted something completely different, something easy and coddling. I had a half-notion that I could read myself back to a state of ice-cream innocence. That if I returned to the books I had read as a hale and Haribo-hearty child, I could restore the old, unthinking way of eating, undo the damage of the illness. Recapture the spirit of childhood crumpet-wassailing and chocolate-carousing. That I could again be the child who read *Harry Potter* on the garden wall with a Toblerone melting in the sun.

I didn't always read *Harry Potter* with a Toblerone. I read the books so often I would have been solid nougat. Not always on the garden wall, either, balanced on the flattest, widest stretch. I read the books in bed, in the bath, at school, at home and on holiday. In the car, more Slytherin-green and bilious with every hump and pothole.

I do not think it dull that the March sisters in Louisa May Alcott's *Little Women* read their Bunyan's *Pilgrim's Progress* every morning before breakfast, without ever tiring of the same chapters, because I did not tire of *Harry*. I would finish one and start another, read to the end of the book most recently published, and start over again. I read with a dragonish appetite. I never could have had too much. There was always room for just one more re-reading, one more stoat sandwich, one more sherbet lemon.

And *Harry* was fatter and fatter with every instalment. Every summer, a new book in the windows. The first three were published while I was at primary school. They went towards my Twenty-Five-Book badges. I read *Goblet of*

Fire in the summer after my first year of secondary school. Harry, Ron and Hermione took their OWLS (Ordinary Wizarding Levels) while I was doing GCSEs, and *Hallows* was published the summer before university.

No author has so hocussed me as J. K. Rowling did. In no other series have I been so absorbed, so entirely transported, so taken out of myself. I had wanted to re-read them for years. After *Deathly Hallows*, going up to university, I put the books away with other childish things. Returning to *Philosopher's Stone* again at twenty-eight, after a nearly ten-year interval, was like a reunion, a falling in with old friends. I felt again that concentration, that whisking away out of myself into another world. There was no Toblerone this time, but as I read, everything else in life – commissions, deadlines, reviews, invoices, bills, appointments, obligations, frets and fidgets – fell away.

When the sweet trolley trundled down the corridor of the *Hogwarts Express*, I remembered how I had coveted Harry and Ron's haul of enchanted tuck. The Bertie Bott's Every-Flavour Beans, Drooble's Best Blowing Gum, Chocolate Frogs, Pumpkin Pasties, Cauldron Cakes, Liquorice Wands and Fizzing Whizzbees. After finishing *Philosopher's Stone* I too was fizzing like a Whizzbee.

I read all the books again, smiling at the bottomless beneficence of Mrs Weasley ('"I don't blame you, dear," she assured Harry, tipping eight or nine sausages onto his plate'), the flagons of pumpkin juice after Quidditch matches, and choco-nut sundaes at Florean Fortescue's ice-cream parlour. I can't bring myself to go back to my old secondary school. I still take detours to avoid it, still suffer stomach lurches when a bus passes the old bus stop. Hogwarts was the school I would have wanted to go to if it had existed, if I wasn't such a Muggle without a magic bone in my body. It was a joy to go back there.

I understood for the first time what Laurie Lee and Mary Francis Fisher had meant by 'voluptuous'. This was voluptuous reading. Not reading for research or reading for a review, but reading for sheer pleasure, indulging a whim, a craving for a childhood favourite. The cauldron had been stirred and, staying with Mum and Dad for a summer holiday, I raided our old shelves of children's books.

First there was Roald Dahl, and his preposterous larder of buttergin, frobscottle, fizzwinkles, glumptious globgobblers and repulsant, disgusterous, slime-wrangling snozzcumbers. There was *Matilda*, the little girl who is rescued from telly-tray suppers with her goggle-box parents by reading, by *Nicholas Nickleby, Tess of the D'Urbervilles, Jane Eyre*, and Pinkie, Pip and Kim.

I read *The Edge Chronicles* again, written by Paul Stewart and illustrated by Chris Riddell. The early books – *Beyond the Deepwoods, Stormchaser, Midnight Over Sanctaphrax* – were great favourites when I was nine and ten and I read the sequels into my twenties with much bookshop subterfuge: 'It's for my cousin. He's a fan. Mad about Banderbears.' The Deepwoods have their own extraordinary harvests: earth apples and delberries, tripweed for pickling, steaks of hammerhorn meat and tilder sausages steeped in a broth of nibblick and orangegrass. With every new helping of seedrusks, pinecoffee, gyle honey and woodgrog, however, I felt more and more deflated. This was as hopeless as the Jolly Sandboys' tripe and sparrowgrass stew in *The Old Curiosity Shop*. What good were Cauldron Cakes, globgobblers and boiled mire cabbage to me?

I was hungry for books that would continue the good

work that Woolf had done, pelican-feeding me new foods
to try, reconciling me to old ones. There wasn't much I
could do with a snozzcumber. Instead, I went back to the
shelves and took down Kenneth Grahame's *The Wind in the
Willows*. That I knew was a munching book. I remembered
Toad's gaolbird bubble and squeak and Ratty and Mole's
picnic luncheon basket:

'What's inside it?' asked the Mole, wriggling with
curiosity.

'There's cold chicken inside it,' replied the Rat
briefly;   coldtonguecoldhamcoldbeefpickledgherkins
saladfrenchrollscresssandwichespottedmeatgingerbeer
lemonadesodawater—'

'O stop, stop,' cried the Mole in ecstasies: 'This is too
much!'

'Do you really think so?' inquired the Rat seriously.
'It's only what I always take on these little excursions;
and the other animals are always telling me that I'm a
mean beast and cut it very fine.'

This was more like it. And it wasn't only the fat wicker
luncheon basket. When Toad sets off for the open road
and dusty highway it is in a caravan stocked with biscuits,
potted lobster, sardines, bacon, jam, baccy, cards and dom-
inoes. At breakfast in Badger's sett there is bacon, eggs,
porridge and buttered toast, and in Mole's cottage burrow
more sardines, Captain's biscuits, German sausages in
silver wrappers and bottles of ale for mulling.

Preparing for the siege of Toad Hall, Rat cooks a
nerve-steeling supper of bacon, broad beans and macaroni
pudding, before loading his gallant band with cutlasses,

pistols, truncheons, handcuffs, bandages, sticking plasters, flasks and sandwich cases. Never go to war without your sandwiches. That night, Toad, Badger, Rat and Mole share a victory supper of guava jelly, cold chicken, tongue, trifle, lobster salad, French rolls, cheese, butter and celery. No wonder illustrator Ernest Shepard inked their waistcoats so tight.

Fortified by sardines, toast and butter (two rivers run through *Wind in the Willows*: one is the otter and kingfisher sort, the other is a river of butter, which sweetens every meal and is laid so thickly onto Toad's hot prison toast that it drips through the holes 'in great golden drops, like honey from the honeycomb'), I started unpacking other favourite childhood picnic baskets. First was *Little Women*, a book of buckwheat muffins, pickled limes, molasses candy and blackcurrant jellies that – confound them – simply won't jell. Alcott used to write with a pen, paper and 'pile of apples to eat' and she has Jo March do the same, writing her stories with a bushel of russets by her side in the garret.

With L. M. Montgomery's *Anne of Green Gables* I feasted on crocks of crab-apple preserve; 'juicy, toothsome, raspberry tarts;' broiled chickens and crisp 'cowcombers'; and chicken pies, mince pies, apple pies, lemon pies, cherry pies, caramel pies and cranberry pies. Susan Coolidge's *What Katy Did* was stocked to bursting with ginger cakes; cold sliced lamb; batter puddings with shiny tops; parcels of dried cherries; and pies with candied edges of 'blissful stickiness'. These are a hit with Katy's younger brother Dory – 'a sort of Dr Livingstone where strange articles of food were concerned'.

Nostalgic and indulgent though it was to re-read these childhood favourites, I realised that I had my ideas in a twist. I'd come to think that if only I could compile an extensive enough index from my reading, a private *Larousse* – from abalone to *zucchini fritti* and everything in between – then I could eat any food bravely.

I need not fear, for example, a dish of Caribbean chicken: don't the kidnapped children tuck into fried chicken when their pirate abductors dock at Saint Lucia in Richard Hughes's *High Wind in Jamaica*? After the chicken come mountain mullet, crayfish, red snapper, land crabs, young turkey, wild pigeons, sweet potatoes, yucca, guavas and cream. All of which is very welcome to the children after some time at sea with nothing to eat but the cargo of crystallised fruits. I could even steel myself for catfish because that's what Mark Twain's Huckleberry Finn has on the Mississippi, haggled open with his saw and smoked over a campfire, on his island of unripe wild strawberries, blackberries and green 'razberries'. And I really ought to be able to do beer, trout and gloriously sticky and steaming marmalade rolls after having them for tea with Mr and Mrs Beaver and the Pevensie children in C. S. Lewis's *The Lion, the Witch and the Wardrobe*.

But it wasn't enough just listing pies and pigeons and plum cakes. The success of the riverbank picnic is only partly down to the contents of Rat's wicker basket. The cold tongue and cress sandwiches and ginger beer and mustard are no good on their own. What makes the picnic is the sun, the first sniff of spring – 'Hang spring-cleaning!' says Mole, flinging down his brush – the river, the dabchicks, the moorhens and the fine-day glory of 'messing about in boats'. Likewise, the bubbling, gurgling, gipsy stew of partridges, pheasants, chickens, hares, rabbits, peahens and guinea fowls eaten by Toad until he is 'stuffed, and

stuffed and stuffed'. It is the best breakfast he has ever had
in all his life, not because every game bird, hare and rabbit
in the county has been sacrificed to it, but because it tastes
of new liberty. 'He was, indeed, a very different Toad from
the animal of an hour ago . . . he was nearing home and
friends and safety, and most and best of all, he had had
a substantial meal, hot and nourishing, and felt big, and
strong, and careless, and self-confident.'

Strong, careless and self-confident – words to chew over.

What I was coming to realise was that all the meals that
appealed to me were invested with some emotion, character or quality. They were none of them eaten for eating's
sake. Just as Virginia Woolf's roast beef and apple amber
worked on me because they heralded a homecoming – off
the Downs, back from the ballet – and the warmth and
familiarity of the kitchen, the smell of Leonard's tobacco,
so it was with Mole, coming back to his burrow after three
seasons away to cobble together a meal from what he and
Rat can find in the cupboards: sardines, Captain's biscuits
and the silver-wrapped sausage.

When the field mice carollers arrive, blowing their
fingers and stamping their feet, Rat thrusts a basket at
one of them and sends him running for fresh-this and a
pound-of-that. Rat meanwhile mulls the ale to warm the
chilblained mice and soon each of them has forgotten 'he
had ever been cold in all in his life'. The errand mouse
returns, staggering under the weight of his basket, and,
in a very few minutes, supper is ready and Mole takes the
head of the table. He 'saw a lately barren board set thick
with savoury comforts; saw his little friends' faces brighten
and beam as they fell to without delay and then let himself
loose – for he was famished indeed – on the provender so

magically provided, thinking what a happy home-coming this had turned out after all'.

That is why the sardines were worth remembering. Not because they are sardines, but because of what they signify: home, comfort, the beginnings of a brightening, beaming winter supper. Thanks to Mole I am now never without a tin in the cupboard, and if I have been away, if I am sitting at Slough on a delayed train, waiting for bags at Heathrow, walking back late from Olivia's flat in Stockwell, I am already, in imagination at least, putting the fish in the pan to warm, turning the pepper mill, lifting the capers from the jar and tipping the fillets onto rye crackers to be eaten at my own table in my own home-sweet kitchen.

Thinking again about Harry and Ron trading Chocolate Frog cards – Circe, Paracelsus, Merlin – in their train carriage, I realised that it didn't matter whether I had the wherewithal, the gold galleons, the silver sickles, the bronze knuts, to buy Pumpkin Pasties and Liquorice Wands and all the rest. What is important is the forging of a friendship, Harry's first chance to be generous after his childhood deprivations at the Dursleys, and the sparing of Ron from Mrs Weasley's corned-beef sandwiches. '"Go on, have a pasty," said Harry, who had never had anything to share before or, indeed, anyone to share it with. It was a nice feeling, sitting there with Ron, eating their way through all Harry's pasties and cakes (the sandwiches lay forgotten).'

Food isn't just company, home and warmth, it is care and kindness. So often, particularly in children's books, food is given not just to build bones or put hair on chests,

but because it is a loving, motherly, fatherly, sisterly thing
to do. There is no ailment, no head-, no stomach-, no
spirit-, no heart-sickness that cannot, in children's books
at least, be mended by pudding. A basin of sugar, rice,
milk, cream, baked in the oven and brought to a lonesome,
homesick, headachey child cures all.

When I was at primary school I had always wanted to
be ill enough to merit a hot posset, much better than the
strawberry-dream of a spoonful of Calpol. In John Masefield's *Box of Delights*, Kay Harker, home from school for
the Christmas holidays, drinks a posset to the recipe of
the local police inspector. You start, the Inspector explains,
with 'a jorum of hot milk; and in that hot milk, Master
Kay, you put a hegg, and you put a spoonful of treacle,
and you put a grating of nutmeg, and you stir 'em well
up, and you get into bed and then you take 'em down hot.
And a posset like that, taken overnight, it will make a
new man of you, Master Kay, while now you're all worn
down with learning.' That night Kay asks Ellen, the cook
at Seekings house, to make up a posset, a big one, because
he is feeling very miserable. He has it in bed from a mug
and 'the comfort seemed to tingle through him, which put
an end to his miseries'. What could be better than a jorum
and posset together?

In children's books there is no nostrum to improve on
a crumble of pears and rhubarb, no sleeping pill to rival
Mrs Peter Rabbit's chamomile tea, no linctus better than
the maple syrup poured so freely over every stack of toast
in the *Anne of Green Gables* books. In *Anne of Avonlea*, the
second in the series, there is a little boy called Davey who
is an imp for maple syrup. He holds the plate upright like
a mirror and licks it clean – 'There ain't any wasted that

way' – and steals jars of yellow-plum jam, the sort reserved for best, and tries just a 'weeny taste' on the end of his finger, before fetching a spoon and 'sailing' in. When it is suggested that he must wait until after supper for plum cake, and in the meantime have a slice of bread and butter, he protests: 'But I ain't bread-and-butter hungry . . . I'm plum-cake hungry.' Anne concludes that Davey has 'no sorrows that plum jam could not cure'.

Mum is very much of Davey's mind. Each year, after the courgette glut, come the plums, baskets of them, barrows of them, more than the four of us can eat in season without pleading for purple mercy. So Mum makes pots and pots of Victoria-plum-and-greengage jam to see her through the parsley-and-chard months, and the lettuce-and-raspberry months, until the plum months come round again. She had been making the jams for three or four years, and each year I had watched the stocks empty and replenish, the jars rinsed out and filled again, and I had not tried so much as a weeny taste on the end of one finger. But plum jam had given Davey such a kick – 'much gooder than I'd ever thought' – and a little of the Davey plum hunger had rubbed off on me.

I was there for a weekend in August 2016, in full plum flood: baskets of Victorias on the kitchen floor and in bowls on the counter, ready for the deepest boiling pot. Mum had timed the eking-out of the previous year's jam harvest to the day. There was a half-inch of Victoria-plum-and-vanilla jam left in the last jar in the fridge. It would be a help if I finished it, liberating a jar for the new batch. I tipped up the jar and hustled the last jam out with a spoon onto a half-slice of buttered toast. I made a cup of tea, very milky. Toast, butter and plum jam. On a saucer painted with raspberries. I don't know about curing all sorrows, but it was even gooder than Davey had promised.

It was telling, when revisiting childhood books, to realise what I had remembered and what I had forgotten. In *Little Women* I had remembered Jo cutting her hair, Amy falling through the ice, Meg burning her fringe with crimping papers and spraining her ankle – 'let us be elegant or die' – in too-tight slippers. I'd almost missed out Beth. She is ill for much of the book: first with scarlet fever, then, after a false dawn when the sisters believe she is on the mend, she suffers a slow, sad decline, becoming weaker and weaker, more listless each day. When Beth dies, the blow falls most heavily on Jo. Her grief only begins to mend when Marmee encourages her to put on her old 'scribbling dress' – a pinafore of a dark, coarse fabric on which to wipe her nibs – and try to write stories again.

I hadn't been a particularly sickly child. Chicken pox as a baby, then coughs and colds, but nothing worse. No sprains, no breaks. Never in hospital. When I first read *Little Women*, aged seven or eight, it was natural not to be interested in frail, fading, angelic Beth when Jo was so headstrong, Meg so appallingly prinked and vain, and Amy so stubborn for all her golden curls. I didn't know what it was to be bedbound and so I took less notice of Beth.

Similarly, I had remembered Katy Carr on the roof of the schoolhouse in *What Katy Did*, playing in the loft, on the swing, but not the staple coming loose from the swing rope and the fall that fractures Katy's spine. I had remembered Eleanor H. Porter's Pollyanna climbing the tree outside her bedroom window, and skipping around town with covered bowls of lamb broth, poached chicken and calf's foot jelly for infirm ladies, and sleeping on the tin roof of her aunt's sun parlour, but not the motor car that hits her or her paralysis after.

Reading these books again – now with some experience of illness – I was struck by how sentimental the invalid chapters of *Katy* and *Pollyanna* are. After the first shock and pain, the girls are darlings. Pollyanna teaches herself to play the Glad Game again. Katy, hair brushed, nightgown trimmed with ribbons, becomes a bustling little housekeeper, directing the dusting and polishing from her sickbed. And because they are so good and uncomplaining in their hours of crisis, both girls learn to walk again as their reward.

This is so much poppycock. Being bedridden does not make you saintly and sweet-natured. It makes you cross and querulous and self-pitying. It is horrible to be cooped up and kept away. You come to hate the four walls of the bedroom, the window, the bedside table, the carpet, the bed sheets, the oppressive nearness and familiarity of things seen all and every day.

I have a horror now of even a day in bed with a cold. Too much of my teens was spent in bed with the anorexia, and with endless coughs that turned into chest infections, and chest infections that turned into bronchitis. Two bouts of it every winter: weeks of choking coughs and a temperature. Being underweight must have made me more prone to bugs and lurgies. I didn't help myself by neglecting the old wives' adage 'Feed a cold, starve a fever', and starving both equally. I was not a dear little Pollyanna, cheerfully ministering to the town from under her quilt. I was lonely, crotchety and scared. Not a Katy Carr, but a Colin Craven.

Colin, as I remembered him from reading Frances Hodgson Burnett's *The Secret Garden* when I was seven, was a wraith in a nightshirt. A spoilt, horrid, tantrumming little princeling. He was nothing like as nice as the Yorkshire lad Dickon, with squirrels in his pockets, a crow on one shoulder and a lamb in his arms. Dickon is a boy of the moor. He is out on the heather and gorse before the sun, a lunch bundle in his pocket: two thick pieces of bread and a 'fine slice o' fat bacon', wrapped in a blue-and-white pocket handkerchief. He digs a deep hollow in the woods beyond the walled secret garden to make an oven for roasting potatoes and eggs 'fit for a woodland king'.

Reading *The Secret Garden* again after twenty years, my allegiance shifted. I understood why Colin was so awful, why he cried in the night and had hysterics and threw fits. To be shut up in the dark with the windows closed, to be told he'd grow a hunchback, that he'd die before he was a man, to feel his spine every day for the first lump . . . all of that would make any child foul and frightened. It takes his cousin Mary to shout sense into him, to feel his poor, thin back and tell him that there is *nothing* there. Not a lump as big as a pin. The pity of Colin's shut-up childhood is that there never was any lump, only a Chinese-whispered misdiagnosis. What has made him so unwell are private fears, never spoken aloud, until Mary prods them out of him:

> If he had ever had any one to talk to about his secret terrors – if he had ever dared to let himself ask questions – if he had had childish companions and had not lain on his back in the huge close house, breathing an atmosphere heavy with the fears of people who were most of them ignorant and tired of him, he would have

found out that most of his fright and illness was created by himself.

Hodgson Burnett is unfairly lampooned for her children's writing – remembered for her moppet creation Little Lord Fauntleroy, a cherub in velvet bloomers – but her account of Colin's illness and recovery is an acute and brilliant one. Colin's weakness, his crippled legs, his hunchback are all his own imagining, a show of what dreadful things the mind can do. It is only when Colin spits it out, articulates his hunchback nightmare, that he can begin to get well.

Writing this book has been a spitting-out, not an easy one by any means. But the more I scribble, as Jo March scribbled, the more I reach for the right words to make sense of a shambled mind, the more certain I am that I am stronger than the illness, and that I can scribble any and all Jabberwocks away.

When Mary has finished shouting at Colin, and when the nurse has given them both beef tea and Mary has promised Colin she will take him to the garden, he is able to sleep, for the first time in many years, soundly without fits in the night. The next morning Colin is a new boy. 'Instead of lying and staring at the wall and wishing he had not awakened, his mind was full of the plans he and Mary had made yesterday, of pictures of the garden and of Dickon and his wild creatures. It was so nice to have things to think about.'

It *is* so nice to have things to think about apart from illness, whether the spasms are in the mind or the back. It was books for me, later art, architecture, walking and writing. For Colin it is the rose garden and the hush-hush picnics, kept secret from his doctor and nurse, which put meat on his skinny spine and weakling legs. Dickon and his mother Mrs Sowerby ferry baskets to the garden from their cottage on the moor: buttered toast and crumpets; pails of good, frothed, new milk with cream on the top; a crusty cottage loaf; oatcakes and heather honey; currant buns folded into napkins and hot potatoes from the wood oven with salt and fresh butter. 'They are plumpin' up,' says Dickon of the formerly wasted Colin and sour Mary. Mary, for her part, embraces the plumpin'. 'I know I'm fatter,' she says agreeably. 'My stockings are getting tighter. They used to make wrinkles.'

With pails of cream and sizzling ham and snow-white eggs and fresh air and garden spadework, Colin recovers not just his legs, but his temper. He becomes no longer a petulant Rajah on silk cushions, but a radish-cheeked Yorkshire boy. 'I'm well! I'm well!' he cheers with 'rapturous belief and realisation'. And you cheer with him, as you don't for Katy or Pollyanna, because it was too easy for them to be nice in their misfortune, their cures too smoothly won. I like very much the doctor's note with which Hodgson Burnett signs off her patient. It is sound advice for anyone who has fought depressions or mind despairs:

> So long as Colin shut himself up in his room and thought only of his fears and weakness and his detestation of people who looked at him and reflected hourly on humps and early death, he was a hysterical, half-crazy little hypochondriac who knew nothing of the sunshine and the spring, and also did not know that he could get well and could stand upon his feet if he tried

to do it. When new beautiful thoughts began to push
at the old hideous ones, life began to come back to him,
his blood ran healthily through his veins and strength
poured into him like a flood . . .

> 'Where you tend a rose, my lad,
> A thistle cannot grow'

If you have never been ill, you cannot know what it is to
realise you are well. Not necessarily cured, not free of every
ghost, every niggling, itching thought, but more well than
you could ever have hoped. Reading Colin's 'I'm well! I'm
well!' made me see how well I had become, how unrec-
ognisable from the sickroom teenager with no company
but books, how different too from the sleepless person I'd
been when I'd first left the newspaper. It had happened
so slowly, with so many false starts and mis-steps and
gains and relapses and better days and worse, that I'd not
stopped to look back across the span of my recovery to see
how far I'd come.

When Dickon and Mary are first in the secret garden
and Dickon is cutting the dead wood from the roses to
show the green sap inside, he tells Mary: 'It's as wick as
you or me.' Mary remembers that Dickon's sister Martha
has told her that 'wick' means alive or lively. Reading *The
Secret Garden*, I wanted to stand up and say not 'I'm well!
I'm well!', but 'I'm wick! I'm wick!' It was a gorgeous
snowdrop, crocus, daffadowndilly thought.

The wrinkles in Mary's stockings had given me pause.
When Mary first arrives at Misselthwaite Manor from
India she is a skinny, sallow creature, yellow as buttermilk.
It is only after a sufficiency of Yorkshire air, toast, 'taters,

crumpets and marmalade that she becomes plump, rosy and cheerful. Skinniness, rightly, isn't prized in children's books. The orphaned Pollyanna, gingham dress gaping against her little body, has never had enough to eat in her life. She and her minister father had been too poor to afford the fuel to cook at home, so they had eaten out – beans and fishballs –longing for roast turkey (too dear at sixty cents) and ice cream.

Anne Shirley, orphaned too, arrives at Green Gables a whippet. 'I am dreadfully thin, ain't I?' she tells her adoptive Aunt Marilla and Uncle Matthew. 'There isn't a pick on my bones. I do love to imagine I'm nice and plump, with dimples on my elbow.' Helped along by Marilla's cakes and crab-apple preserves and a first ice-cream picnic – 'Diana tried to explain what it was like, but I guess ice-cream is one of those things that are beyond imagination' – Anne loses some of her pickishness. Still, for all the ice cream she eats – 'so lovely and dissipated' – she remains a toothpick next to Diana. 'But you have such dimples,' she sighs at her best, dimpliest friend, 'lovely dimples, like little dents in cream. I have given up all hope of dimples. My dimple-dream will never come true.'

What's the opposite of a dimple dream? A bone craving? A skeleton wish? I still inspect my back in the mirror. Can I feel my spine and a run of ribs? I like to be able to see them through my skin. I harbour no dimple dreams. But something has changed since I was most ill. Then, I aspired only to bone. Now I am less sure. I hate the idea of putting on weight. I do feel a thrill when my hip bones stand prouder after a cold or a stomach upset. But I look at very thin women and find little beauty in their bones. What misery has driven them to it?

I know now that when I do lose weight, when my bones start to jut again, I don't feel the old adrenaline high of starvation: the rush and delirium of hunger. Now I feel only dog-tired, bone-tired. I go cold and can't get warm. I get pins and needles in my hands and nettling headaches.

I am not a doctor, I don't understand the mechanics, but it is as if my body has had its limit of hunger. It has been through it too many times, and when a new starvation threatens it shuts down, conserving every scrap and reserve of energy. It is a bad state to be in. I used to be more casual: starve on Monday, make it up tomorrow, starve on Tuesday, make it up on Wednesday, and on and on through the week, putting off eating today what I might eat tomorrow. Now, if I miss a meal, skimp on breakfast, skimp lunch, skimp again in the evening, my limbs turn lead-heavy and the life, the wick goes out of me.

This lassitude of hunger is caught most convincingly in an unlikely book. I had remembered Roald Dahl's *Charlie and the Chocolate Factory* only for what I had most swooned for as a child, and that was: C H O C O L A T E. I remembered the chocolate river, sailed in a boiled-sweet boat, the chocolate-milk cows, the Wonka bars hiding Golden Tickets. I had remembered Everlasting Gobstoppers and Wriggle Sweets and Whipple-Scrumptious Fudgemallow Delight and Strawberry Juice Water Pistols (Ed would have liked one of those) and Luminous Lollies for Eating in Bed at Night (handy for after-lights-out reading.)

What I had forgotten was the hunger of the Bucket family before Charlie finds the Golden Ticket. Bread and margarine for breakfast. Boiled potatoes and cabbage for lunch. Cabbage soup for supper. Then it starts to snow and Charlie's father loses his job, and then, slowly but surely,

the Bucket family begin to starve. Charlie grows thinner
and thinner, his face white and pinched, the skin drawn
tightly over his cheeks:

> And now, very calmly, with that curious wisdom that
> seems to come so often to small children in times of
> hardship, he began to make little changes here and
> there in some of the things he did, so as to save his
> strength. In the mornings he left the house ten minutes
> earlier so that he could walk slowly to school, without
> ever having to run. He sat quietly in the classroom
> during break, resting himself, while the others rushed
> outdoors and threw snowballs and wrestled in the snow.
> Everything he did now, he did slowly and carefully.

This is Dahl at his most solemn. No swashboggling, no
gobblefunking. Only a quiet and mournful anatomy of
starvation, the sapping of strength and will. No child de-
serves his Golden Ticket more than Charlie.

I say I don't see any beauty in the bones of others, that I
don't like to think of the undertaker's scene in *Oliver Twist*
or skinny Anne or Pollyanna or Charlie, thin not through
choice but poverty, but I still expect thinness of myself.
It's very hard to shake. The fifteen years I have kept myself
hungry have now outrun the thirteen jam-and-teacake
years of childhood. I obsess about balancing the scales: not
eating so much that I gain an ounce; not eating so little
that I lose my mind and wick and strength.

One of the questions Martha asks Mary in *The Secret
Garden* is: 'How does tha' like thysel'?' Mary thinks about
it for a moment, then: 'Not at all, really. But I never
thought of that before.' By the end of the book Mary does

like herself, and others like her too. Martha's question was a prompt. How do I like myself?

I used not to like myself at all. I hated myself. Hated my greed, my sloth, my stupidity, my clumsiness, my face, my body, my weight. Hating became habit. Always some new inadequacy to despise. Martha's question came at a useful moment. I was away at Mum and Dad's for a holiday, reading, walking, sleeping well, more and more certain that the decision to go freelance was the right one. The weather was clear, blue and sunny. 'How does tha' like thysel'?' – I think I do like myself. Not every day, not without gripe or reservation, but I no longer think I am hateful, not really greedy or slothful or stupid, or any of those things that used to echo in my head and still do at bad times.

A different question now: 'Are thou kind to thysel'?' This is more difficult. Often I am not kind. I beat myself out of bed at five in the morning. I feel guilty for 'lying in' to quarter past. I still let myself get cold and hungry and run down, and then it's a scramble to right myself before the pins and needles start. It is not kindness to treat the beginnings of a cold with a two-hour walk on a wet, freezing morning. I could always have worked another hour, walked further, eaten less. The flat could always be tidier, even when to visitors there isn't a paperclip out of place. Why can't I follow Mole in discovering: 'the joy of living and the delight of spring without its cleaning'? I'm not ready to 'learn to love myself', as the self-help books would have me do. But to like myself and to try to be kind to myself is a good and sensible aim, as Martha is a good and sensible Yorkshire girl.

One last word of Martha's wisdom – and she is wiser than any self-help book on the shelves. When Mary will not eat her breakfast because, she says haughtily, 'I don't know what it is to be hungry,' Martha is indignant. 'Well, it would do thee good to try it. I can see that plain enough. I've no patience with folk as sits an' just stares at good bread an' meat.' There was, as I read those words, the leftovers of a blackcurrant and almond cake, purple and sugar-blistered, under a wire dome on the kitchen counter. Mum had baked it with blackcurrants – after the courgettes, but before the plums – grown on teepees in her own secret garden.

I went to the kitchen and stared at the cake and the cake stared back at me with blackcurrant eyes. It would, to use Martha's words, do me good to try it. I had walked that day: two hours after breakfast, an hour after lunch. No one could begrudge me a pea-stick's width of cake. Even two pea-stick's widths. So that is what I had: a two-pea-stick's width's slice, in the garden, in the sun, feeling more wick with every bite and currant.

The first sign of Colin's recovery is curiosity. His hunger for Mary's stories of India, elephants, ivory and mahout-men tips into a hunger for muffins: 'Those muffins look so nice and hot. Tell me about Rajahs.' This is the lesson for anyone who has been ill. Stoke your appetite for new stories, pictures, landscapes, sights and music, and the other appetites – for food, for friends, for life – will follow.

There's another name to add to Martha Sowerby's on the cover of my fantasy self-help book and that is Merlyn's, the Merlyn of T. H. White's *The Once and Future King*. It wasn't a book I'd read as a child. Dad had often recommended the four books, starting with *The Sword in the Stone*, that make up White's telling of the legend of Arthur, but they had sat and sat on the shelves and I'd never got around to them. Then, the Christmas after I went freelance, when it rained every day for a week (it never does this in books: it's snow for the Cratchits, snow in *The Tailor of Gloucester*, snow in Narnia, snow in *The Box of Delights*, snow at Hogwarts), and every walk was a galoshes walk, I found myself needing a thick, sustaining book to see me into the new year.

I had put it off for so long partly down to a feeling that it was a boys' book. That it would be all tilts and jousts and fewters and morions and habergeon chain mail. There is a bit of that. No lack of crusading, if you like that sort of thing. But White also has a pleasing, antiquarian, almost maiden-auntish interest in all the bits and bobs of the age of the Round Table: Arthur's embroidered coronation hand-kerchiefs, Merlyn's teaspoons, Guenever's hairnets strung with pearls. He doesn't just tell you that the knights went in search of the Questing Beast or a unicorn, he tells you the really important things. What did they pack? What did they wear? And where did they stop for their picnic?

White makes mischief with the old legends about vil-leins living fatly in the woods. When our hero Wart, who will become King Arthur, is lost in the forest he decides he will forage for berries. Then he remembers it is July, too early in the season. The best he can find are two wild strawberries, which don't go far in filling up a boy. If only he had his goshawk Cully, the bird could catch him a rabbit, which he could cook, if only rubbing sticks to-gether would make a fire. But Cully has flown off. When Wart later mucks in with Robin Hood and his men he finds them eating an unvarying diet of venison patties, or cold venison and bread, with mead at every meal.

Civilisation is represented by Merlyn, who lays the

table in his cottage in the woods for the perfect breakfast: peaches, melons, strawberries, a brown trout piping-hot, grilled perch, 'chicken devilled enough to burn one's mouth out', kidneys and mushrooms on toast, fricassee, curry, boiling coffee and best hot chocolate with cream. There is a mustard pot that struts from place-setting to place-setting, lifting its lid as if tipping a courteous hat.

Merlyn has much to teach Wart, transforming him into a perch, a merlin falcon, an ant, an owl and a badger as he does so. The sagest of Merlyn's advice, however, needs no jiggery-pokery. It is given to Wart as the wizard smokes his pipe:

> 'The best thing for being sad,' replied Merlyn, begin-ning to puff and blow, 'is to learn something. That is the only thing that never fails. You may grow old and trembling in your anatomies, you may lie awake at night listening to the disorder of your veins, you may miss your only love, you may see the world about you devastated by evil lunatics, or know your honour tram-pled in the sewers of baser minds. There is only one thing for it then – to learn. Learn why the world works and what wags it. That is the only thing which the mind can never exhaust, never alienate, never be tortured by, never fear or distrust, and never dream of regretting.'

This is the trick. It is what works for Colin Craven and it is working for me. There are too many self-help guides that say: get fit, lose weight, make friends, find a hobby, revamp your wardrobe. Clear the clutter to clear your mind. Eat right – and right is always avocado, chia and other whatnot – to 'improve your mood'.

Better that they should say: feed your mind. Learn something, read something, see something new: a painting, a church, a bird, a rose garden, a park, a monument, a castle moat white with swans and hidden perch, a mews of hooded merlins, an elephant with ivory tusks and a palanquin throne on his back. Fill your thoughts with the world and what wags it. Plant roses so that thistles may not grow. Be as curious as you were as a child, as curious as the Wart, helping himself to Meryln's breakfast and gasping: 'Oh, I love the mustard-pot! Wherever did you get it?'

'Curiouser and curiouser!' says Alice when she eats the cake that opens her out like a telescope. Curiosity drives children's books. It is what tips Alice down the rabbit hole into Wonderland, and the Pevensie children through the wardrobe into Narnia. It is what launches the Swallow – 'With an island like that within sight, who could be content to live on the mainland and sleep in a bed at night? – and has Mary following the robin that uncovers the secret garden door.

The most curious of book children is Bevis, boy-hero of Richard Jefferies's summer-holiday stories. Bevis wouldn't like to think of me reading his book. I am, after all, that most disagreeable of things: a girl. When Bevis and Mark find one of these offensive creatures on their island, and being very hungry after failing to cook the ducks they have shot, they seize her. 'Make her fetch the water,' they cry. 'Chop the wood.' 'Turn the spit.' 'Capital; we wanted a slave!' 'Just the thing.' 'Hurrah!' 'But it's not so nice as a tiger.' 'Oh! No!' 'Nothing like.'

That is the lot of a girl in a boys' book: to cook the dinner and be less exciting than a tiger. Handicapped as

I am, I enjoyed every page of *Bevis*. It wasn't a book I'd read before. But his name kept cropping up in other books – he was on the shelves of Virginia Woolf's nephews at Charleston – as a model of outdoors, devil-may-care mischief and restless imagination. When Bevis packs a picnic he takes the usual tea, biscuits and bacon, but also a harpoon, a boomerang, a telescope and an astrolabe. He draws maps and dots out battle lines. Every piece of driftwood is a Spanish galleon, every breeze a tornado, every bird a desert genie, every campsite a place for gold-prospecting, every gardener guarding her fruit bushes a gooseberry witch.

Imagining is hungry work. Plotting and geometrizing make his stomach thunder. Bevis builds his raft with cherries in his mouth, bent over canvas sails with a pencil, working out measurements: 'It took over forty cherries to get it out properly.' Potatoes and campfire 'dampers' – flour and oatmeal cakes baked in the embers – are good thinking foods. So, too, are mushrooms, charred duck wings, streaky bacon and potatoes.

Bevis was a boon to me. I'd got it into my head that I was only allowed to eat if I had walked, that physical activity was the only exercise that burnt fat and calories. Mental exertion, desk work, being still and sedentary, did not justify a square meal. I couldn't understand why I stood up reeling and light-headed from hours writing at my desk. All I had done was sit there. Why was I so ravenous?

Bevis's brain hisses and steams because he feeds it: with huge double slices of bread and butter, and legs of roast duck stolen from the house, and anything he can throw on the campfire. On the island, exhausted by the effort of terrifying each other with ghost stories about ghouls and vampires and satyrs and 'huge creatures, with prickles on their backs', Bevis and Mark are revived by buttered biscuits and tinned condensed milk.

Bevis galvanised me to eat when I am hungry with work and writing. He loosened my dependence on walking to 'earn' the right to eat. And he made me madly wish for cherries. Now, because I have read *Bevis*, when I am stumped on any paragraph, stuck in the reeds, I can fetch cherries from the kitchen, or an apple in honour of Jo March, and chew around stones and stalks and pips until I am out of the shallows and in open water again.

Even when the boys' morale flags badly, after their bacon has been got at by a tiger or a Red Injun or possibly a panther (they never think to question Bevis's spaniel Pan), all can be righted with a raid on the remaining provisions. The campfire is lit. The kettle put on. 'A good supper and strong tea restored their strength.' That is the line that stuck like a linseed. Bevis's good supper and strong tea seemed to sum up so completely, so simply everything I had been reading my way towards. That good food would give me the strength for life and living: for rafting, for harpooning, for treasure-diving, for hunting tigers, for walking, reading, writing and imagining.

I had to think again about the words to keep me fighting. Good supper. Strong tea. On.

7

'The names are entrancing'

'What would you like best to eat?' says the White Queen to Edmund in *The Lion, The Witch and the Wardrobe*. 'Turkish Delight, please, your Majesty.' The witch, for she is no queen, magics a box from the air, a round box, tied with a green silk ribbon. Edmund has never had anything so delicious and the more he eats the more he wants to eat.

What would you like best to eat? Every child in a children's book has his or her favourites. A favourite dessert of gingerbread and whipped cream. Favourite muffins for breakfast. Favourite cream pudding for tea. Favourite monkey-face cookies before bed. It was a game Ed and I had played in the car as children, divided and subdivided into ever more categories. Your favourite meal? Your favourite pudding? Favourite ice cream? Favourite fruit? Favourite berry? Favourite chocolate? Favourite sweet? Favourite flavour Fruit Pastille? Favourite colour Smartie?

If you asked me today to name my favourite biscuit, favourite sandwich, favourite anything, I wouldn't have a ready answer. I am so out of the habit of having favourite, petted foods. I may have edged away from thinking that all foods are bad foods, could concede that there are some foods that are not bad, but a favourite food, a loved food, a last-supper food ... If pressed, the best I can come up with is porridge, but that is too monastic, too hair-shirt. Davey Balfour's uncle in R. L. Stevenson's *Kidnapped* is fanatical about porridge, indeed he is fanatical full stop: a crabbed miser in a storm-blasted castle somewhere north of the middle of nowhere. His only pleasures are hoarding his nephew's inheritance and 'parritch' for breakfast, lunch and supper: 'I could never do mair than pyke at food.'

Worse, my favourite parritch is plain parritch. Not porridge with jam or honey, or treacle and sugar as Martha tells Mary to have it *The Secret Garden*: 'Tha' doesn't want thy porridge! ... Tha' doesn't know how good it is.' Nor do I have it with whole milk, washed down with a Thermos flask of boiling cocoa, as the Swallows and Amazons have their porridge after the storm, rowed across from the mainland by Mrs Dixon, the dairy farmer's wife. My porridge is just porridge as it is with milk and water, and sometimes, when I'm feeling very daring, with sunflower and pumpkin seeds. After Mrs Dixon has disembarked, she gives the children her philosophy of breakfast: 'There's no room in anybody for a cold if they're full up with hot porridge, I always say.' She sloshes in whole milk from the can. She's already put in the sugar at the farm. It goes scalding down six throats. 'Good for you, Mrs Dixon,' says Captain Flint, arriving in his own boat. 'I ought to have thought of that. Porridge was the very thing.'

The very thing. But not a favourite thing.

What if I were Mr Toad, locked up for stealing a motor car, and told I may have a last favourite meal before my prison life sentence began? Could I really look the pretty gaoler's daughter in the eye and say: 'I'll have a bowl of

porridge.' I have to do better than that. Perhaps, and I'm
thinking aloud now, I could ask for a leg from one of Mum's
roast chickens, skin as crisp as parchment, flesh falling
from the bone. Perhaps, too, lemon, fennel and shallots,
cooked in the tray, softened with the heat and the juices
from the bird. Also, peas podded from the garden, spring
onions and mint. And, on the side of the plate, just one
or two frabjous new potatoes with parsley and wholegrain
mustard. Yes, I think that would be it. A favourite supper.

I have had to ginger myself up to admit it, to overcome
the feeling that it is shameful to say: I like this best of all.
More: that I like every part of it. The scrape of racks pulled
in and out of the oven. The aniseed sweetness of fennel,
distinct the minute you walk in the hall. The plates with
their patterned coveys of pheasants and partridges. The jar
of last year's redcurrant jelly rescued from the fridge just
in time for carving.

There, that is my favourite supper. I will give my order
to the gaoler's daughter. There'll be porridge enough
behind bars.

It is not a simple thing for me to say: I am eating this
because I like it. Not because it is on the doctor's menu
plan. Not because I must eat something to keep body and
soul together. Not because I read it in a book. But for its
own sake. Because it is delicious.

What do I like to eat? Over the years I have lost sight
of the answer. I could more easily say what I do not like.
I have told myself that I do not have a sweet tooth. That
I prefer bitter things, sour things, pickled things. That I
will sit cross-legged on a stool and pick Peter Piper-like at
pecks of pickled anything: pickled ginger; pickled plums;

pickled cabbage; pickled cocktail onions; outrageous pickled gherkins and polite pickled cornichons; pitted olives;
capers in brine; anchovies in salt; rollmop herrings; sul-
phurous piccalillis and black-as-pitch miso. If it is soused,
pickled, steeped in vinegar, if it makes my eyes water and
lips pucker, I will be first to the jar with a Triton's anchovy
fork.

When Winnie-the-Pooh gets his head stuck – 'there
was a little left at the very bottom of the jar, and he pushed
his head right in, and began to lick . . .' – in a jar of honey,
I wonder: was it worth it, Pooh? All that trouble for just a
lick of hunny? But if it had been anchovies at the bottom
of the jar, those pale, mercury-light Spanish ones called
boquerones, with parsley and garlic and white-wine vinegar,
well, that is a jar worth getting stuck in. I can see myself
fishing for the last fillet and getting my wrist caught and
going about the rest of the day with a Heffalump for a
hand.

Is it ladylike to choose garum-grey Gentleman's Relish
over dainty strawberry jam? To prefer men's college and
clubhouse fare – Welsh rarebit, Scotch woodcock, devilled
and cayenned savouries – to the white doilies, scones,
cream and antimacassared frills of the tea party? I like – I
am getting into my stride now with liking – Marmite on
blackest rye toast, ear-steaming horseradish, kippers 'n'
capers at Sunday brunch. I think I could make a better
fist of the hunting breakfast in R. S. Surtees's *Mr Sponge's
Sporting Tour* – 'a disorderly table, further littered with
newspapers, letter backs, County Court summonses, mustard pots, anchovies, pickles – all the odds and ends of a
most miscellaneous meal' – than I could a village fete of
iced fancies and buttercream cupcakes.

When very young, perhaps three or four, I had a passion for cold sliced tongue, salami and beef brisket. I would pilfer slices from any packet left open on the kitchen counter. Later, there was a mania for cheese on toast with Worcestershire sauce, fuelled by an advert then much on television for cheddar, sliced bread and Lea & Perrins. On screen it seethed and flared like Etna. It was the first thing I learnt to cook. I would drag a chair into the kitchen so I could stand eye-level with the grill and watch the cheese hiss and geyser, and the Worcestershire sauce turn to lacquer.

Dad, asked to get up our tea one afternoon, made bubble and squeak, which, like toad in the hole, had a pleasing slugs-and-snails-and-puppy-dogs'-tails ring. That was another one worth standing on a chair to watch in the pan. I'd not thought of Dad's bubble and squeak for years before I re-read *The Wind in the Willows*. It is bubble and squeak that the gaoler's daughter brings Mr Toad: a portion of her own dinner, set aside for him and kept hot between two plates. 'Its fragrance filled the narrow cell. The penetrating smell of cabbage reached the nose of Toad as he lay prostrate in his misery on the floor, and gave him the idea for a moment that perhaps life was not such a blank and desperate thing as he had imagined.'

Was cabbage ever so tempting? Toad had made me want to try stuff-of-life bubble and squeak again. The recipe I followed – and really I shouldn't have needed a recipe for this cabbage-and-bacon-and-'taters throw-it-all-in supper – came from Nigel Slater. He borrows the Scottish name 'rumbledethumps'. It's as simple as that: rumbling the pan to keep the brawl of cabbage and potatoes from burning, and thumping it to stop the bacon sticking. If Elizabeth

David's break, beat, butter, shake omelette recipe has a
dancing elegance, then rumble, thump, bubble, squeak
was a meal made in the boxing ring. What came out was a
hash, a muddle, a frying-pan fist-fight of savoy, mash and
streaky bacon. Salty, hearty, a bruiser of a dish. Very good.
I liked it, as I had liked it years before.

If I could eat bubble and squeak, what about cheese on
toast, my other childhood favourite? The clean eaters had
made me wary of cheese. They had banned it and so had I.
Two encouragements, coming close together, pressed me
to try again. The first was an overheard brunch order given
to a waiter, while I waited for a girlfriend in a café. The
woman at the next table – and certainly she was a siren,
very pretty, very tanned, very slim – asked: 'Can I get the
cheese on toast? But can I get it with vegan-soy cheese?
And gluten-free bread? And can I get a latte? But can I
get it decaf with almond milk? And can I get a "Meaner
Green" juice? But a small one?' Was there anything warm,
fun, easy about this woman? I looked at my own menu,
considered my options, and when the waiter came to the
table I ordered a breakfast of boiled eggs and buttered soldiers, and tea with real milk, and felt tall and defiant.

The second cheese-spur was a watercolour by Beatrix
Potter, seen in an exhibition catalogue when I was writing
an article for the 150th anniversary of her birth in 1866.
Potter gave the sketch the title: *A Dream of Toasted Cheese*.
The *Dream* was done for her uncle Sir Henry Roscoe to
celebrate the publication of his 1899 textbook *First Steps
in Chemistry*.

A great Bunsen burner rises through the centre of the
sketch, tall as a totem pole. Perched on the collar con-
necting the gas tube to the chimney is a mouse, in round

spectacles, frowning in concentration over his copy of *First Steps*. Behind him his lab assistants, all of them mice, are inspecting test tubes, flasks and pestles and mortars for their suitability in toasting samples of yellow cheese. Three mice have got hold of a glass stirring-rod and, having skewered a piece of cheese on its end, are poking it into the hottest part of the Bunsen flame. It looks as if it is toasting very nicely, for a circle of mice have gathered below it, holding up their paws as if in prayer. Those mice, I thought, are having a high time of it with their experiments and glass pipettes. The woman in the café: was she having as much fun as the lab mice? I couldn't convince myself that she was.

Potter's mice had set me cheese-day-dreaming. I planned cheese-on-toast suppers. Sunday would be a good night, I'd say. Then Sunday would come and go and I'd have contrived some reason not to have cheese. I was in the mood for a soup. There were leftovers to be used up. Wednesday, then. Cheese on toast with gem lettuces and radishes. And Wednesday would come and go and I'd have had sardines and soft, quartered artichoke hearts. I'd buy milk and yogurt and think: 'Well, that's all in this aisle,' and scarper, not stopping to look back at the chilled cheese cabinets. Week after week I bottled it. Feeble, feeble, namby-pamby, niminy-piminy.

In the end, the choice was taken out of my hands. I was briganded by cheese on toast. We had gone out walking, Andy and I, one Sunday in early October, blue skies, sun, showers, sun, blue skies, showers again – John Constable weather – on Hampstead Heath. The Heath was once a place of highwaymen and I should have known to be on my guard. We walked up for a view of St Paul's and the Shard, and down to the ponds, and were rained on and dried out in the sun, and ate apples on a bench on Parliament Hill.

Walking back to the bus stop on Fitzjohn's Avenue, we stopped to pick up lunch. I asked for the day's salad: pearl barley, French beans, courgettes. But they had sold out. I asked for the avocado on rye. They had sold out. Andy asked for the double-cheese toastie – Cheddar and Red Leicester – with red-onion relish, and I said in a voice that didn't sound quite my own: '*Two* double-cheese toasties.' Our toasties came in foil to keep them hot. We opened them on the bus. Two slices of sourdough streaked and branded by the grill. A slice of tansy-yellow Cheddar. A darker, Penguin-paperback-orange slice of Red Leicester. A layer of pickle as thick again as the cheese. I liked the pickle. I very much liked the pickle. The pickle was the best of it. The ingredient that stole the show.

Can I do better than that? Deep breath and courage to the sticking place. I liked the sandwich. I liked the pickle. The bread. The Cheddar. The Red Leicester. I liked the company, the sense of being a partner in crime, the day, the sky, the city. It had been – all of it – a dream of double-toasted cheese.

I say my tastes are savoury, that my palette is a soused and soured and pickled one, that I haven't a sweet tooth in my head. But it's not quite true. I have confessed my childhood sugar sins: Bounty-lust, Iced-Gem gluttony, wrath at the unshared Rolo. Yet I pretend now that nothing sweet – not the smallest comfit, not a Hundred-Thousand, not a Polo Mint, not a caterpillar cake nor Mini Egg – could excite me as much as a single wrinkled, pickled walnut.

Over the years, I've done a complete job of convincing

myself that sugar, cream, sweet pastry, candies and cara-
mels aren't for me. That my palette is more sophisticated.
It calls for the whip of vinegar, the eye-twitching squeeze
of lemon. There have been moments of rebellion. The
Mantua ice cream was the first. The *tarte tatin* another.
The plum jam. The blackcurrant cake. But always afterwards a craven return to white sauerkraut and sliced
beetroot.

I have tried experiments. What would happen if I did
have my porridge with treacle? Would a thunderbolt really
come through the kitchen ceiling to strike me down? There
had been a tin of Lyle's Golden Syrup in my cupboard for
years, bought and left behind by a boyfriend who'd had his
syrup with porridge in the mornings. Very much that way
around: a lake of syrup, an island of porridge. Stamped on
the lid was the date: 'Best Before February 2014'. The relationship had ended long before then, but Golden Syrup
lasts and lasts.

They are very gorgeous, the Lyle's tins. Golden lion. Ever-
green enamel. A stamp: 'By Appointment to Her Majesty
The Queen', and the motto: 'Out of the Strong Came Forth
Sweetness.' On the day of the syrup experiment, I made
my morning's bowl: dull, dour Scottish parritch with sunflower seeds – begging for adulteration. I levered the lid
off the Lyle's tin with a butter knife and drizzled, let us say
a brook, as a lake would be a fib, of syrup over the top of
the oats. I added a Swallows-and-Amazons slosh of whole
milk – whole milk, not skimmed, not semi-skimmed, not
soya, not almond – to the bowl. I had a first spoonful and
kept on until the bowl was empty. I waited for the thunderbolt, the flash of divine retribution. None came. It gave
me a fillip, a Lyle's lion roar of courage. I wouldn't want

syrup every day, but to know that I can eat it, that I am not scared of my own kitchen cupboards, is important. When the Jabberwock roars, I know now I can roar back.

More and more, I have edged towards sweetness with sharp, wincing desserts: a tangerine granita, a blood-orange sorbet, a rhubarb fool. These are sour, I say, not sweet. Sour is allowed. If I were being bold I might ask for my last chicken supper to be followed by a bowl of Mum's gooseberry crumble. Gooseberry, though, or rhubarb, not pear. The fruit has to be tart, has to make me wince. It's the way tartness wakes you up, like opening the bedroom window on a morning of frost.

When I'm in a bullish, confident mood, I chance an ice cream. I thought when I had the Mantua cone that I'd never do it again. Recently, though, I have summoned the Mantua spirit in London. On a very hot day, I find ice creams sickly. But in April, with a blue sky and a breeze, a first day without coat (and gloves and scarf and hat), I cannot see a curious flavour on a menu, the curiouser and curiouser the better, without wanting just a melon-ball scoop. Myrtle berry and pear. Pumpkin and amaretto. Banana, cardamom and ginger.

There is something to me wildly exciting – a small act of rebellion – about sitting on a high stool, bag and coat and abandoned woollens piled on my lap, sculpting a scoop of sour cherry with a tiny plastic mason's trowel, and gossiping with Olivia, and leaping down every other minute to rescue a glove that has fallen on the floor. Yes, I feel fretful and wracked on the walk home. I shouldn't have done it. No one needs ice cream. It is a want, not a need, and wanting is wrong. But I am getting better and more determined at quashing that feeling of wrongness

and telling myself that, for one April evening, I am allowed to be Empress of Ice Cream.

There is one flavour of ice cream, however, that I never
have. Never even think of having. My choice is never chocolate. Never *cioccolato fondente*. Never *cioccolato bianco*. Never
stracciatella. Never *gianduia*. Never *bacio*. Never chocolate
under any circumstances. Not since I was fifteen.

Then, coming back from a holiday at the end of a year in
which I had eaten less and less, and when I had eaten nothing for the two weeks abroad but muesli, tomato salads
and pale, cured fish, my resolve broke as we waited at the
airport. There was no café open, nothing to eat. Only a
vending machine and only junk inside it. I fed my last
currency coins into the slot and a Mars bar dropped into
the metal gully. It was the first chocolate I'd had in more
than a year. With a long flight ahead, I was already shaking
with hunger. I scraped my teeth along one end of the bar,
taking off little channels of chocolate, caramel and nougat.

I didn't manage even a third of it before shame caught
up with me. What made me think I had any right to eat?
And to eat something so disgusting? A Mars Bar. An ingot
of sugar and fat. I folded the rest of the bar into the wrap-
per, neatly, because lord knows I like things to be neat, and
threw it in a bin.

Some combination of voices, my own, the Jabberwock's,
decided that was the end of it. I would never eat chocolate
again. Never be so weak-willed, such a pig. That was early
in January 2003. Never since a Bounty or a Rolo. Never a
brownie or a chocolate mousse. Never a slice of chocolate
cake or a dusting of cocoa powder. Not a bar, not a button,
not a choc-chip. Chocolate is the last unconquerable.

I may be nervous about cheeses, cakes, red meat, puddings, breads and bagels, but I will eat them. I can quiet my nerves, the more so if politeness – at a dinner, in company – demands it. I may not seek out rich or heavy foods, or sugar and treats, but they are no longer impossible. Chocolate, though. Chocolate is impossible. I can't fully explain it. This last intractable. What do I think will happen if I eat a single chocolate-covered raisin? I used to eat Poppets by the two-dozen on the way home from swimming in a chlorine-and-chocolate fug in the back of the car. What would one Poppet do to me? Would the sky fall? Would the world end?

I have a superstition that so long as I cleave to this last denial, then I will always know that the old discipline is keen and oiled. That if ever again I was determined to stop eating, I could do it. I don't want to starve myself, I don't, I don't. But if I did. Chocolate is the last taboo. Stuck and stubborn as toffee.

A trail of dropped chocolate papers runs through all my reading. Chocolate was there in one of the first of the Dickens novels, *A Tale of Two Cities*, read early in the bicentenary year. Monseigneur has his breakfast hot chocolate carried to him by four lackeys. One to carry the chocolate pot, one to mill and froth the chocolate, a third to present the napkin, a fourth to pour.

The Great War was fought and won on chocolate. Rouen – 'a damn depressing spot' – is made less so when Siegfried Sassoon's Sherston finds a supply of chocolate to munch. Edmund Blunden eyes up chocolate *bouchées* in silver paper in the windows at Festubert, and buys chocolates from an old woman peddler at Cambrin – 'where had she sprung from?' Givenchy is an Arcadia because the men can get chocolate and beer, while at Senlis they buy life-restoring sugar beet and chocolate before bedding down in the straw of a barn. David Jones eats chocolate when his fingers are too numb to turn the thin India paper of his books. He overhears a conversation between public-school officers: 'I say Calthrop, have a bite of this perfectly good chocolate.'

Stanley Spencer wrote a piqued letter to a friend on Easter Sunday 1917 to say that he had missed his hot-cross buns. He begged for chocolate from home in compensation, failing that biscuits or a cake. Anything except gingerbread: 'I don't like that.'

Laurie Lee, starving in Spain in *A Moment of War*, is rescued by a Red Cross parcel of chocolate that arrives in time for Christmas. He eats the two-penny bar of Cadbury's Milk Chocolate 'with almost erotic excitement'. It tastes of home. In the years after, Christmas always sets him off in search of chocolate. He goes to Germany for the Wolfsgarten Christmas fairs, where he eats chocolate cakes wide as cartwheels.

Paddy Leigh Fermor nudges bars of chocolate into the corners of his rucksack. They are iron rations to be raided later, pulled out with rotting apple cores and dismembered garlic cloves. What, I wonder, is the Bulgarian for chocolate?

M. F. K. Fisher amasses dragon hoards of chocolate: boarding-school chocolates, chocolate truffles and anisette to settle her stomach, cold chocolate inside hot baguettes on February walks with the Club Alpin of Dijon – 'Never eat chocolate without bread, young lady!' says a Dijon doctor. 'Very bad for the interior, very bad.' She cannot resist a look at the pastry trays in cake shop windows, always on the lookout for the perfect *Sachertorte* or the dream *cassata all siciliana*. They never live up to her mind's image. Better to read about these Hapsburg and Palermo cakes, she concludes, than to eat them. Kinder, too, on the liver. She and her siblings had been delighted when her uncle George married a woman called Georgetta who made cookies with walnuts and dark chocolate and even darker fudge frosting. She cannot, however, be persuaded of the merits of the all-American chocolate brownie. Delicious, she says, but indigestible.

Elizabeth David makes the case for the *petit pain au chocolat*, beloved by French children but little known in England, she wrote, in 1977. One needs coarse cooking chocolate, she writes, baked until it is just about to melt. She first had them from a bakery in Paris, eaten for breakfast on the tram from Passy to the Boulevard Saint-Michel, before lectures at the Sorbonne. Ed and I clamoured for these on holidays in France. *Pains au chocolat* dipped and baptised in bowls of *chocolat chaud* for breakfast, then rounds of baguette with chocolate Nutella and sugared *citrons pressés* for tea.

Elizabeth David doesn't stop at *pains au chocolat*. 'Ginger with chocolate,' she writes, 'if it is good ginger and very bitter chocolate – is one of the happiest of inventions.' She gives a recipe for a 'marvellous chocolate confection called Mohr im Hemd or moor in a nightshirt'. I looked this up. *Mohr im Hemd*: a chocolate and almond bread pudding, not unlike our Christmas pudding, made in Austrian patisseries. Soaked in red wine, glossed with hot chocolate and topped with whipped cream. Typically shaped like a *Gugelhupf*. I looked that up, too. *Gugelhupf*: a *Bundt* cake. And that. *Bundt* cake: a type of ring-shaped teacake baked in a fluted mould.

The teenage Virginia and Vanessa Stephen, before a country walk on holiday in Bognor, laid in stocks of biscuits and chocolate 'in case we were benighted'. No map, no watch, no knowledge of the country, but they had chocolate so all would be well. A book-shopping trip became a chocolate-shopping one when Virginia bought half a crown's worth of simple square drops at a sweet shop, and seven shillings' worth of Leopardi, John Stuart Mill and Max Beerbohm. She has rissoles and chocolate custard at Monk's House; cold salmon and chocolates at Sissinghurst; a chocolate roll from Thomas Hardy's tea table; chocolates after listening to the wireless, but before bed.

On the *Hogwarts Express*, Harry and Ron dive into tuck-trolley chocolate frogs. Ron is more interested in the chocolate; Harry is mesmerised by the cards. In their third year, their Defence Against the Dark Arts teacher Professor Lupin administers enormous slabs of chocolate to help the Gryffindors recover from a first encounter with the soul-sapping Dementors. 'Harry took a bite and to his great surprise felt warmth spread suddenly to the tips of his fingers and toes.' Madam Pomfrey, the school matron, has a special chocolate hammer for breaking apart whole boulders of chocolate – antidote to a Dementor's attempted death-kiss.

My childhood books were chock-full of chocolate: chocolate profiteroles in the windows of Fattypuff bakeries; French hot chocolate that won't froth in time for Amy's party in *Little Women*; a Golden Ticket unwrapped with a Wonka Bar in *Charlie and the Chocolate Factory*, and the factory chimneys that smell of 'roasting coffee and burnt sugar and melting chocolate and mint and violets and crushed hazelnuts and apple blossom and caramel and lemon peel';

the Punch and Judy man in *The Box of Delights* eating a supper of eggs and bacon and hot toast and a jug of sweet chocolate, with good meaty bones for Toby the dog.

There was no chocolate in T. H. White's *The Once and Future King*, no chocolate at all in the age of Arthur. But there was chocolate in White's *Mistress Masham's Repose*. When Maria finds a colony of Lilliputians, refugees from *Gulliver's Travels*, on an island in the grounds of her ancestral home, she brings a bag of tribute to the People:

> The final glory was in a paper bag. Maria opened it herself, the People standing back in wonder, and laid the contents out in rows. It was a shilling's worth of chocolate creams.

> She had gone through a tussle with the Professor about these. He, with his giant's obsession about choosing small things for small people, had wanted to buy an old-fashioned sweet which was sometimes used on cakes, called Hundreds and Thousands. They were tiny pellets of hard sugar, coloured pink or white or blue. Maria had insisted on full-sized chocolates. Which would you have preferred, then: a hard piece of sugar about the size of a toffee apple, or a chocolate cream the size of a pram?

Maria has judged the people of Lilliput well. They cut the chocolates into slices with razor blades and in less than a minute every man, woman and child is nodding, smiling, rubbing his waistcoat and taking another bite.

It's a wonderful set-piece, absurd in its contrasts of scale: the smiling Lilliputians gathered around the vast chocolate cream, unwieldy as a Silver Cross pram, the razor blades as long as broadswords. I admired Maria's chocolate wheeze very much, thought it wonderfully clever. Who likes Hundreds and Thousands sprinkles anyway? They were never so nice topping tea-party fairy cakes as angelica, or glacé cherries, or silver balls, or orange and lemon sugar segments.

Did Maria's chocolates work? Did I try a Lilliputian bite of chocolate? A razor-paring of Dairy Milk? You will be expecting me to say that, inspired by Maria and the Lilliputians, I closed the book and struck out for the chocolate shops of Marylebone. That there I treated myself to one silky, tempered chocolate cream. That the tissue paper crinkled winningly. That I couldn't wait until I was home but that I chose a bench outside the Wallace Collection, that I sat in late, low September light and let the chocolate melt on my tongue.

You know how it ought to go. The boiled eggs. The Christmas pudding. The Sussex Yorkshires. The *tarte tatin*. The omelette. The mushrooms. The crystallised ginger. The blackcurrant tart. The plum jam. The bubble and squeak. The cheese on toast. All conquered because I had read about them or seen them painted. But in this case, there has been no victory. For all my reading, I still cannot eat so much as a chocolate drop. The airport Mars Bar has cast a long shadow. Even when a restaurant ended its menu with a flourish: 'Elizabeth David's *St Emilion au Chocolat*', I cried chicken. No, not even for Elizabeth David.

So I eat around it. Easy enough. I needn't tell a hostess in advance, as I would if I were vegetarian or allergic to dairy. If pudding is chocolate soufflé, I can claim to be too full of the main. 'Delicious, but I couldn't eat another bite.' If there is chocolate fondue, I can pick the fruit from its skewer and leave the chocolate to others. Most people don't mind, or don't notice, but the odd person takes this chocolate resistance badly. It's strange. No one ever minds when I say I am not much given to blue cheese, or that I am indisposed when it comes to scallops. But not eating chocolate is outrageous, perverse.

Once, at a party, after a conversation about Jaffa Cakes and marquee baking shows, a woman I had just met was so vexed by my admission that I didn't eat chocolate that she followed me into the loos to remonstrate. What was the matter with me? I must like chocolate. Everybody liked chocolate. Cornered against the hand-dryer, I mumbled excuses. From her perch on the edge of the sink, she told me that I *had* to read Joanne Harris's *Chocolat*. It was her *favourite* book, about her *favourite* food. That would fix me. And, boy, her disbelieving look said, did I need fixing.

She had been so serious, so insistent, that the next time I went to the library I looked up Harris and took a copy home. It sat on the hall table for weeks. '*Choc-o-lat*', it breathed every time I walked past. '*Choc-o-lat.*' I put a pile of Muriel Sparks on top of it. Then a couple more. Shush. *Tais-toi.* '*Choc-oh!-lat.*'

Why was I letting it pester me? I'd read *Chocolat* before, when it was first published. My last year at primary school: 1999. I had it in hardback with a Cadbury's-purple cover. It was one of the first 'grown-up' books I read. There was a love scene – great excitement – between the sorceress-chocolatier Vianne and the gypsy Roux. He smells of paint and soap and chocolate and tastes of chocolate when Vianne kisses him. It was a melting sort of book, hazy at the edges, heady, sleepy. It lingered and made Rolos bought from the corner shop taste muddy. More than muddy, it made them taste childish. Chocolates could be more sophisticated than that, corrupted with coffee, rum, *crème de cassis*. Hot chocolate could be made with a dash of Kahlua – a dark cocoa-bean liqueur. Vianne's sugar lumps were laced with calvados.

Chocolate, with an E, was the stuff of Christmas stockings, party bags, midnight feasts and long car journeys. *Chocolat*, said coquettishly, done with an accent, was temptation, sin, seduction, love in the long grass. I was eleven, about to go to an all-girls school. This was potent stuff. I have remembered the book ever since as smelling like a Terry's Chocolate Orange, the nearest thing I knew to a fruit liqueur. There's no sign of it on the shelves at Mum and Dad's. It must have gone to the charity shop in one of my teenage book purges. I suppose it would have been a taunting reminder of what I could not have.

Choc-o-lat.

The library copy had started to annoy me. Bad enough being frightened of the real thing. I couldn't now develop a complex about the fictional stuff. I shifted the Muriel Sparks and moved *Chocolat* to my bedside table. It took another two days of excuses – this book to review, that one to finish – before I started reading. 'We came on the wind of the carnival. A warm wind for February, laden with the hot greasy scents of frying pancakes and sausages and powdery-sweet waffles cooked on the hotplate right there by the roadside.' It is a book that gives no quarter. To pancakes in fewer than twenty words and waffles in under thirty. So suspicious was my imagination, so braced for sweet things, that I read the first sentence as: 'We came on the wind of the caramel.'

Vianne Rocher opens her chocolate shop – *La Céleste*

Praline – at the beginning of Lent. 'The traditional season of self-denial,' pouts the village *curé* François Reynaud. He is not impressed. While others have their breakfast *chocolats chauds*, he recites the contents of the window display to himself as if they are ungodly matins: chocolates, pralines, truffles, candied fruits and rose petals, hazelnut clusters, chocolate seashells, sugared violets, *guimauve* – long, twisted marshmallows – and plump, pressing, unchaste brandy-and-chestnut chocolates called Nipples of Venus. There is just the faintest suggestion of *Carry On Curé* as he blushes before the *Capezzoli di Venere*.

Reynaud does what I would do faced with such a chocolate shop: he fasts. He will touch only bread, soups, salads and a single glass of wine on a Sunday. He believes it cleanses him: guts and soul. He confesses his tortures: 'The sight of the butcher's window appals; scents are heightened to a point of intensity that makes my head reel. Suddenly the morning odour of baking from Poitou's is more than I can bear; the smell of hot fat from the rotisserie in the Place des Beaux-Arts a shaft from hell.' He may be the villain of the book, but I sympathise. I know what it is like to stand outside windows, to feel that you want, more than anything in the world, to join in, and at the same time to know that you would despise yourself if you did. So you stand on the pavement and try to silence with clear soups and salads the come-hither whispers of *marrons glacés, amourettes* and *huîtres de Saint-Malo*.

There is, of course, only so much 'Get thee behind me, Satan' a man, even a man of the cloth, can manage. What undoes Reynaud in the end, after he has broken into the shop with a cudgel to destroy the Easter display, isn't the scent – cream, vanilla, a bouquet like fine wine, the

richness of ground coffee beans – but the *words*. 'The name
of each piece is lettered on the lid in fine cursive script.
The names are entrancing. Bitter orange cracknel. Apricot
marzipan roll. Cerisette russe. White rum truffle. Manon
blanc. Nipples of Venus.' He lingers over each name. *Crème
de cassis*. Three-nut cluster. Eastern Journey. *Pêche au miel
millefleurs*. The names are his downfall. The first truffle
he tries, having not tasted chocolate since he was a boy,
having never touched a woman, is the *Capezzoli di Venere*.
Wouldn't you? If you'd been celibate all your life?

What is the greatest sin of that first chocolate? The las-
civious name? The carnal cocoa? The surrender to a pagan
goddess? Once Reynaud starts he cannot stop:

> It is like one of my dreams. I roll in chocolates. I imagine
> myself in a field of chocolates, on a beach of chocolates,
> basking-rooting-gorging. I have no time to read the
> labels; I cram chocolates into my mouth at random.
> The pig loses his cleverness in the face of so much de-
> light, becomes a pig again, and though something at
> the top of my mind screams at me to stop I cannot help
> myself. Once begun it cannot end. This has nothing to
> do with hunger; I force them down, mouth bulging,
> hands full . . .

This is what I fear. That one chocolate would not be
enough. One would mean another, and another, and another. Chocolates first, and then anything and everything
else. That one chocolate would break my will and I would
eat until I was smeared with food, sick with it, pigged with
it. That is why I do not tip flurries of powdered chocolate
from canisters over pancakes, or pick Celebrations from

the tin, or ask for a Flake with a soft-scoop ice cream. One drop of molten chocolate and I might drown in the flood.

I don't miss it. Not really. I can pass a chocolate shop without a pang. I am incorruptible as marble.

Ed and I used to be fascinated by the 'Death by Chocolate' pudding that appeared on the menu at the local Italian restaurant. It was the rule that since we were being taken out for pizzas, and had tall glasses of peach iced tea with our *margheritas* and *funghis*, we could do without dessert after. We used to speculate, though, about Death by Chocolate, taking it in turns to plot ever more sticky murders.

A chocolate cake.

With white chocolate icing.

And dark chocolate filling.

And milk chocolate topping.

And chocolate sauce.

And chocolate ice cream.

And chocolate chips.

And chocolate sprinkles.

And chocolate powder.

And chocolate biscuits round the edges!

And chocolate milk to wash it down!

And a chocolate-dipped cherry on top!

We proved that invented chocolate can be more indulgent, more improbable than the real thing, rather as Mary Frances's *Sachertorten* were always better in imagination than on glass patisserie shelves.

There is a type of ornate still-life painting called *pronkstilleven* – 'pronk' is parade, pomp, flamboyance – which was much in vogue among Dutch artists of the seventeenth century. All the most expensive, rare and exotic stuffs and treats and kickshaws that merchant money can buy are piled on tables that become altars. They have the dazzling bling of Christmas windows: sparkling Venetian glassware, antique *roemers* of wine, mince pies spilling their fruit, silver salt cellars, shrimps in their shells, saltwater crabs, grapes, peaches, bone-handled knives, a gilded stand for a pigeon pie, Delftware jugs, Chinese dishes piled with olives. Such a painting would have hung in the best rooms of private houses, something to gaze at over frugal bread and herrings.

Our Deaths by Chocolate then were *pronk*-puddings: improbable pilings of richness on richness. Better, really, eaten in imagination than queasy reality. So I don't miss chocolate. Not really. Not at all. Perhaps a little.

I miss it only in one form. I would like to drink hot chocolate again. I loved hot chocolate – loved, not liked – when I was little. We had it made in the microwave with three heaped teaspoons – never were there such Boffin-high heaps – of chocolate powder and milk. We made it when the weather was cold, when our fingers were stiff through gloves after the park and the playground. When I read Monseigneur's breakfast in *A Tale of Two Cities*, with its hot chocolate served by four cocoa flunkeys, there is a twitch of longing. How many teaspoons of chocolate does he have in each cup? Siegfried Sassoon's Sherston insisted on not more than two spoonfuls of cocoa to each man. Ed and I would have thought this very scrimped. We would have had four, five, six teaspoons if we'd been allowed.

Then there is Sir John in *Barnaby Rudge*, breakfasting in bed, chocolate and toast at his elbow, books and newspapers to hand. The chocolate gives him an air of 'tranquil satisfaction'. He dallies lazily with the teaspoon. He finishes the cup with 'infinite relish'. Sir John is the most languid of breakfasters: his chocolate a symbol of late-to-bed, long-to-lie-in hedonism. As a chocolate puritan I have more in common with his opposite, the industrious locksmith and lark Gabriel Varden. Varden is a tea man. His kettle sings and chirps. His tea table, laid with a service painted with mandarins and their umbrellas, makes him 'the rosiest, cosiest, merriest, heartiest, best-contented old-buck, in Great Britain or out of it'. Very nice, very jolly, but the mind drifts back to layabout Sir John reading the news in bed and ringing the bell for more chocolate when the first cup goes cold.

I try to tell myself that tea with milk is just as warming. And it is. Ish. If Bevis can imagine a breeze is a genie, then I ought to be able to convince myself that Earl Grey is hot cocoa. Horlicks does a passable impression of hot chocolate. But it is Fool's Gold. It has some of the character of chocolate, its warmth, its pillowiness, but it is a bran-coloured drink and tastes a little too much of stable and manger ever to be really decadent.

At the same exhibition as the Monet *galettes* at the National Gallery, there was a painting by Renoir: *La Tasse de Chocolat* – The Cup of Chocolate. Some catalogues call it *La Tasse de Thé*. But it is not tea she is drinking. She would not sit so close to the table if it were only tea, not have taken such pains with the rose at her breast, her coiffure. Who dresses up for tea? There is a plaited napkin folded across her lap. Tea won't do much damage to silk. But a spill of hot chocolate? That will ruin a dress. It is a very small cup she is stirring. A *demi-tasse*. I hesitate to admit it, but I do, I do, I do crave a tiny blue-and-white cup of hot chocolate on a blue-and-white saucer, the sort that Renoir painted and Monseigneur and Sir John had brought in for their breakfasts.

I read books and write CHOCOLATE in capital letters in the margins where it appears and draw stars at the tops of pages and copy the words of chocolate-eaters into my notebooks. It is 'Indian nectar', *'Jocolatte'*, *'Chocolat Délicieux à Manger'*, 'choc' and 'choccy'. There are the double-chocolate 'jiggers' eaten at a Princeton ice-cream-sundae shop by Amory Blaine in F. Scott Fitzgerald's *This Side of Paradise*, and bargaining-chip chocolates offered by Henry Higgins to Eliza Doolittle in George Bernard Shaw's *Pygmalion*: 'You shall have boxes of them, barrels of them, every day. You shall live on them.'

But no matter how many books I read, no matter how many exhibition catalogues I go through, no written or painted chocolate has yet made it from the page to my kitchen. I am stumped. Chocolate is so tangled up in my mind with ideas of sin, greed and loss of control. The more I try to untangle these thoughts, the longer the time I have gone without chocolate, the tighter that particular knot is drawn. If I have managed without for this long, why weaken now?

It isn't just me. Chocolate-makers and their advertisers love to play on chocolate sin. The Flake girl in her overflowing bath. The Milk Tray man stealing into the bedroom at night. *All Because the Lady Loves . . .* The Galaxy bar that asks: 'Why have cotton when you can have silk?' Naughty chocolate. Forbidden chocolate. Chocolate for affairs and anniversaries. St Valentine's chocolates. Chocolates on the pillow. 'Fond lovers' ways and flowers and chocs.' I shouldn't, I couldn't, I mustn't. Don't tempt me! Just one then. Don't tell!

The language is vice and virtue, trespass and atonement.

I notice it talking to friends or in meetings. Because I have
not had the chocolate pudding or the Kit-Kat biscuits that
come with tea, someone will say: 'You're so restrained' or
'You're so good.' How unappetising this is: good if one
doesn't eat, bad if one does. Kale saints and chocolate sin-
ners. By these standards, then, I am saintly. I do not dither
over the box of praline seashells and say: 'Just one more.'
And: 'This is the last one.' And: 'Just this one last.' Yes, I
can see they are pretty – the marbled seahorse, the *noisette*
clam – but I do not want them. I have forgotten how to
want them. I do not announce, penitent after chocolate
cupcakes or an Aero or a brownie pudding: 'My diet starts
tomorrow.' I have a different addiction.

I do often tell myself, looking at the pile of books by
my bed, on the hall table, on the windowsill behind my
desk: 'No more books. You are stuffed to the gills. Your
eyes are bigger than your stomach.' Forty minutes later I'll
find myself in Marylebone, or on Piccadilly, or in front of a
second-hand bookstall on the Portobello Road balancing a
piled-up, triple-decker, knickerbocker, banana-split glory
of books. If you were to ask me what I was doing among
the Portobello bookstalls at half past five in the morning,
I would have to invoke the defence of the late-night fridge
raider caught with a tub of chocolate-chip ice cream:
'I couldn't help myself.' Do I feel guilty for my lack of
self-restraint, my bookshop binges? Not really. Worried,
perhaps, about the expense. Chocolate is cheap; hardbacks
expensive. But not guilty, no.

When I take the top book from the pile – 'What a lark!'
– and press the covers and smooth the spine and start reading – 'What a plunge!' – it is with a sense of wonderful
possibility, of immersion and escape. G is for Gluttony.

Here is something better, to me, than *quail financière* and
flapjacks, Flakes and Galaxy bars. No calorie repentance.
No chocolate remorse. I may bankrupt myself, the shelves
may buckle, but I could never be sated, never be too fat,
full, gorged with books.

If I were to paint a modern *pronkstilleven*, I'd put a box of
chocolate truffles, salted caramel ones perhaps, at its centre.
All those Dutch still-life paintings of fruits, flowers and
meats are very sensual: look at me, touch me, taste me. But
often, among the tulips, the apricots, the eel on a silver
salver, perhaps half hidden behind a vase, you find a skull.
Enjoy the spoils of this life, if you must, say the paintings,
you'll pay for it in the next. We call them *vanitas* paintings
or *memento mori* – reminders of the vainglories of greed,
gluttony and buying, spending, shopping. Whatever you
accumulate, however rich you are – all will decay. Even
you.

The Dutch may have gone in for such thou-shalt-not-
buy, thou-shalt-not-gorge paintings more than most. But
they were not the only ones. Vincenzo Campi, a painter of
mostly religious subjects, from Cremona in northern Italy
is the author of a painting known as *The Ricotta-Eaters*.
In this group portrait, a *quartetto* are gathered around a
heaped, just-turned-out molehill of ricotta. In another setting they could be musicians crowded around a stand.

Each has his or her spoon, one has got hold of a deep
soup ladle, and they are caught red-handed, white-handed
even, scooping great snowdrifts of cheese. The man in the
middle tips his head back as far as it will go, opens his
mouth wide, about to drop a dollop from a height. The
man with the soup ladle already has more than a mouth

full. He simply cannot cram in any more. The curds are falling from his lips. Campi paints himself into the scene, second from the right, with a telling speck of white on his moustache. The woman taps her spoon on the tablecloth. 'Me next,' she might be saying. 'My turn.' Tilt your head, look a little closer, and you see that the ricotta has been scooped into the shape of a skull – a warning against too much cheese-liberty.

Instinctively, I am against the gluttonous ricottees. Grotesque, I say, joining the moral finger-waggers. *Vanitas vanitatum.* Gross to have so much between just four and to eat with such scooping cupidity. Why couldn't they have it nicely, neatly crimped into ravioli, the barest teaspoon of ricotta to each parcel? My trouble is that I see eating in opposites and extremes. I could not eat a snowball of ricotta, so I must have no ricotta. One chocolate would mean never stopping eating chocolate. If I am not skeletal, I must be obese. I know these are rash leaps of logic, that I am not being sensible. There are happy mediums. What is there between Campi's ricotta and no ricotta?

A half-spoon of ricotta in a courgette flower. A white bud of ricotta on late-summer figs. A catch-up supper of butternut squash and soft ricotta baked in one of Olivia's Stockwell lasagnes. I am learning by degrees to eat rich things, sweet things. Finding confidence that one taste of ricotta is not the first slip on the slope to Campi gluttony. The more I look at Campi's four *mangiatori di ricotta*, the more a dissenting, excited voice pipes to be heard. You must admit, it says, they are enjoying themselves. You must admit, it looks like fun.

8

'A very valiant trencherman'

The Ricotta-Eaters are trenchermen. No opportunity lost, no spoon left behind. Campi catches them – catches himself – at it. They've hardly yet made a dent in the ricotta mound. You do not doubt for a moment that they'll do it: finish the cheese between four. One of them, I'd put a bet on it, will lick the plate clean and fall asleep with the ladle in his mouth to dream strange whey dreams.

'He is a very valiant trencherman,' says Beatrice about her once and future lover Benedick in *Much Ado About Nothing*, 'he hath an excellent stomach.' She says it with some asperity, with raised eyebrows. Men may prize their stomachs if it amuses them. When I read of trenchermen – and women – or them on gallery walls, it is with some awe and not a little disbelief. When Mary Frances Fisher has her lunch by the watermill or the ricotta-eaters scoop drifts of white cheese, I think: very clever, most ingenious. But how was it done? Where was the sleight of hand? Where did they put it all?

Trencherman eating is like a conjuring trick. The card disappears up a sleeve. The rabbit trembles in the false top of a hat. The sequinned assistant escapes the three-sword-box through a trapdoor. They cannot really have eaten it. There has been some trick. It was there on the supper table

. . . and now it is gone. You don't mean to tell me they actually swallowed it?

When I have given others a potted summary of this book – reading as a cure, meals from the page – the response has been largely a chop-licking one. Eyes light with trencher greed. They start to give their fantasy dinner-party lists of gourmandising authors and their hungry creations. But of course you have read Parson Woodforde? But of course you know Trimalchio? But of course Gargantua and Pantagruel? But of course Pickwick and Proust?

A confession: I have not read Proust. He's on the list, the long list of books to be read, but other authors, pushier authors, always edge in front. I know the much-anthologised *petites madeleines* passage with its *décoction* of lime-blossom tea. But I cannot pretend to any profound madeleine moments. I have only once eaten madeleines and they came from the oven of a restaurant on Commercial Street between Spitalfields market and Brick Lane. My *petites madeleines*, fluted and scalloped like pilgrim's shells, were Cockneys.

As for the others, I have been working my way through them, course by course. The man who was all praise for Parson Woodforde, eating a full English breakfast with teak-stain tea as he made his recommendation, was insistent. I could not write about appetite without having read about the Parson and his table.

James Woodforde is a very different sort of churchman to the praline-fearing Monsieur Reynaud. Woodforde, a curate in Somerset and then Norfolk, and a lifelong diary-writer, is a clergyman with a modest interest in his parish and an immoderate interest in his supper. The diaries open in 1758, when Woodforde was eighteen. He kept them until

October 1802, three months before his death. They start
reasonably enough: 'Our entertainment was thus, one Lobster of a Pound, a half-pennyworth of Bread, and the same of
Cheese, half of an Old Bottle of Ale, Half a Bottle of Wine,
and a Bottle of Lisbon.' That is May 1760. As the years go
on, as his collar and cassock stretch tighter, the lunches and
suppers take up more and more space on the page:

*{October 1770}: I gave them for dinner a dish of fine Tench,
which I caught out of my brothers Pond in Pond Close this
morning, Ham, and 3 Fowls boiled, a Plum Pudding, a
couple of Ducks roasted, a roasted neck of Pork, a Plumb
Tart and an Apple Tart, Pears, Apples and Nutts; White
Wine and red, Beer and Cyder. Coffee and Tea.*

*{January 1780}: We had for dinner a Calf's Head, boiled
Fowl and Tongue, a Saddle of Mutton, rosted on the Side
Table, a fine Swan rosted with Currant Jelly Sauce for the
first Course. The Second Course a couple of Wild Fowl called
Dun Fowls, Larks, Blamange, Tarts etc. etc. and a good
Desert of Fruit after amongst which was a Damson Cheese.
I never eat a bit of a Swan before, and I think it good eating
with sweet sauce.*

*{March 1795}: We gave them for Dinner a Couple of boiled
Chicken and Pigs Face, very good Peas Soup, a boiled Rump
of Beef very fine, a prodigious fine, large and very fat Cock-
Turkey rosted, Maccaroni, Batter Custard Pudding with
Jelly, Apple Fritters, Tarts and Raspberry Puffs. Desert,
baked Apple, nice Nonpareils, brandy Cherries and Filberts.
Wines, Port & Sherries, Malt Liquors, Strong Beer, bottled
Porter &c.*

The last words of his last diary entry – 17 October 1802 – when he was sixty-two and increasingly unwell, were these: 'Dinner to day, Rost beef &c.' He protested that he had lost his appetite, but to outsiders it sounds robust to the end.

He suffered, though, for his codlings and calf's pluck, wigeon and bullock's heart, frilled oysters and roast ox. From time to time there would be a violent pain in his great toe – a warning of an imminent attack of gout, bad enough to leave him hobbling. It was very much the age of gouty pains. James Gillray published his cartoon *The Gout* – a fire-breathing beastie clamped to the swollen foot of a sufferer – in 1799. This was the same year that Parson Woodforde attended the annual Tithe Banquet and recorded: 'Two Legs of Mutton boiled & Capers, Salt-Fish, a Sur-Loin of Beef rosted, with plenty of plumb & plain Puddings &c.'

He is often dyspeptic, his insides uncomfortably disarranged, and on one occasion he gives himself a violent attack of the 'Hickupps' by laughing too much over a dinner of mackerel, boiled chicken, bacon, neck of roast pork and hot gooseberry pie. He puts his hopes in home remedies: stewed and strained rhubarb before going to bed, cleansing cucumbers, a rind of alder stick steeped in hot water. He introduced a system of fines, like a modern swear jar – a shilling a time – to be paid when he overdid it on giblet pie and flummery.

I read the Woodforde Diaries (in my notebook I have several times written 'Parson Woodcock', all that game having gone to my head) with a half-frown, not a critical one, more incredulous. It was so offal-y, so boiled and sweetbreaded, so improbable that any man or woman could eat like that. Sometimes even the Parson gets bored with it. Entries trail off into etceteras and ellipses: 'We had for dinner a Breast of Veal ragouted, a fine Piece of boiled beef, a Pidgeon Pye, Custards, Puffs, and some Lemon Cream. For Supper, a young Chicken, cold tongue etc.'

Reading Woodforde, I felt like an explorer in a straw hat and linen suit parting the vines for a glimpse of a last surviving member of a distant, lost-world tribe: 'The Eighteenth-Century Parson-Trencherman at Table. Now Extinct.' There was a part of me that wanted to disapprove of a man who could write: 'Before we went to Church there was Chocolate and Toast and Cake with red wine and white,' and an hour later, 'After our return from Church we had Cake and Wine and Chocolate and dried Toast carried round.' But I couldn't summon the old outrage. My lips just wouldn't purse.

His is not a lonely, self-indulgent greed. The supper words that appear most frequently in his diary are not custard or jelly or veal, but 'merry', 'gave', 'treated'. 'We were very merry,' he remembers of one port-and-madeira supper, 'and pushed the bottle on very briskly.' He begins his long dinner lists: 'I gave my company . . .' He treats friends to dinner at the Bear Inn in Dropping Lane. He treats family, friends, servants, parishioners, and the poor children of the parish. He treats right, left and centre.

Parson Woodforde's most distinctive characteristic is not his gluttony but his generosity. Greed is tempered by the desire to share. On a trip to London with friends and family he writes: 'After regaling ourselves with chocolate &c. we then walked to the Shakespeare Gallery filled with beautiful Paintings. We afterwards went to the Poets Gallery filled also with fine Pictures.' Chocolate, friends, gallery-hopping. I copied the Parson's day out in my note-book, highlighted 'chocolate', drew a circle around it and put an asterisk in the margin. I'm still thinking about it.

The next one was: but of course you know Trimalchio? I didn't. I bluffed, though, and said: 'Of course,' and sprinted to the library to mug up. Trimalchio does give dinners, he does treat his guests, but no one is merry as they are at the Parsonage. Trimalchio, the nouveau-riche lout of Petronius's *Satyricon*, doesn't give dinners to be convivial, only to show off. His Roman guests could never say, as Woodforde does after the Tithe Banquet, 'everything harmonious and agreeable', or 'all well pleased and merry'. Our fly-on-the-wall narrator at Trimalchio's feast admits that when the last dish of the evening is brought in – what looks like a fat goose surrounded by every kind of fish and bird, all sculpted from minced pork – the assembly conclude that death by starvation would be preferable.

Woodforde's suppers may be massive, but they are honest, till-the-soil suppers. Cucumbers from his own frames, tench from his brother's pond, melons brought by his neighbour Mr Custance with a note to say that Mrs Custance had that morning at two o'clock been safely de-livered of another son.

Trimalchio's brag-banquets are something else. The entrée arrives on the back of a donkey made of Corinthian bronze. Soldered silver dishes carry dormice dipped in honey and poppy seeds and plates of ripe plums and pom-egranate seeds. The meal is gimcrack and riddles. Peahen's eggs contain whole, plump little fig-pecker birds dipped in peppered egg yolk. A hare is given wings to make it a Pegasus. A roast boar suckles pastry piglets. Cakes squirt staining yellow saffron juice when touched. Tiny pastry thrushes are stuffed with raisins and nuts and served for pudding. Quinces are pierced with thorns to look like sea urchins. Trimalchio is ringmaster of this supper-circus. He arrives wearing his dressing gown, clinking with gold and ivory bangles. He hacks at his teeth with a silver tooth-pick, swears, makes jokes about the chamber pots in the corridor. He may have money, but he's an oik, and noth-ing, no amount of Roman silverware, could persuade me to have a meal with such a man.

I had the same feeling about the giants Gargantua and Pantagruel. 'Most noble boozers . . .' begins Rabelais, wel-coming readers in his author's prologue. Gargantua is born under a greedy star. Hours before his birth, his mother, the giantess Gargamelle, eats more *godebillios* than any woman, even a giant one, can safely stomach. *Godebillios* are the fatty tripes of *coiros* – oxen fattened on meadow grass. The infant Gargantua does not mew and cry as a baby should, but bawls 'Drink! Drink! Drink!' and is suckled by 17,913 cows. By the time he is ten months old he has eighteen chins. Pantagruel, Gargantua's son, eats whole bears as if they were no more a meal than a chicken. At university he borrows books from the library with titles such as *The Goad of Wine*, *The Gluttons' Cavity*, *The Fat Paunch of the Presidents* and *Of Peas and Bacon.* I tried, I really did, to like Gargantua and Pantagruel, to want them at my dinner parties, but the book is too slobbering and I am too prim. As I read, I thought to myself too much, too much, and, eventually, *enough*.

I suppose what I was doing in reading these trencher books was testing my limits. Yes, I had an interest now in food writing. Yes, I wanted to know who these giants of literary feasting were. But I could not admire feasting for feasting's sake, of eating until one's body was heaving and crop-sick.

Mary Frances Fisher had nominated Rabelais among her heroes, imagining his ghost haunting the dining room of the *Trois Faisans* at Dijon and ordering the nine-course *dîner de luxe au prix fixe*. But neither Fisher nor Elizabeth David is obscene or vulgar. They do not forget their table manners or belch with Gargantuan satisfaction. There is always a sense of respect for food: the effort that goes into planning and shopping, washing and dicing, sweating an onion, skimming the top off a *rouille*. When they sit down to eat it is as if they say a grace, not to God, but to the chef. There is nothing of that pause and contemplation with Trimalchio or the giants of Rabelais, only a rush to swill and scoff and wipe greasy lips on the tablecloths.

Trimalchio, Gargantua and Pantagruel I had struck off my dinner-party list. The Parson I had found very merry. Proust I still have not read. That left Pickwick, the last guest at the table.

I had a guilty sort of feeling about Mr Pickwick, as if I had not given him a fair trial. *Pickwick Papers* was the book I had enjoyed least in the year of Dickens. In many ways it was wasted on me. After 600 pages, I wanted to leave *Pickwick* to unbuckle its belt and sleep things off by the fire. I had, I'm afraid, lost interest in the Pickwick Club – Mr Pickwick, Mr Winkle, Mr Tupman, Mr Snodgrass and honorary member Sam Weller – barrelling from inn to inn on their lads-on-tour trip around England. I had had enough of their eating, drinking, napping, duelling, bedroom-farcing and cod-fish-wrangling.

But, as I say, wasted on me. The fault was mine and not *Pickwick*'s. It was my failings that make me resist the book's bumpers and hampers, toasts and wassails, punches and brandies, hot pineapple rums and endless etceteras. The Pickwickians, like Parson Woodforde, are great ones for etceteras. I don't think I can have drunk in my whole life what a Pickwick Club member would put away in an evening. At university, once a term, I'd try a glass of cider, feel briefly chipper, then get a headache and go to bed. Later, at leaving parties for newspaper colleagues I'd venture a Bellini, be happy enough for a quarter of an hour, before the familiar headache and home to bed.

I've rather given up now. I do wonder if I'm missing something. It gives others such pleasure. 'Uproarious was the mirth of the round table,' we hear of the Pickwick Club at Christmas. 'Long after the ladies had retired, did the hot elder wine, well-qualified with brandy and spice, go round, and round, and round again; and sound was the sleep, and pleasant were the dreams that followed.' Mr Winkle dreams of Miss Arabella and her winter boots with fur round the tops.

Having taken against Mr Pickwick first time around, when others started telling me he was their veal-eating, ale-swilling literary hero I tried him again. I liked the Club – 'as brisk as bees, if not altogether as light as fairies' – more on their second outing. I was so much better in my mind, so much more tolerant of food and festivity. This time I could smile at the Fat Boy, cheeks quivering like blancmange, seated in Jack Horner majesty in a corner and devouring a Christmas pie. I warmed to the snackish Mr Bob Sawyer, who cannot pass a roadside hostelry without stopping:

'I say, we're going to dine here, aren't we?' said Bob looking in at the window.

'Dine!' said Mr Pickwick. 'Why, we have only come nineteen miles, and have got eighty-seven and a half to go.'

'Just the reason why we should take something to enable us to bear up against the fatigue.'

I am grateful to the friends who sent me back to the book. It made me realise how much my thoughts had changed in the four years since I'd first read *Pickwick*. I was not only more forgiving of the travelling party and their pies and oysters and whole, huge cod-fish, but I realised that I also no longer inwardly tutted at friends for cinema popcorn or bags of Maltesers or burgers and chips. Far from reproaching Pickwick tendencies, I wanted to applaud them in others. Better Pickwick bonhomie than mineral-water-and-chia-seed nicety. Dickens takes a very dim view of the lawyer Mr Fogg, who has brought a case against Mr Pickwick: 'An elderly pimply-faced, vegetable-diet sort of man.' More and more, I am on the side of the Pickwicks over the Pimples.

Perhaps the distinction is between ordinary greediness – Parson Woodforde, Mr Pickwick, Mary Frances Fisher – and the extraordinary greediness, the diabolical greediness of Trimalchio, Gargantua and Pantagruel. The difference between eating with gusto, with bold knife and fork, with friends, and eating grossly, rudely, obscenely. I once thought that to eat anything at all was to be Gargantuan. Now I see the Pickwick side of things: liking food, looking forward to it. I am heartened by the Club's walk on a frosty, bracing evening, driven on by the supper comforts that await them, and feeling so light of heart that, at any moment, Mr Tupman might challenge Mr Pickwick to a game of leapfrog in the snow.

Overwhelmingly, it was men who recommended these books. Women were more inclined to make pitches for the *manon blancs* of *Chocolat*, or for Jane Austen's picnic of strawberries on Box Hill in *Emma*, or for F. Scott Fitzgerald's *Great Gatsby*. They reminisced, as if they had been there, about parties at Gatsby's: the crates of oranges for squeezing, the harlequin salads, the lemon cakes from the delicatessen. It says something about men and women and the foods we expect them to eat that while the men were for whole roast ox and spitted boar, the women were for marzipan, orange juice, salads and drizzle cakes.

In Virginia Woolf's *Orlando*, there is a scene soon after Orlando has become a woman when she is offered a slice of corned beef by the captain of the ship taking her back to England. 'A little of the fat, Ma'am?' he asks. 'Let me cut you just the tiniest little slice the size of your finger nails.' There were never such endearments when Orlando was a man. 'Well, she would, if he wished it,' Orlando agrees, 'have the very thinnest, smallest shiver in the world.'

Why should women eat like this? Why should they be helped to the tiniest, thinnest, smallest shivers of food and blush for daring – so bold, so forward, so sluttish – to want more than teaspoons and *soupçons*? Why is a man's appetite valiant and a woman's a shock and scandal? Why was I so surprised by Mary Francis Fisher and Elizabeth David? Women who eat, cook, drink, lay down wine, call for more, shout: 'Another glass!', stretch for the cream, help themselves, who write about appetite without shame or apology. Orlando, left to her own devices, unlaced from crinoline bondage, eats like a man: 'She cut herself a slice of bread and ham, clapped the two together and began to eat, striding up and down the room . . . After five or six such turns, she tossed off a glass of red Spanish wine.' Three cheers for Orlando, you want to shout, and down with corsets.

They meant to be helpful, the men who championed Trimalchio and Gargantua. But they had misunderstood – perhaps I had not explained it well enough – what reading had done for me. They imagined the books on my shelves turning me from timorous mouse, afraid of a rind-paring of cheese, into a great snake – a 'boa constructor', as Sam Weller calls the Fat Boy in *Pickwick Papers* – capable of swallowing a herd in one gulp.

It was never my ambition to be a Pickwick. When I started reading Dickens, I had no certain aim in mind. I wanted to mark the anniversary, tick off the novels, fill a gap in my knowledge. I read because I'd always read, and stealthily, at first without my realising, the books I read found a place in my mind's book room. It started with single words, copied onto scraps of paper, pressed between the leaves of the books: jorum, pottle, dixy, zestfully, twist. Then came whole scenes that, weeks after finishing a book, were begging, badgering to be recreated: the Cratchits' Christmas pudding, Robert Graves' S'nice S'mince S'pies, Sherston's boiled eggs.

I didn't want to recline, comatose, in front of a peacock made out of pork at Trimalchio's banquet, or to eat until I was gouty, red-faced, beyond the help of rhubarb, straining the buttons of my waistcoat. I wanted to be eating on the march with Laurie and Paddy or up in a church tower with Tom Birkin. Pacing the room with one of Orlando's ham sandwiches. I wanted to cook with guts and dash and skirlings of butter with Mary Frances Fisher and Elizabeth David. To make a new sort of life for myself, as Virginia Woolf did, of mushrooms on toast, reading, writing and walking. I wanted to recover some of my childhood relish in eating. Relish, that was it. Not Rabelesian, Trimalchian greed.

In the year that I read the war poets, I also read the *Memoirs* of the eighteenth-century engraver Thomas Bewick, known for his folios of cuckoos, larks and cormorants, so lifelike they might leave feathers between the pages. Edmund Blunden, a literary journalist and academic after the war, had written an introduction to the book and it was this that put me on to him. Bewick remembers working on the family's allotment as a boy in the 1760s and being sent out to the fields by his father all day. 'Very hungry work,' he wrote, 'and often made me think dinner was long in coming, & when, at last, it was sent to me, be what it would I sat down on the lown side of a hedge & eat it with a relish that needed no Sauce.'

A relish that needed no Sauce with a capital S. This was the relish I was searching for, not relish that comes from salt or pepper, mustard or mayonnaise, pickles or gravy, or Heinz Tomato Ketchup. The relish is all Bewick's. It comes from his own appetite, sharpened by exercise and air. It is a relish made by his hungry mind and stomach. He doesn't tell us what was sent for his midday meal, eaten in the lee of a hedge. It doesn't matter. At least it doesn't matter to me. The emotion, the looking forward to, the relish in eating is what has stayed in my mind. What I have found in reading isn't a dictionary of foodstuffs – A is for apple amber, B is for beautiful soup, C is for cheese on toast – but a whole library of reasons to eat, share, live, to want to be well.

Mutton chops to cheer a downcast heart. Plum pudding – 'Oh, a wonderful pudding!' – for Christmas, for family, for fireworks of steam and flaming brandy. Boiled eggs for zestful mornings. Frizzled bacon to keep you fighting. Mackintosh toffees for brothers-in-arms. A Yorkshire pudding to give a man hope again. A gleaming trumpet of golden couscous with an oldest friend. Beef broth to cure the flu. Saffron buns on Cornish holidays. Blackcurrant cake to be wick and strong. Cherries to set the brain whirring. Cheese toasts for hill-climbing. Golden Syrup to make you roar.

Reading has also given me spells to say under my breath, charms against Jabberwock voices. Galoshes. Courage. Good Supper. Strong Tea. Learn something. Learn how the world works and what wags it. On.

Epilogue

'The only thing that never fails'

A long illness. I was thirteen when it started. Fifteen when Mum took me to the doctor. There were steps in the right direction. Ground gained and lost. Better days and worse. Relapses and braver beginnings. Now, at thirty, I am an almost-trencherman. Not quite there, but trying.

As a teenager I had held up fashion models as my idols, pinned their photos to my walls and counted the ribs that could be seen through silk slips. Now I fill the flat with books that say: 'Come dine with us.' They offer a thousand invitations: a chophouse supper, a Mont St Michel omelette, a river picnic. When the old voices return and I feel I cannot eat, I know reading will help. For here is Claudia Roden simmering a *ragù* sauce *'da sole a sole'* – from dawn till dusk – and spiking her dishes with hot red chillies called *diavolilli* – little devils. And here is the gamekeeper Mellors offering Lady Chatterley a lunch of boiled ham and pickled walnuts with the appeal: 'Shall t'eat a smite o'summat, if I bring it thee?'

I don't think I'll ever be rid of them completely, the voices that say you are worthless, you have no right to eat, you don't deserve a life. There will be things that will call them back, disappointment, heartbreak, grief. They will crowd at the book-room door and call and taunt, beat

Jabberwock wings against the wood. I will have to shore
up the door, stopper the keyhole and say: there is no place
for you here. It is my book room, my mind. You are not
welcome. There is no room for you among the novels. Nor
in biography. Those shelves are full. No space among the
art books, I have propped postcards in all the gaps on
the shelves. There is not an inch to spare on the history
shelves or among the recipe books.

I have covered the tables in paperweights and notebooks.
Put busts of Dickens and Woolf on the windowsills. Hung
prints of Bewick's birds and Monet's *galettes* and Renoir's
Tasse de Chocolat and William Nicholson's mushrooms and
Lely's and Kneller's court beauties and Stanley Spencer's
leaping bacon on every spare inch of wall. Beatrix Potter's
Dream of Toasted Cheese is framed above the mantelpiece.
Better that than a mirror. So there is no room. No place for
a Jabberwock.

Writing this book has been a release, a catharsis. A
wrench at times, sad, and painful, but a release more than
anything. There have been thoughts I have been able to
express in writing that I've never been able to say out loud.
I don't think I'd understood them until I came to write
them here. Writing has made sense of an illness that takes
much of its power from nonsense. Anorexia destroys your
sense of reason. It thrives on looking-glass logic. It up-ends
your thoughts, turns bone into flesh, makes life unlivable,
death seem glorious. What you see and hear are not real;
but how real they look, how real they sound.

I hope it is a book that will give courage to anyone
whose mind has ever been more enemy than friend, who
has found that depression, exhaustion, hopelessness con-
spire against them. It was a solace to me to have Dickens

write: I could not sleep. And Woolf: I was mad. These are not easy things to say. We like to keep up appearances as far as we can, to smile, to make ourselves useful, to put on a brave face.

What has given me the most difficulty has been to say: I have heard voices. I have read back over paragraphs just written and thought: shall I cut it, soften it, not reveal so much of myself? I have hovered the cursor over these paragraphs and felt my fingers twitch for the delete key. Better, I think, to be honest. One of the challenges of being ill is the feeling that you are a freak. Why am I laid low by noise in my head, ghouls that no one else can hear? But other people do hear such voices, their own Jabberwocks, different in each case, the noise getting louder at times of crisis or depression and illness.

When I came to read Virginia Woolf, it marked the difference between feeling a coward and failure because I let myself be bullied by these voices, and drawing strength from knowing that others have had their demons, their galloping horses, their aches low down in the back of the head. Better to write about these things, then say: it is not a life sentence. It will not always be like this. When you hear nothing but Bedlam noise, do not believe you will never be quiet.

I remember one night, in the first months after diagnosis, taking the shoes out from the bottom of my wardrobe and getting in under the bottom shelf and shutting the doors because I thought I could shut out the noise. I remember lying in the dark and crying because the voices would not be shut out, had followed me in, because they were in my head and nothing would drive them off. I cried until I was sick, the voices howling louder and louder. It

seemed then that they would always win. If you had pulled
me out from my hiding place and dusted me down and
said: you are losing the battle now, no doubt about it, but
you're going to win the war. If you had said that, I would
have thought you were the mad one. I would not have believed it, and I did not want to go on if all the future had
for me was noise.

It is now nearly fifteen years later, and I do not cower
in dark corners. Then, I was never quiet, never alone for a
minute. The only escape was sleep – and I could not sleep.
Now, days, weeks, months go by and my mind is my own.
This is what is so hard to understand about anorexia, what
makes recovery so long. It is not a battle about thin and
fat, eating and not eating. Those are the things that obsess
you, distract you, but the fight is for quiet, for having your
mind to yourself again, wrested from Jabberwock noise.
More than any new potato, it is this quiet that makes me
shout: 'O frabjous day! Callooh! Callay!'

I want a life and a future. I want to make plans. I buy
travel books and ask: where next? Japan to walk the pil-
grimage paths. Hastings to see the sea. I remind myself
that if I am going to travel, I am going to have to eat. No
cereal bars, no niminy-piminy fear. I'm still on the hunt
for Robert Graves's Carlsbad plums to eat at the top of a
mountain.

I pull more books from the shelves. I limber up. I read
Kakuzo Okakura's *Book of Tea*. Okakura writes of the man
who 'has no tea in him', that is, the man who is weak,
insipid, humourless. A man needs strong tea in his veins
– Japanese Samurai and tiger-hunting schoolboys alike. I
read, too, the diary of a cook and travel writer. He writes
of epicure breakfasts quite unlike porridge mornings at

home, of *shiro*, *enoki*, *kabocha*, *tarako* and *shichimi togarashi*. I say to myself: 'The names are entrancing.'

If it is Hastings in December, that calls for fish'n'chips behind a windbreak. Here I have Davey Copperfield for my model. In the Peggotys' ship-house he dines 'in a sumptuous manner off boiled dabs, melted butter, and potatoes'. The fish are small and bony, the potatoes are burnt, but he is safe and warm and welcome and no boy ever dined so gladly. Fish and chips it is then, sumptuous ones. And mushy peas.

Since I am determined to be honest, I must be honest, too, that there are still bad days and bad weeks. I'll have a good run, days of skipping, hopscotch energy, my mind my own, the world mine for the walking. Then I'll overdo it, grind my mind and body down with hours of work, too little sleep, a supper that is not quite good enough. I let myself get tired and hungry, let the pins and needles start. That's the warning. And if I don't take notice of it, the voices come next. Quiet turns to jabber.

When I am sieged by noise I forget why I ever wanted to travel, why leave the house, why eat, why go on. It is then very difficult to see how I can bear to live in a body that will make demands every day, three times a day for food. How will I eat meal after meal, year after year, when starving seems so much easier? At such times, the future looks a long, old slog and I worry that my boots are not up to it. But the only way to know is to try. Boots, courage, on.

In writing this book, I want to say both that is possible to get better from an illness, to make for yourself a life worth living, but also that there will be days when it seems impossible. There will be times when you think: I cannot sleep, I cannot eat, I cannot hear myself think. I cannot remember how to be happy. I cannot keep going.

I say: keep going.

I can't tell you to go away and read my books, borrow my pair of galoshes, fill the kettle for a cup of my blend of strong tea. If you are to pull your boots out of the mire of depression, or anorexia, or any other head illness or heart sickness, you have to do it your own way. I only say that it is possible, not that I have the cure, the cold compress for anyone and everyone who is struggling.

If you remember the words of only one person in this book, let it be Merlyn. Learn something. It is the best medicine. It is the only thing that never fails. In my case that has meant reading, most of all. Galleries and church-haunting, too. But it needn't be book-learning, it might be a language, an instrument, the names of wildflowers, the calls of town-garden birds, fifty years of county cricket scores, or how to make bread, mix watercolours, thread a needle, anything that takes you out of yourself. That is the real magic, not Merlyn's mustard-pot sorcery.

My illness has been a particular one, an extreme one. My anxiety about food, eating, my body is more exaggerated, more distorted than most. I am troubled, though, by what strikes me as a wider set of fears about food. Every newspaper, every magazine, every blog and recipe book has its philosophy of how we should eat. Each of them contradicts the other. Each is more extreme, more absurd, more fad-dish, more tub-thumping than the last.

We in the West have never been so fat. We are whales. We are monsters. We are in crisis. The health service cannot hold. Obesity is an epidemic. Diabetes will ruin us. We must weigh and shame. We must have gastric bands.

We must have a sugar tax. We must punish the supermarkets, fine the manufacturers, banish sweets at the tills.

We do an about-turn. Our daughters have never been thinner, nor more unhappy. We fear for skinny teenagers. We deplore the actress who cannot pinch an inch and the fashion girls who say that nothing tastes as good as skinny feels. We call for catwalk models to be checked and measured. We demand 'real women', condemn air-brushing, thigh gaps, size zero and thinspiration.

We say: wear a pedometer. Walk 10,000 steps a day. Walk 20,000 steps. Walk 25,000 steps. Jog. Sprint. Sign up for a marathon, a triathalon, an iron man. Prove yourself a Tough Mudder. Get up early for bootcamp. Get your money's worth at the gym. Swim, spin, step, but do not eat afterwards. Do not undo the calories-burnt good you have done. We say: drink isotonic, drink hypotonic, drink hypertonic water. Drink coconut water. Drink protein shakes. Drink two litres a day. Drink for hydration. Drink for long life. Hydrate, refresh, repeat.

Juice. Don't juice. Eat five a day. Eat kale. Eat quinoa. Eat clean. Eat lean. Eat green. Eat local. Eat organic. Eat biodynamic. Eat vegan. Eat for wellness. Eat superfoods for superhealth. Watch your weight. Fast two days in every seven. Eat nothing after five p.m. Chew, chew and chew again. Eat on a smaller plate. Eat with a smaller spoon. Say no to carbs. Go dairy-free. Go gluten-free. Go sugar-free. Go half mad with guilt with every bite.

This is lunatic eating.

We are so confused about food. I look at the shelves and I see not recipe books but collections of the bizarre. Each page is like a sideshow at an Edwardian circus, except that instead of the Siamese Twins, the Strong Man, the

Bearded Lady, you have the cake with no wheat or sugar, the immune-boost turmeric smoothie, the courgette dolled up as linguine. This isn't food, this is freakery. The emphasis is all askew. Instead of agonising about what we eat, stretching ourselves on racks of calories, sugar and fats, we might think about why we eat, when we eat, where we eat and who we eat with.

Eat with relish. Eat cold cherry tart after cricket. Eat a gipsy stew to make you strong. Eat an hegg in a posset to nurse a cold. Eat haystacks of buttered toast when there is company for tea. Eat up to your knees in the waves on holiday. Eat sardines and sausages for winter carols. Eat stir-fries with new friends and steamed dumplings with old. Eat ice creams on high stools. Eat with others. Munch, treat, share, be merry. Talk with your mouth full if the talk is good. Splice the last rasher of bacon between two. Eat buttered rolls on top of hayricks. Drink cider under them with Rosie, if she's willing.

When I read of 'mindful eating', that is, really concentrating, meditating on every bite, I wonder if it isn't better to grab and dodge and pass and snatch with Laurie Lee and his brothers and sisters like kitchen pelicans. To help yourself to absent-minded bread and cheese, up on a scaffold, absorbed in your work.

Try not to turn eating into a solitary pursuit, a private communion with an irritable bowel and neurotic digestion. Don't make a Marshalsea prison of rules for yourself – no biscuits at tea, no meat in the week, no pudding, not ever. Don't trap yourself in lonely habits. Don't be Amy Dorrit alone at the mantelpiece when you might be Pickwick dividing veal pie between friends.

I say this not because I have mastered all these don'ts

and dos, but because I have to remind myself of them at every meal of every day. If I forget my better rules, neglect them, allow hungry, lonely eating to take hold, there is a solution: back to my books to remind myself how I must try to eat. I have bad habits still. I will turn down an invitation to dinner if it means I can have soup at home. I take fright at some puddings and leave others to their cheese. I am no further along with chocolate. But I keep reading and finding new encouragements to eat, because friendship, company, chatter and good suppers are worth having.

What makes anorexia such a dangerous illness, so difficult to treat, is that it isolates you. It makes you believe that no one minds you if you starve and waste yourself, no one would miss you if there were an empty place at the table. If I am well enough to have written this book it is because people did care, did mind, did convince me that I would be missed if I was not there for the opening of the bottle, the lighting of the candles, the cutting of the cake. I owe much to Dickens and Woolf and Laurie and Paddy and every writer in these pages. But I owe more still to family and to friends who have shared meals with me and coaxed and chivvied and distracted me from my nerves with jokes and gossip and plans and games.

Not all of my friends knew I had been ill. Those I met at university and after, I met when I was well enough to put on a good show. When Adam, who had bought the Prussian-blue egg cups, took me for lunch in the East End and ordered Cockney madeleines he did not know as he nagged and jostled me to try one. 'The best!' he said. 'You can't not!' And so I did. He had five and I had one and it was a wonderful one and he was right to have jostled.

When Hermione invited me for a Freshers' stir-fry

supper she did not know what she had done for me. She
ended a week of eating oatcakes alone in my room. What
sizzled from that wok was more than prawns and noodles
and cut red peppers, it was chatter, confidence, belonging. The others I met that night have remained among my
closest friends; they have taken me out for ice creams and
stood me barbecues and birthday dinners and a hundred, a
thousand, cups of strong tea.

I would never have eaten those Michaelmas chips if the
others from the paper had not been there, arguing the toss
of mayonnaise against ketchup, vinegar against salt. There
would never have been a first and second helping of golden
couscous if I had not had Camilla sitting with me. Never
steamed mushroom dumplings if Olivia had not suggested
Chinatown. Never Tess and her dairy if Katy had not added
her voice to Sherston's and said: 'When are you going to
read Hardy?'

I have had Andy's company at chicken-of-the-forest
dinners and for double-cheese toasties. He walked with
me for miles in the sun for saffron buns, and hours in the
rain for Yorkshire puddings. His invincible appetite for
life, walks, books, plays, scrambled eggs and buttered toast
have given me strength and great happiness. He has gone
uncomplainingly to Great Yarmouth and Broadstairs when
I was obsessed with Dickens, and St Ives and Sussex when it
was Virginia Woolf. He has had first, second and third
helpings of my cooking, and met kitchen triumphs and
disasters just the same. For him it is worth cooking with
life and bite and dash.

Always I have had Ed to remind me that I once ate with
complete freedom. That we swapped Rolos, and compared
the fatness of our Christmas stockings, and plotted Deaths

by Chocolate. Was I ever more content than reading my *Harry Potter* while Ed read his, each of us breaking our teeth on bars of Toblerone?

When I could not laugh I had Dad to bring me Molesworth. 'Hurra for the botany walk!' gave me hope when life seemed hopeless. He set me Dickens quizzes: which book Mr Turveydrop? What fate Mr Carker? Who gets their head stuck in the railings? He took me antique-shopping and together we found Bamboo plates and Grasshopper bowls. It was his copy of *The Once and Future King* that introduced me to Merlyn.

To Mum I owe everything. She took me to the doctor when I was starving and shouldered the whole burden of keeping me alive. She sat with me for meal after meal, for hours if that was what it took, and said: 'Eat a little more, eat enough to keep body and soul together.' She sent cereal bars to Italy, and drove bolognaise to the Fens. 'She worked out how it was with me': my awkward mind, my Jabberwock fears. She lent me her Patrick Leigh Fermors and Elizabeth Davids. She consulted on calvados and what to do with a hundred courgettes. Mum's minestrone, her roast chicken, her rhubarb crumble – there is a supper to restore your strength.

Anorexia tells you that you cannot eat, that you do not deserve, that you may not have or hope for. It tells you that you are worthless. Always it deals in nos and nots and nevers. It's a way of thinking that is hard to break.

I wrote that I could not have done as Laurie Lee did and eat feathery shrimps at the fish counters of Madrid, or rings of calamari, or belly of lamb. Craggy oysters – no. Fresh lobsters – no. Mussels – no. Snails – no. Squid – no.

I wrote that if a waiter had put before me a crock of whole roast kid and beans, I'd have run hell-for-boot-leather for the first boat back home.

No. Not. Never.

Between writing the fourth and fifth chapters of this book, I did go to Spain. To Segovia, Ávila, Salamanca, Madrid. In Segovia Andy ordered the proud local special *cochinillo asado* – roast suckling pig, snout, ears and all. I had a taste from his plate and a mouthful too of his pudding: *flan de crema pastelera* – custard flan. In Ávila he had *chuletón de ternera* – a steak as wide as the Meseta – and, emboldened by his choice, I ordered chorizo and *huevos flamencos* – the oil-spitting eggs Laurie had listened to with his head in his arms. In Salamanca, we waited for slices of Ibérico ham while the butcher told us in his best Spanglish that *Romeo and Juliet* had been filmed in the city: 'More beautiful, you see, than Verona.' We shared a great stew of roast kid and beans in the cave-like cellar of a restaurant and I did not run wailing for the boat.

All those nos, nots and nevers. Defeated one by one. Defeated because I had read Laurie and he had quickened my appetite. Defeated because I had someone there to eat and share with, to talk to about books we'd read and would read.

On our first morning in Segovia, hot in the sun, chilly in the shade, we went church-hunting. We took photographs of columns carved with herons and salamanders, baboons and wombats, and prophets with beards to their knees. We read about Knights Templar in our guidebooks, and dropped coins in boxes below painted martyrdoms. We sat on an outcrop below the Church of the Vera Cruz so that I could sketch, and we shared between us a *cruasán de almendra* – a custard croissant – stolen from the breakfast table and folded in a napkin.

Sitting there on that very blue morning eating pastry and custard and chatting and sketching the bell tower, I could almost hear the rock and clatter of a cart, could imagine the mules coming over the hill behind the church, rolling nearer and nearer, and giving up the first sight of a figure in the back. A boy from Gloucestershire, very sunburnt, very lean with walking and eating little but figs and goat's cheese. Beside him a violin, and in his hands carob pods, given by the driver, to tide him over until that night's supper, a good supper, of beans and mutton, eaten in a cloud of woodsmoke.

Acknowledgements

I would like to thank not only those who have brought this book into being, but also those who have knowingly and unknowingly helped my recovery, who have shared meals and walks, recommended books, and said: 'write!'

To my agent Will Francis, best of *consiglieri*. To Michael Steger and Kirsty Gordon at Janklow & Nesbit.

To Bea Hemming at Weidenfeld & Nicolson, who commissioned this book, and Holly Harley, who edited the manuscript with wit and grace. To Steve Marking, who designed this beautiful cover. To Virginia Woolstencroft, press mastermind. To Alex Mayland, who kept me going through seventeen hours of audiobook.

To Leaf Kalfayan, editor of editors. To Andrew Morrod, Andrew Yates, Neil Darbyshire, Simon Heffer, Heather McGlone, Sandra Parsons and Susie Dowdall. To Sophia Money-Coutts, Rachel Shields, Katherine Spenley, Emma Rowley, Jenny Coad, Alice-Azania Jarvis and Laura Pullman. To Jane Fryer, Jan Moir, Harry Mount, Christopher Stevens, Leo McKinstry, Quentin Letts and Tom Utley whose words, arriving at six o'clock, were a joy.

To the late Paul Carter. I never write a sentence without asking: 'What would P.C. say?'

To Neil Armstrong, stalwart friend.

To Guy Walters, Annabel Venning and Oliver Kamm

who introduced me to Will.

To Fraser Nelson, Freddy Gray, Mary Wakefield, Igor Toronyi-Lalic, Sam Leith, Camilla Swift, Lara Prendergast, Max Pemberton and Danielle Wall at the *Spectator* for wonderful, distracting commissions when chapter-writing weighed heavy.

To Daniel Johnson at *Standpoint* and Gail Pirkis and Hazel Wood at *Slightly Foxed.*

To Michael Stothard, Hugo Gye, Rob Peal, Anna Trench, Laurie Tuffrey and Emma Mustich for *Varsity*. To Dan Hitchens for early office mornings. To Zing Tsjeng, Paul Smith and Laurie again for Michaelmas chips in Market Square.

To all at Daunt on Marylebone High Street.

To Michael Gormley and Caroline Meindl.

To Camilla Fawcett for golden couscous. To Hermione Wace for first-court stir-fries. To Olivia Bright for Chinatown dumplings and Stockwell lasagnes. To Katy King for Thomas Hardy. To Adam Smith for Cockney madeleines. To Emma Hogan for endless encouragement.

To my parents Clara and Michael, and my brother Edward – this book is dedicated to you.

To Lorraine Jenks, for mince pies and so much else.

To Andy Ryan, the Invincible One.

Book Room Bibliography

Louisa May Alcott, *Little Women* (1868), Penguin Classics, 2009

Thomas Bewick, *Memoir*, Longman, Green, Longman and Roberts, 1862

Edmund Blunden, *Undertones of War* (1928), Penguin Modern Classics, 2010

Charlotte Brontë, *Jane Eyre* (1847), Penguin Classics, 2008

Emily Brontë, *Wuthering Heights* (1847), Penguin Classics, 2008

Craig Brown, *This is Craig Brown,* Ebury, 2003

Richard Carline, *Stanley Spencer At War*, Faber, 1978

J. L. Carr, *A Month in the Country* (1980), Penguin Classics, 2000

Lewis Carroll, *The Annotated Alice: Alice's Adventure In Wonderland and Through The Looking-Glass* (1865) *and What Alice Found There* (1872), ed. Martin Gardner, Penguin, 1970

Lisa Chaney, *Elizabeth David*, Macmillan, 1998

Susan Coolidge, *What Katy Did* (1872), Wordsworth Editions, 1994

Artemis Cooper, *Writing at the Kitchen Table: The Authorised Biography of Elizabeth David*, Michael Joseph, 1999

Patrick Leigh Fermor: An Adventure, John Murray, 2012

Alan Coren, *The Alan Coren Omnibus*, Robson Books, 1998

Charles Gibson Cowan, *The Voyage of the Evelyn Hope*, Cresset Press, 1946

Roald Dahl, *Charlie and the Chocolate Factory* (1964), Puffin, 1985

Matilda (1988), Puffin, 1989

Elizabeth David, *Spices, Salts and Aromatics in the English Kitchen*, Penguin, 1970

English Bread and Yeast Cookery, Penguin, 1977

An Omelette and a Glass of Wine, ed. Jill Norman, Penguin, 1986

Harvest of the Cold Months: The Social History of Ice and Ices, ed. Jill Norman, Michael Joseph, 1994

Is There a Nutmeg in the House?, ed. Jill Norman, Michael Joseph, 2000

Charles Dickens, *The Pickwick Papers* (1836), Penguin Classics, 2003

Oliver Twist (1837), Penguin Classics, 2009

Nicholas Nickleby (1838), Penguin Classics, 2003

The Old Curiosity Shop (1840), Penguin Classics, 2001

Barnaby Rudge (1841), Penguin Classics, 2012

Martin Chuzzlewit (1843), Penguin Classics, 2012

A Christmas Carol (1843), Penguin Classics, 2010

Dombey and Son (1846), Penguin Classics, 2012

David Copperfield (1849), Penguin Classics, 2014

Bleak House (1852), Penguin Classics, 2011

Hard Times (1854), Penguin Classics, 2011

Little Dorrit (1855), Penguin Classics, 2012

A Tale of Two Cities (1859), Penguin Classics, 2011

Great Expectations (1860), Penguin Classics, 2008

Our Mutual Friend (1864), Penguin Classics, 1997

The Mystery of Edwin Drood (1870), Penguin Classics, 2012

Gerald Durrell, *My Family and Other Animals* (1956), Penguin, 1976

M. F. K. Fisher, *As They Were*, Chatto & Windus, 1983
A Cordiall Water, Chatto & Windus, 1983
Consider the Oyster, North Point Press, 1988
Long Ago in France: The Years in Dijon, Touchstone, 1991
With Bold Knife and Fork, intr. Prue Leith, Vintage, 2001
Love in a Dish, ed. Anne Zimmerman, Penguin, 2011

F. Scott Fitzgerald, *This Side of Paradise* (1920), Penguin, 2010
The Great Gatsby (1926), Penguin, 2010

Mollie Gillen, *The Wheel of Things: A Biography of L. M. Montgomery, author of Anne of Green Gables*, Harrap, 1976

Victoria Glendinning, *Leonard Woolf: A Life*, Simon & Schuster, 2006

Kenneth Grahame, *The Wind in the Willows* (1908), Penguin Classics, 2005

Richard Perceval Graves, *Richard Hughes: A Biography*, Deutsch, 1994

Robert Graves, *Goodbye to All That* (1929), Penguin Modern Classics, 2000
I, Claudius (1934), Penguin, 1953

Valerie Grove, *The Lives and Loves of Laurie Lee* (1988), Robson Press, 2014

Thomas Hardy, *Tess of the D'Urbervilles* (1891), Penguin Classics, 2008

Joanne Harris, *Chocolat*, Doubleday, 1999

Frances Hodgson Burnett, *The Secret Garden* (1911), Heinemann, 1911

Penelope Hughes, *Richard Hughes: Author, Father*, Alan Sutton, 1984

Richard Hughes, *High Wind in Jamaica*, Chatto & Windus, 1929

  In the Lap of the Atlas: Stories of Morocco, Chatto & Windus, 1979

Richard Jefferies, *Bevis: The Story of a Boy*, Puffin, 1974

David Jones, *In Parenthesis* (1937), Faber & Faber, 1978

Jacob Kenedy and Caz Hildebrand, *The Geometry of Pasta*, Boxtree, 2010

Miles Kington, *Let's Parler Franglais!*, Penguin, 1983

  Let's Parler Franglais One More Temps, Penguin, 1984

D. H. Lawrence, *Lady Chatterley's Lover* (1928), Penguin Classics, 2009

Stephen Leacock, *Nonsense Novels* (1911), The Bodley Head, 1958

Hermione Lee, *Virginia Woolf* (1996), Vintage, 1997

Laurie Lee, *A Rose for Winter* (1955), Penguin, 1977

  Cider With Rosie (1959), Vintage, 2014

  As I Walked Out One Midsummer Morning (1969), Penguin Modern Classics, 2014

  A Moment of War (1991) Penguin Modern Classics, 2014

Patrick Leigh Fermor, *A Time to Keep Silence* (1953), John Murray, 2004

  Mani: Travels in the Southern Peloponneses (1958), John Murray, 2004

  Roumeli (1966), John Murray, 2004

  A Time of Gifts (1977), John Murray, 2013

  Between the Woods and the Water (1986), John Murray, 2005

  The Broken Road (2013), John Murray, 2014

C. S. Lewis, *The Lion, the Witch and the Wardrobe* (1950), Harper Collins, 1990

John Masefield, *The Box of Delights, Or, When the Wolves Were Running*, Heinemann, 1935

André Maurois, *Fattyputts and Thinnifers* (1930), Vintage, 2013

Alexander McCall Smith, *Portuguese Irregular Verbs*, Polygon, 2003

At the Villa of Reduced Circumstances, Polygon, 2003

The Finer Points of Sausage Dogs, Polygon, 2003

A. A. Milne, *Winnie-the-Pooh* (1926), Methuen, 1987

Nancy Mitford, *The Pursuit of Love* (1945), The Reprint Society, 1947

L. M. Montgomery, *Anne of Green Gables* (1908), George G. Harrap, 1929

Anne of Avonlea (1909), Vintage, 2013

Anne of the Island (1915), Harrap, 1943

The Alpine Path: The Story of My Career, Everywoman's World, 1917

Anne's House of Dreams (1917), Constable, 1917

Anne of Ingleside (1939), Harrap, 1946

Kakuzo Okakura, *The Book of Tea* (1906), ed. Christopher Benfy, Penguin Classics, 2010

George Orwell, *Keep the Aspidistra Flying* (1936), Penguin, 2014

Sylvie Patry and Anne Robbins, *Inventing Impressionism: Paul Durand-Ruel and the Modern Art Market*, The National Gallery Company, 2015

Petronius, *The Satyricon*, trans. P. G. Walsh, Clarendon Press, 1996

Eleanor H. Porter, *Pollyanna*, George G. Harrap, 1927

Beatrix Potter, *The Tailor of Gloucester* (1903), Frederick Warne, 2002

The Complete Tales, Frederick Warne, 2012

Antony Powell, *A Question of Upbringing* (1951), Fontana, 1980

Terry Pratchett, *Monstrous Regiment*, Doubleday, 2003

Rabelias, *Gargantua and Pantagruel* (1534, 1532), ed. J. M. Cohen, Penguin Classics, 1975

Arthur Ransome, *Swallows and Amazons* (1930), Red Fox, 2010

Joan Reardon, *M. F. K. Fisher: Poet of the Appetites*, North Point Press, 2004

Byron Rogers, *The Last Englishman: The Life of J. L. Carr*, Aurum Press, 2003

J. K. Rowling, *Harry Potter and the Philosopher's Stone*, Bloomsbury, 1997
Harry Potter and the Chamber of Secrets, Bloomsbury, 1998
Harry Potter and the Prisoner of Azkaban, Bloomsbury, 1999
Harry Potter and the Goblet of Fire, Bloomsbury, 2000
Harry Potter and the Order of the Phoenix, Bloomsbury, 2003
Harry Potter and the Half-Blood Prince, Bloomsbury, 2005
Harry Potter and the Deathly Hallows, Bloomsbury, 2007

Siegfried Sassoon, *Memoirs of a Fox-Hunting Man* (1928), Penguin Classics, 2013
Memoirs of an Infantry Officer (1930), Penguin Classics, 2013
Sherston's Progress (1936), Penguin Classics, 2013
The Old Century and Seven More Years, Faber, 1938
The Weald of Youth, Faber, 1942

Peter Sawbridge (ed.), *William Nicholson: Catalogue Raisonné of the Oil Paintings*, Modern Art Press, 2011

Will Self, *A Report to the Minister: Bushy Park*, Strange Attractor Press, 2009

George Bernard Shaw, *Pygmalion* (1913), Constable, 1925

Nigel Slater, *Tender Vol. I: A cook and his vegetable patch*, Fourth Estate, 2009

 A year of good eating: the kitchen diaries III, Fourth Estate, 2015

Frances Spalding, *Vanessa Bell* (1983), I. B. Tauris, 2016

Paul Stewart and Chris Riddell, *Beyond the Deepwoods*, Doubleday, 1998

 Stormchaser, Doubleday, 1999

 Midnight Over Santaphrax, Doubleday, 2000

Wallace Stevens, 'The Emperor of Ice Cream' (1922), in *The Collected Poems of Wallace Stevens*, Faber, 1955

R. L. Stevenson, *Kidnapped* (1886), Puffin, 1973

Anne Stevenson Hobbs, *Beatrix Potter: Artist and Illustrator*, Dulwich Picture Gallery, Frederick Warne, 2005

John Stuart Roberts, *Siegfried Sassoon*, Richard Cohen Books, 1999

Claudia Roden, *The Food of Italy: Region by Region*, Square Peg, 2014

Timothy Shy and Ronald Searle, *The Terror of St Trinian's*, Max Parrish, 1952

J. T. Smith, *Nollekens and his Times* (1828), Turnstile Press, 1949

R. S. Surtees, *Mr Sponge's Sporting Tour*, Evans Bradbury, 1852

Claire Tomalin, *Thomas Hardy: The Time-Torn Man*, Viking, 2006

 Charles Dickens: A Life, Viking, 2011

Mark Twain, *Huckleberry Finn* (1884), Oxford World's Classics, 2008

Evelyn Waugh, *Men at Arms* (1952), Penguin Classics, 2001

Officers and Gentlemen (1955), Penguin Classics, 2001

Unconditional Surrender (1961) Penguin Classics, 2001

Barry Webb, *Edmund Blunden: A Biography*, Yale University Press, 1990

Geoffrey Willans and Ronald Searle, *The Compleet Molesworth,* Parrish, 1958

T. H. White, *Mistress Masham's Repose* (1946), Jonathan Cape Ltd., 1947

The Once and Future King, (1958), Flamingo, 1984

P. G. Wodehouse, *Blandings Castle, and Elsewhere,* (1935) Herbert Jenkins, 1957

James Woodforde, *Diary of a Country Parson 1758–1803*, ed. John Beresford, Oxford University Press, 1949

Leonard Woolf, *Beginning Again: An Autobiography of the Years 1911–1918*, Hogarth Press, 1964

Virginia Woolf, *The Voyage Out* (1915), Vintage, 2004

Night and Day (1919), Vintage, 2000

Jacob's Room (1922), Vintage, 2004

Mrs Dalloway (1925), Penguin Classics, 2011

To the Lighthouse (1927), Vintage, 2004

A Room of One's Own (1928), Penguin Classics, 2014

Orlando: A Biography (1928), Penguin Classics, 2011

The Waves (1931), Oxford World's Classics, 2015

The Years (1937), Vintage, 2004

Flush (1933), Oxford World's Classics, 2009

Roger Fry: A Biography (1940), Vintage, 2003

Between the Acts (1941), Oxford World's Classics, 2008

A Haunted House (1944), Penguin, 1973

A Writer's Diary (1953), ed. Leonard Woolf, Persephone, 2011

The Diary of Virginia Woolf (five volumes), ed. Anne Olivier Bell, Penguin, 1981–1985

The Common Reader, Vintage Classics, 2003

The Common Reader: Second Series, Vintage Classics, 2003

Moments of Being: Unpublished Autobiographical Writing, ed. Jeanne Schulkind, Chatto & Windus for Sussex University Press, 1976

A Passionate Apprentice: The Early Journals 1897–1909, ed. Mitchell A. Leaska, Hogarth Press, 1990

Travels with Virginia Woolf, ed. Jan Morris, Pimlico, 1997

Selected Letters, ed. Joanne Trautmann Banks, Vintage, 2008

Selected Essays, Oxford World's Classics, 2009

The London Scene, intr. Hermione Lee, Daunt Books, 2013

Jenny Uglow, *Thomas Bewick: Nature's Engraver*, Faber, 2006

Copyright Acknowledgements

The author wishes to thank the following for their generosity in granting permission for copyright material to be printed in this book (see bibliography for full details of publication):

For quotations from Edmund Blunden, with permission of David Higham Associates, London on behalf of the Estate of Edmund Blunden, Copyright © Edmund Blunden; from Roald Dahl, reproduced with permission of David Higham Associates, London on behalf of the Estate of Roald Dahl Copyright © Roald Dahl; from Elizabeth David, reproduced by permission of the Elizabeth David Estate; from M. F. K. Fisher, reproduced by permission of the MFK Fisher Literary Trust; from Robert Graves, with the kind permission of Carcanet Press Limited & The Trustees of the Robert Graves Copyright Trust; from Richard Hughes, reproduced with permission of David Higham Associates, London on behalf of the Estate of Richard Hughes, Copyright © Richard Hughes; from Laurie Lee, reproduced with permission of Curtis Brown Group Ltd, London on behalf of The Estate of Laurie Lee, Copyright © Laurie Lee; from Patrick Leigh Fermor, with permission of the Estate of Patrick Leigh Fermor; from T. H. White, reproduced with permission of David Higham Associates, London on behalf of the Estate of T H White, Copyright